Fugger Newsletter

Edited, with an introduction, by

GEORGE T. MATTHEWS

Department of History,
Columbia University

CAPRICORN BOOKS NEW YORK

Library of Congress Catalog
Card Number: 59-9113
MANUFACTURED IN THE UNITED STATES OF AMERICA

CONTENTS

8

1598-1604

INTRODUCTION

I

In 1655, Emperor Ferdinand III offered to purchase from Count Albert Fugger the valuable library which for generations had been one of the most famous ornaments of the Fugger mansion in Augsburg. The proposition was an uncommon one, for in the long history of Hapsburg-Fugger relations, it had been more usual for the "Lords of Austria" to borrow money from the Augsburg bankers than to buy books.

The first transaction of such nature of which we have definitive record, was in 1487 when Jakob Fugger II (1459-1526) made a loan of 23,627 florins to Siegmund, Archduke of the Tyrol, against the security of a mortgage on the silver mines of Schwaz. On this modest foundation Jakob II—affectionately called "The Rich"—built the House of Fugger, for a hundred years the preeminent financial institution of Europe. Jakob's operations were many and diverse, but they all followed an essentially simple pattern: The loan of ready cash, at high rates of interest, against guaranteed sources of revenue of the kind only princes, kings and emperors had at their disposal. In its heyday, the Fugger firm—always a family partnership—dealt with nearly all the dynasties of Europe. It financed the purchase of titles and benefices, provided funds for the gorgeous ceremonies so essential to the exercise of authority at the time, raised the money that bought the election of emperors, and enabled the potentates of Europe to fight the wars that shaped the history of states and religions. But among the power-holders who depended upon the Fuggers for credit, those of the House of Hapsburg were the first and the last. As the Hapsburg dominions expanded beyond central Europe to the Netherlands, Italy, Spain and the New World to reach an apogee with Charles V (1500-1558), the scope of Fugger business widened. The Hapsburgs never had enough money to pay for their vast political and military commitments. Loan followed loan: As Austrian archdukes, as kings in Hungary, as emperors in Germany, the Hapsburgs pledged silver and copper mines and feudal revenues to

13

the Fuggers; as kings in Italy they mortgaged the fiscs of Naples and Sicily to the Augsburg bankers; as kings in Spain they leased to the German financiers the revenues of the ecclesiastical military orders and added the mercury and silver mines of Almaden and Guadalcanal. By 1525 the Fuggers' financial and business operations reached from Poland to Spain, from Brussels to Naples. Already branches of the firm were reaching into Spanish America and into the Portuguese Far East. The Fuggers dominated the international trade in metals and spices. They were preeminent in Antwerp, greatest money-market of the world. Half the royal houses of Europe were in their debt. Jakob II was the genuine genius of the family, yet even after his death in 1526, Fugger affairs continued to flourish. However, the traditional caution of the firm gave way to rasher policies. Huge sums were advanced to Charles V without adequate security while the Fuggers themselves borrowed on their own credit to raise more money for the Hapsburgs. By 1546 various members of the partnership were already anxious to liquidate and to retire to their landed estates to enjoy the prestige of their purchased titles of Imperial Counts. But with the bulk of their capital frozen in debts on which the Fugger partners could not demand payment, there was no alternative but to lend more. The crisis came in 1557-1559, years in which most of the great princes and kings of Europe, their treasuries emptied by the expenses of war, declared bankruptcy and defaulted. The losses were enormous but they were not fatal, and the Fugger family survived. But now they were bound even closer to their regal debtors than ever before. By the death of Anton Fugger in 1560, the firm had passed its zenith and had entered its period of slow, dignified decline. The decline was halted temporarily by brief periods of relative prosperity, enviable interludes always brought to a close by the Spanish royal bankruptcies which punctuated the history of the late sixteenth century. By the end of the century the power of the House of Fugger was considerably diminished. By the mid-seventeenth century all that remained was some landed property, devasted by war and heavily mortgaged, and a paltry 615,000-florin claim against the Imperial House that bore five per cent interest per year, collectable whenever the Emperor could be induced to pay.

Thus when the Emperor Ferdinand III proposed to buy his family library in 1655, Count Albert Fugger welcomed the opportunity. He was more than willing to part with his precious heirloom for the modest sum of 15,000 gulden because he needed the money more than the books. So the deal was closed and in due course—after some initial difficulty on the part of the Imperial Treasury to scrape together the 15,000 gulden, and of the Imperial Librarian to secure release of the goods from numerous Fugger creditors in Augsburg—the great collection of books, works of art and manuscripts was baled and crated and sent by the rivers Lech and Danube to the Court in Vienna.

The library thus acquired by Ferdinand III was a princely possession. Its central treasure was rich in erudition; there were nearly fourteen thousand volumes in Latin, Spanish, Italian, French and German. Its collection of *objets d'art* was distinguished; there were sculptures, scientific instruments, busts, medals and the numerous sorts of curios in which every respectable library of the period abounded, including two shoes belonging to a Red Indian and a tooth from a salt-water fish. No doubt it was principally this wealth of learning and art which the Emperor had wanted when he paid over his 15,000 guldens. However, the library also continued another treasure whose worth was only dimly recognized in 1655 but which came, in time, to be regarded as at least of equal value to the scholarly tomes. This was the great accumulation of unbound, unsorted manuscripts which had also made the journey from Augsburg to Vienna, along with the Latin writers and the tooth from a salt-water fish.

The credit for being the first scholar to appreciate the value of the Fugger manuscripts belongs to Johann Benedict Gentilotti von Engelbrunn who died, full of years and honors, as the Bishop of Trent in 1735. In the early eighteenth century, Gentilotti sorted the loose sheets and bound them in volumes. He made extracts of some four thousand of the manuscripts which appeared most interesting to him and, understanding their general nature, coined the name by which they have been known ever since: *Fugger-Zeitungen* or, in English, Fugger News-Letters. Gentilotti quite correctly ascribed the word *Zeitung* to the Fugger manuscripts, for in the German of his day, *Zeitung* meant simply "tidings." But in so doing, he unwittingly gave to the world an erroneous impression of the News-Letters' origin and purpose. In the nineteenth century, *Zeitung* came to be the common German word for newspaper or gazette and this fact, combined with the published writings of certain antiquarians whose imaginations were more active than their sense of historical accuracy, produced a myth concerning the Fugger manuscripts that was difficult to dispel. It was widely held that the News-Letters actually were early examples of professional journalism, edited and sold as newspapers by the House of Fugger in the days of its decline. It took a century of scholarship to lay low this ghost and to determine the real character of the Fugger manuscripts and the circumstances of their collection.

In origin the Fugger News-Letters go back to the days of Count Philip Eduard Fugger who was born in 1546 and died in 1618. The Count admirably combined the banking talents of his ancestors with the bookish tastes of a late Renaissance gentleman. Together with his brother Octavian II, Count Philip Eduard directed a branch of the family firm which, unlike other parts of the House of Fugger at that time, enjoyed a brilliant prosperity. But he was more than an astute financier. He was a born collector—many of the books purchased by the Emperor in 1655 bore his initials—and a man possessed of a positive craving for the news. Only few private persons in his age could have been in a more favorable position to gratify both passions.

Even in the second part of the sixteenth century, the Fugger interests were world-wide in scope. Partners, factors, clients and servants of the firm were located in nearly all the commercial and political capitals of Europe, Spanish America, Mediterranean Africa and the Orient. In the normal course of business, these agents were in regular communication with the home-office. Couriers for the Fugger, traveling the dangerous roads and seas of the sixteenth-century world, bore a heavy burden of correspondence from nearly every part of the known globe to Augsburg. It would seem that when the Fugger representatives abroad learned of the Count's extraordinary interest in the news, quite routine dispatches were fleshed out with whatever information on whatever subject the agents could obtain. Count Philip Eduard apparently saved every letter until the collection grew to formidable proportions.

But Count Philip Eduard's thirst for news was not quenched by the information obtained through the ordinary channels of his business correspondence. He turned to other sources present in his native Augsburg. In the German cities, accounts of happenings of all description were hawked in the streets in the form of broadsides, called *Neue-Zeitungen*. In the sixteenth century, *Neue-Zeitungen* on every conceivable subject were printed and sold: miraculous storms and royal weddings, the death of popes, reports of scandal in places high and low, songs, religious polemics, descriptions of public executions, all are subject matter for the thousands of *Neue-Zeitungen* of which we have knowledge. Given Count Philip Eduard's curiosity, it is not surprising to find evidence in the Fugger manuscripts that he added to his collection of letters from his business agents the wealth of news and rumor to be found in the readily available *Neue-Zeitungen*.

In addition to *Neue-Zeitungen*, Augsburg possessed still another source of current news. There was in the city at the time, an agency, headed first by Jeremias Crasser and later by Jeremias Schiffle, which specialized in the professional editing and sale of news-reports to a list of paying subscribers. These *Nouvellanten*, as Crasser and Schiffle described themselves, supplied their clients with information drawn from a great variety of sources, from the simple gossip of market towns to copies of such *Neue-Zeitungen* as fell into their hands. Crasser and Schiffle, genuine, if none too scrupulous, newsmen, naturally counted among their customers the news-hungry Count Philip Eduard, who added their reports to his accumulation of dispatches, letters and *Neue-Zeitungen*.

Although it is conjecture, it seems safe to assume that at some time Count Philip Eduard, impressed by the value of the papers he had amassed and perhaps overwhelmed by their sheer variety, resolved to have them copied the better to preserve them for the future. For this labor he employed the firm of Crasser and Schiffle, which hired scrivners as needed to keep up with the volume of copying work fed them across the years by the Count. As the materials were copied—in at least fourteen different hands—they were deposited in the Fugger library to form the bulk of that manuscript collection which finally found its way to Vienna in 1655.

Thus the mass of manuscripts which, since the time of Gentilotti, has been called the Fugger News-Letters, represents at least three different sorts of news-sources, the whole being copies of originals rather than originals themselves. It is difficult, if not in most cases impossible, to determine to which category—genuine Fugger dispatch, *Neue-Zeitung* or Crasser and Schiffle report—any particular document belongs. A few of the longer letters can be identified with reasonable accuracy: the letter from Cochin in India, for example, is clearly from a Fugger agent stationed on business in the Portuguese Far East. Some of the documents are recognizable as *Neue-Zeitungen:* The account of the judgment against the witch Walpurga Hausmännin, for example, is among their number. Most of the shorter dispatches are probably from Fugger correspondents; some, however, were supplied by Crasser and Schiffle. But as a whole the identity and history of the originals is lost in the anonymity of the copyists.

The News-Letters bear datelines from places all over the world. Most often the shorter dispatches came from commercial centers, always prime sources of the news: Antwerp, Middleburg, Seville, Hamburg, Venice are conspicuous, but Amsterdam, already in the closing years of the sixteenth century a busy port, is absent. Political capitals are also well represented: Madrid, Paris, Rome, Prague, Brussels and Vienna are prominent, but London, with which the Fuggers had only tenuous connections at this time, appears but infrequently.

The News-Letters are not only copies but, in many cases, translations. Hence it is difficult to discover the original language of any given report: the bulk of the manuscript News-Letters are in German, yet Italian documents fill an entire volume. French is rarely used, Latin less frequently still, while Spanish is almost entirely absent, although there is good evidence that many of the reports from Madrid, Lisbon and the Spanish Américas were originally in that language.

Although the News-Letters deal with every subject from the wonder-working of alchemists to the assassination of kings, there are certain lacks. *Autos-de-fé* in Spain are described with relish: the plays of Lope de Vega are never mentioned. The pillage of the Caribbean by English sea-dogs is duly recorded: Shakespeare, Marlowe and Jonson do not appear. Although the occult world of magic, black and white, is amply reported, nothing is said of science, art or technology. Although the general conditions of trade as affected by war and the bankruptcy of ruling monarchs give rise to rejoicing or to lamentation, nothing important is revealed of the business activities of the Fuggers themselves.

The Fugger correspondents, whoever they may have been, display a certain consistency of attitude toward the great questions of politics, war and religion. Hawkins and Drake are not depicted as heroes, but as wild pirates preying upon the peaceful trade of Spain. The Huguenots of France are heretics and rebels, while the Sea-Beggars of Holland are outlaws. This is only natural, for the Fuggers were Catholic. They were loyal subjects of the Hapsburgs in Spain and in the Empire. They were bankers committed to the finance of states and the trade of regions, threatened by the eruption of the new powers of England and the Dutch into an established commercial world which they had for decades dominated. The Fugger News-Letters were not objective pieces of reporting, and their writers frankly disclose their biases and interests, their joy or despair over every turn of events.

It is evident that the Fugger News-Letters—of the vast manuscript collection of which only a part is published in this edition of *News and Rumor in Renaissance Europe*[1] —are not what historians would call primary sources of evidence for the establishment of fact in the realms of political, economic or religious history. They are not state papers, or even letters, journals or memoirs of participants in events. For the most part they are not even the reports of eye-witnesses of great events, but rather the reports of

---

[1] In 1923 Victor Klarwill edited a German edition entitled *Fugger-Zeitungen: Ungedruckte Briefe an das Haus Fugger aus den Jahren 1568-1605* (Rikola Verlag, Vienna). In 1924 this work appeared in an English translation by Pauline de Chary as *The Fugger News-Letters* (G. P. Putnam's Sons, N.Y.). In 1926 Victor Klarwill made an additional selection of materials which, translated by L. S. R. Byrne, appeared as *The Fugger News-Letters, Second Series* (G. P. Putnam's Sons, N.Y.). All of these editions have been long out of print. This present edition contains about one half of the News-Letters found in the two English editions.

those who have heard the echo of events as they rever-
berated through the markets of the world. Moreover, as
the manuscripts are found in the Vienna collection, the
Fugger News-Letters are not organized according to any
sequence or filed under subject headings. There is no way
to tell when, or in what order the various sorts of reports
reached Augsburg. The selections published in this book
have been arranged, with few exceptions, in as strict a
chronological order as information concerning the date of
the writing of each piece permits. But it should not be assumed that it was in this order that they were read by
Count Philip Eduard. Although Augsburg and most of
south central Germany were relatively peaceful places
between 1568 and 1604, the terminal dates of the News-
Letters, the routes to the city were long and dangerous.
The best postal service covered only eighty-five miles a
day; the swiftest Mediterranean galley could make but
one hundred and twenty-five miles a day. It took a letter
from Madrid one to three months to arrive in Augsburg.
Moreover, the news-reports arrived haphazardly, with the
narrative of one event crossed with the stories of others.
One day one might read of the return of Captain Drake
from a voyage of rapine and discovery; the next of the
execution of a Bohemian nobleman for common robbery
in the streets of Prague; on the next again of the rich gifts
which Drake had made to his queen. The story of the fate
of the Spanish Armada of 1588 took almost six months
to unfold in the inland city of Augsburg and even then
there was doubt as to just what had happened in the
waters off England and Scotland.

Thus if the Fugger News-Letters are not primary
sources for a full reconstruction of past events, they also
are not to be regarded as organized, edited news. Rather
they represent the news as it might appear on the uned-
ited, continuously moving tape of a press agency's tele-
type: true reports and false rumors, trivial occurrences
and important events follow one upon the other without
interruption and without discrimination. The Fugger
News-Letters exhibit history not as it has been organized
for rational discourse by the scholar—in other words not
as past event, classified and pinned down—but history as
it was experienced by a contemporary, disorganized, uncertain, a thing of many variables, each one of equal, im-

mediate import. The Fugger News-Letters reveal a confused "present" before it became an ordered "past."

II

The events reported as news in the Fugger News-Letters have now receded far into the past. At the time of their receipt in Augsburg, a reader would have understood them as part of a familiar world: intelligent reading of the "news" always depends upon some sense of its "background." In order to make meaningful a reading of the News-Letters four hundred years after their writing, it is necessary to have some formal, reconstructed knowledge of the chief drift of events in the late sixteenth century. The first News-Letter to be found in this volume is dated Brussels, 1568, and deals with the execution of the Counts Egmont and Horn for the crime of treason against Philip of Spain and the Netherlands. The last letter is from Vienna, 1604, and concerns the extraordinary appearance of a white dove at the court of the Emperor Rudolph II. What was happening in Europe between these two apparently unrelated episodes?

The second part of the sixteenth century was comparatively peaceful in Central Europe. The storm of the Reformation was blowing itself out in minor squalls, and the hurricane of the Thirty Years War had not yet formed on the German horizon. The Baltic and Slavic worlds were stirring to the rise of Swedish military strength and the emergence of Muscovy from medieval obscurity, but events in these regions impinged only faintly upon the rest of the continent, even upon Germany. On the middle Danube, Turkish power, which in the first half of the century had threatened Vienna itself, was quiescent. But for Western Europe this same period was a time of turmoil and war.

An appreciation of the key position held by Spain is important to an understanding of this situation. Throughout most of the period under consideration, Philip II (1527-1598), son of the Hapsburg Emperor Charles V, bore the crowns of Spain. He was king of a country whose profound sense of national destiny was identical to its deep sense of Catholicity. Spanish nationalism was imperial and proud; Spanish Catholicism was militant and fanatic. No king ever typified his country more completely than Philip II. But Philip's dominions were more than Spain, his native land. He was also lord of the Netherlands, an active complex of cities, headed by Antwerp, which was, at this time, the commercial and financial center of Europe's rapidly expanding capitalist economy. Far to the south, Philip ruled the duchy of Milan and the kingdoms of Naples and Sicily, from which positions he dominated the peninsula of Italy. Over the Alps, in central Europe, Philip's Hapsburg cousins were archdukes of the Austrias, emperors in Germany and kings in Bohemia and Hungary. Far across the Atlantic, Philip was master of Peru, Mexico and the Antilles. It was Philip's ambition to make Spain the heart and the head of this great constellation of states and regions and from its strategic positions to dominate the continent. Between 1568 and 1604, Europe was alive with Spanish armies and navies, with Spanish diplomats and priests, with Spanish governors and generals all directed by Philip from Madrid or from his strange monastery-palace of the Escorial. Philip II sought a Spanish hegemony in Europe, an hegemony powerful enough to restore the Catholic unity of Christendom which the Protestant reformation had disrupted.

However, Spain's predominance did not stand unchallenged. Philip confronted savage opposition all over the world. Only in the Mediterranean could he claim any real success. There at Lepanto in the Gulf of Corinth in 1571, a Venetian-Genoese galley fleet, commanded by Philip's bastard brother Don John of Austria, crushed the Turks at sea, turning back a Moslem threat to the coasts of Italy. Philip, not without setbacks, thereupon assumed the task of clearing the waters for Christian commerce. Elsewhere Philip was not so fortunate. The great war which finally opened along the Atlantic seaways between Spain and a rebellious Northern Netherlands aided by a resurgent England and seconded by a regenerated France, never brought Philip to his knees, but his inability to finish it signaled Spain's eventual exhaustion and defeat.

The chronic warfare on the Atlantic, which is the subject of so many of the Fugger News-Letters, resulted from a convergence of many economic, religious and political factors. In economic terms, it was in the latter half of the sixteenth century that the consequences of the discovery of America made their first massive impact upon western Europe. A new pattern of world commerce was emerging based not upon Italy and the Mediterranean, but upon a triangle that connected the Netherlands and England with the Americas on one side and with Africa and India on the other. In this configuration the role of Spain was crucial. For Spain monopolized the New World and after 1580, when Philip made good his claim on the crown of Portugal, added to it the Portuguese monopoly of the Far Eastern spice trade. As the sixteenth century wore on, the colonial market for African slaves and commercial products expanded far beyond the capacity of Spain to supply. Simultaneously, Mexico and Peru were revealed as the greatest sources of precious metals the world had ever known. Beginning about 1545 an ever-mounting volume of silver crossed the Atlantic to the port of Seville in Spain. In the circumstances, interloping and piracy were as inevitable as Philip's attempt to enclose his colonial system by ever tighter nets of administration and military power. But the problem he confronted was more than a simple matter of casual smuggling and robbery. In an age of rapid economic growth, the continued prosperity of England and the Netherlands depended absolutely upon access to a share of the American treasure. So long as English merchants could deal peacefully with the Netherlands, Spain's financial center, bullion could be obtained by the sale of English goods. But as Philip's restrictive measures grew more stringent after 1568, when he faced rebellion in the Netherlands itself, the need for a money supply grew more urgent. English, Netherlandish and French business men took to the sea in an attempt to pry open the American market. Thus the Englishman Hawkins sailed to Africa, bought slaves with trade goods, and transported them across the Atlantic for sale in Spanish colonial markets for silver. Obstinately Philip refused to license Hawkins' activities or those of others, of many nationalities, who followed in his wake. Since the needs of the colonies themselves far outstripped the ability of the Spanish economy to satisfy, the Spanish system soon lost touch with reality. Philip's policies laid open his coasts, his exposed sea-routes and his colonies to an unremitting pressure from Englishmen who, scenting profit, were not scrupulous in their means to obtain it. Interloping led to piracy, piracy to pillage. The need to force the market contributed greatly to the state of open warfare that broke out between Spain and England in 1585.

It would, however, be a mistake to think that these economic considerations alone account for the struggle that consumed western Europe in the last part of the sixteenth century. The commercial rivalries just described operated in an atmosphere of bitter religious animosities and savage political antagonisms. In the late sixteenth century Protestant Europe faced Catholic Europe across a gulf of mutual hate and suspicion. It was a time when religion supported patriotism and rationalized economic interest. Piracy was more easily condoned by Protestant Englishmen, when the victims were Catholic Spaniards. But by like token, religion often subverted patriotism and ignored economic reality. It was an age when many men served a "higher" cause than political loyalty. Many did not scruple to seek aid from foreigners against legitimate kings when their faith conflicted with that of their rulers. The Calvinist Netherlands revolutionaries sought the aid of Protestant England against their lord, Philip of Spain, and, indeed, against such of their neighbors as refused to rebel or to leave the Catholic fold. Catholic Englishmen appealed to Spain for support and fermented rebellion at home. French Huguenots turned to Protestant England and to their coreligionists in the Netherlands for military assistance; French Catholics welcomed Spanish arms and money in their battle with fellow Frenchmen. The regicide of heretic kings was openly advocated by Jesuit publicists; Calvinists could not tolerate Catholic princes. Religious assassination became a mode of political action. Calvinist William of Orange and Catholic Henry III of France were both assassinated, and many lesser personages fell by knife and bullet. The late sixteenth century was an age of ideological conflict that recognized no borders. It was also an age of revolution.

In the Netherlands, a dynamic Calvinism fostered a spirit of rebellion among nobles and bourgeois, basically engendered by Catholic Philip's attempt to bind his rich lordships tighter to his Spanish monarchy and to impose upon them a version of the Inquisition. Spanish religious-political terror only encouraged the dissidence it was designed to suppress. By 1568 much of the Netherlands was in revolt and the movement had found its first martyrs in Counts Egmont and Horn, its first leader in Prince William of Orange and its first heroes in the Calvinist Sea-Beggars who struck at Catholic trade at sea while Spanish armies, successful in the area south of the Scheldt river, vainly attempted to curb the rebellion in the low lands to the north.

If Philip was frustrated in his attempt to quell rebellion in the northern, Calvinist parts of the Netherlands, his policies received encouragement in the contemporary situation in France. It had been the existence of an aggressive France, the most compact and powerful single state on the continent of Europe, standing between Spain and Germany, that had thwarted the ambition of Philip's father, the Emperor Charles V, to drive the Turks from the Danube and to crush the Protestant revolt in Germany. But between 1562 and 1593 the massive French monarchy collapsed and almost foundered in a series of religious-civil wars of unprecedented violence. The Valois dynasty came to an end in the person of a weak and childless king. Long before the assassination of Henry III, last of the Valois, the anticipated vacancy of the throne, combined with the king's own lack of strength and will, unleashed all the forces of religious and political disunity that had been held in check only by the power of the royal house. Catholics and Huguenots flew to arms to attack and to defend, while rich cities and whole provinces fell to rival factions of the great nobility. All sides enlisted sectarian passions in the struggle for political power. The Catholic Guise family, client of Philip II, aimed to establish itself as a new dynasty upon the death of Henry III. The Huguenot Bourbon family sought to secure the royal authority for its head, Henry of Navarre, who had a legal right to the throne. For thirty years France was a scene of strife in which the massacre of Huguenots by Catholics on St. Bartholomew's Eve in 1572 was but the most spectacular episode. In this anarchy the interest of Catholic Spain was clear. A weakened France, purged of the Huguenots, with a Catholic dynasty dependent upon Philip of Spain, would assure the Spanish hegemony.

Thus England emerged as the key to the situation. For the growing weight of the strategically located island kingdom, thrown either way in the Netherlands and in France, could be decisive. Without English support, the success of the rebellion in the Northern Netherlands was dubious; without English support, Henry of Navarre's journey to the French crown was immensely difficult; without English support, Protestantism might well be lost on the continent. But until about 1572 England's policy was ambiguous. Elizabeth I was an imperious woman of great intelligence and absorbing patriotism who commanded the respect and loyalty of the bulk of the English people. But the character of her Protestantism was undogmatic and her conduct of foreign affairs was cautious in the extreme. Moreover, she was a master of deceit. Until the true weakness of France was revealed after 1572, she had no real desire for war with Spain. But the pressure of economic necessity, coupled with a natural greed, pushed her to patronize the English freebooters' privateering on the Spanish Main. When Spain protested, she pleaded innocence and disclaimed responsibility. Although clearly she had no intention of preventing English raids on Spanish commerce, she equally had no intention of declaring war on Philip. Conversely Philip, although exasperated beyond measure by her duplicity, had everything to lose by forcing the matter to open hostilities. Therefore, he chose the weapon of subversion. Between 1568 and 1572 Elizabeth's reign was pock-marked by treasonable plots aimed at her life and throne. All were traced to the Spanish ambassador in London. All involved Catholic Englishmen. All seemed to revolve around the person of Mary, Queen of Scotland who, since she had been driven from her homeland by Calvinist revolutionaries, was a virtual prisoner in England. Mary was Catholic, a relative of the French Guises; she had once been Queen of France. What was more important to Elizabeth, she was the heir-apparent to the English throne. These events, taken in conjunction with the success of the revolutions in the Northern Netherlands and with the St. Bartholomew's Eve massacre in France, inclined Elizabeth to an undercover support of Protestantism abroad as a counter to the Catholicism that threatened her at home. But the support was meager and desultory until 1584 when the assassination of the Prince of Orange forced Elizabeth's hand. For the first time she openly intervened in the Netherlands to prevent the failure of the revolution and in France to assure the accession of Henry of Navarre to the throne.

Thus by 1585 open if undeclared war existed between England and Spain. Further plots upon the English queen's life, fatally involving Mary of Scotland, forced Elizabeth to send her relative to her death in 1587. The failure to gain his ends by subversion forced Philip to muster every resource to crush England in one massive campaign. But the invincible Armada of 1588, the mightiest fleet ever to put to sea, was a failure and the dread Spanish infantry mobilized in the southern Netherlands never boarded the ships that were to carry them to England. The defeat of the Armada did not end the war. Spain's resources were vast. But England's strength, forged by exuberant Protestant nationalism upon an anvil of growing commercial power, was also great. During the last decade of the sixteenth century Elizabeth fought Philip in the Netherlands, in France and in Ireland, where the Spanish monarch supported Irish Catholic rebellion. At the same time, English sea-captains carried the struggle to the Spanish coasts and to the New World. By the end of the century, English and Dutch merchantmen, armed and scornful of the Spanish-held monopoly, were already rounding Africa for direct trade with the Portuguese Far East and laying the foundation for seventeenth-century Dutch and English economic supremacy. Gradually the Spanish giant was worn down. Philip II died in 1598, the same year that peace was established between France and Spain. The new king, Philip III, refused to recognize the independence of the United Provinces of the Northern Netherlands and nominally that war dragged on until 1609. But Elizabeth I died in 1603 and her successor, James I, son of Mary, Queen of Scots, finally brought the English-Spanish conflict to an end in 1604. Shortly after the signing of the treaty of peace, a Fugger correspondent in Vienna reported that at the court of the Emperor, people were surprised at the sudden and unusual appearance of a beautiful white dove.

George T. Matthews
Columbia University

1. Execution of Count Egmont and Count Horn in Brussels

Tidings of how Counts Egmont and Horn were executed on the 5th day of June of the year 1568, what they spoke and what came to pass.

On the 4th day of June of this year 1568, Count Egmont and Count Horn were taken on a special conveyance from Ghent to Brussels. They were accompanied by twelve back. When Count Egmont beheld the town of Brussels, troops of Spaniards on foot and several hundreds on horse-he said: "I am in good hopes that the Duke of Alba will of his mercy allow me to sup with my spouse and my children this night." They had been with him of late and had brought him consolation. But as soon as they entered the town, (it was at three o'clock in the afternoon), they were taken to the King's Bread-House, which stands in the market-place opposite the Town Hall, and thereupon Count Egmont said: "Now I have lost all hope!" The same evening at seven o'clock, their sentence was read out to the two counts, thereupon Egmont on that evening and during the night oft repeated: That the wrongs he had committed against His Majesty might graciously be forgiven him and his life spared in return for the services he had rendered; that he should be punished with lifelong imprisonment and be treated not as a count, but as a poor nobleman. The King should be implored thus on his behalf. The Grand Prior likewise, it is rumoured, has thrown himself on his knees before the carriage of the Duke, but it has availed him nothing. The Duke is reported to have said that the sentence of both gentlemen is to be carried out. Therefore the Bishop of Ypres has been sent to them as Confessor, and, in addition to him, the Duke's Chaplain and a Spanish priest. These remained with them until their death. In the morning a stand, which is called here a scaffold, was erected in the market-place, and on either side a pole with an iron point was nailed thereto. The said scaffold was draped with black cloth and two black cushions were laid upon it. The market-place was guarded by the twenty troops which had come from Ghent and by ten from Brussels. At eleven o'clock Count Egmont was first brought from the King's Bread-House to the market-place. He was unbound and accompanied by the Bishop of Ypres and the two Spanish priests and the Maistre de Camp. He was attired in a black velvet doublet, cut low at the neck, wide black velvet breeches, and brodequins, or white Spanish boots. Over this he wore a red damask night-robe, and an ordinary black cloak, both edged with gold braid. He also wore a hat with black and white plumes thereon. He walked from the said Bread-House to the scaffold. He carried his cloak over his shoulder and had his hands crossed upon his breast. And so he walked in orderly fashion and with a proud face as he had formerly been wont to go to the Council.

He carried himself bravely, though his face looked melancholy and afflicted. He held his cloak before his mouth, thrown over his shoulder, and looked around him; then he laid it aside, composed himself for death, and was about to unrobe himself. The Maistre de Camp said to him: "Oh, there is no haste, take time for reflection. Time and to spare will be given to you and this vouchsafed right willingly." Thereupon he slung the cloak once more round his shoulders and again looked around him, but without saying a word or making a sign. Only his right hand he stretched out from under the cloak and gazed upon it fixedly. Therefore the Bishop of Ypres addressed him in these words: "Sir, do not take thought now of any worldly matters, but bethink yourself of the salvation of your soul." At that he asked: Whether the salvation of his soul could prevent him thinking of his wife and his children? The Bishop answered: "Nay, since our Lord Himself, as He hung upon the Cross for the remission of our sins, committed His mother to the care of John." Thereupon the Count made reply: "Then there is naught that troubles my heart or lies heavy on my conscience." With these words he put down his hat, laid aside his cloak, likewise his night-robe. The Maistre de Camp once more bade him not to hurry, but the Count made answer that, as it was ordained he must die, he wished to do so. He knelt down with the Bishop and spoke privately with him for the space of two paternosters. Thereupon he himself motioned him aside with his hand, lifted a gilt cross from where it lay on the scaffold, and knelt before it. Likewise he pulled the white cap or bandage which he had on his head over his eyes, and thus remained kneeling for some time while the executioner made ready. Meanwhile the Bishop inquired of him whether he would permit his bandage to be made tight. "Nay," he replied, "I will die right valiantly and deport myself in seemly fashion." Thereupon the executioner carried out his appointed task with the sword. Immediately this was done the two Spanish priests bore away the dead body and the head, and placed them under a black cloth at the side of the scaffold. They then fetched Count Horn from the Bread-House. He also was unfettered, and when he stepped out upon the market-place he doffed his hat and bade the soldiers on both sides good-day in the Spanish tongue. These did likewise. Then he went bravely, bareheaded, hat in hand, to the scaffold. He wore his usual garments, a doublet of white linen and laced black velvet breeches, and thereover a cloak. As soon as he mounted the scaffold he spoke to all and sundry, saying how much it grieved him that he had so acted against the King and not served him better. He craved the pardon of His Majesty and of whomsoever he should have offended. This same he was willing to grant to all. He begged that every one should say a paternoster for him. Thereupon he fell on his knees with the Bishop and thus remained the space of two paternosters, or thereabouts. The hat he held in his hands all the time. Then he arose once more, thanked everybody in a strong and manly voice, and made obeisance to all the soldiers, who did likewise. Thereupon he laid aside his cloak and knelt down unbound. After this the executioner did as he was ordered. When both gentlemen had been executed, their heads were placed on two iron spikes where they remained till the afternoon at three. But the corpses were guarded by six monks, who, clad in grey, and as is the custom here, bury the dead. The bodies were unrobed under a linen cloth that was spread over them and each was laid in a special chest, in which they remained for about an hour upon the scaffold. Thereafter, they, as well as the heads, were carried in a four-cornered separate little box to the Church of St. Gudule. There the heads were sewn to the bodies and Count Egmont transported to St. Claire, and Count Horn to another convent. Thereafter Egmont was embalmed and buried in his own domain at Gottegem, and Horn likewise at Weert.

2. The Death of Queen Elizabeth of Spain

From Madrid, the 5th day of October 1568.

I have reported to Your Serene Highness that the Queen of Spain is pregnant once more. Because last year nothing came of her pregnancy, many people have on this occasion cherished doubts likewise. Several women have presented her with jewels and given her flower-water to drink in order that she might the sooner conceive and retain what had been vouchsafed to her. Others say that in the past year when she miscarried, she, according to the reported custom in France, did not cleanse herself properly that she might again soon become pregnant. Be that as it may, Her Majesty hath been weakened mightily by long swoons. Some have it that she is half paralysed and cannot use one arm and one thigh as easily as formerly. Therefore the leeches hold a grave opinion of her illness, and it has been said that she could not live longer than four or five months. These swoons have affected Her Majesty more and more, so that since the Feast of St. Michael she has lain mostly abed. On the second day of this month the physicians gave her two purgatives and bled her. That night Her Majesty, who was very weak, confirmed her former Will, and early in the morning received Extreme Unction. She is said to have commended her daughter to the care of the King, and she sent once more for the Ambassador of France. Him she ordered to tell the King, her brother, and the Queen, her mother, that she besought them to continue and keep the friendship with the King of Spain. If they would do so, God would bestow upon them the help of the King of Spain. They say that the King went to her with frequency and was much affected at her great weakness. On that day, about ten o'clock in the forenoon, the pains are said to have become very grievous until she gave birth to a young Prince. Some assure us that he came alive from the womb of his mother and received baptism, others that he was taken from her dead and in pieces, as he could not have been older than five months. In order to be exact, it must be said that she is only supposed to have become pregnant in last May when she was with the King in Aranjuez. After she had suffered from heavy swooning and great weakness, God our Lord called her unto Him, about two hours after the birth of the child at noon. She is said to have passed away in a most Christian manner. May Our Lord God give her eternal peace. The King has shown great sorrow on account of this and has withdrawn himself to San Geronimo, the convent outside the city. In 1558 we lost here in Spain the Emperor Charles and two Queens. In this year '68 we have lost two Princes of Spain and the Queen. May God turn His wrath away from this land!

Rumour already secretly betroths our King to the eldest daughter of His Imperial Majesty and adds thereto that if His Majesty is not minded to wed a fourth time, then His Majesty will bespeak the eldest Infanta for Archduke Rudolf.

Then His Highness would remain here, renouncing all his concerns abroad, in order to become, after the demise of His Majesty, King of Spain. It is also affirmed that His Majesty wishes to betroth the Archduke Ernst to the youngest Infanta and to give them Flanders as a dowry. These are the views commonly held. What, however, will happen, time alone will disclose.

According to my opinion His Majesty will not omit to marry again.

3. Hawkins Trades Slaves for Silver

From Seville, the 21st day of January 1569.

There have arrived several English letters from Vigo in Galicia, wherein is written as follows: "In the past year an Englishman with eight well-equipped ships has sailed from England to Guinea into the sea territory of the King of Portugal. After he had exchanged his wares for one thousand five hundred negroes, he has made his way with them to New Spain. In order that he might do this without opposition and in a manner to suit himself, he has occupied a small island called San Juan de Lua near Vera Cruz, where the Spanish fleet was wont to load and unload and by which the Spanish ships must always pass. There he has blocked the water with ships and guns so that the Spanish fleet of thirty ships, which arrived there shortly after him, was unable to get into the harbour of Vera Cruz without his permission. The Spanish General had perforce to make a pact with the said Englishman, that he might sell his negroes freely and take away the money thus gained. A written contract was drawn up as to this, and they delivered unto each other twelve hostages. Several days after the Spanish General had come into the harbour of Vera Cruz, either because he held the contract unfair or out of anger at the overbearing demeanour of the Englishman, he broke the treaty, if not openly and by word of mouth, yet secretly by deed. At his instigation, seven old ships were stealthily set alight and driven from out of the harbour among the English ships. In this manner it was desired to burn all the English ships and that the captains thereof might perish. But when the Englishman espied this and realized the deceit practised upon him, he became wrathful and has, with his other ships, thus pressed the Spanish fleet that four of their ships were sent to the bottom. But as his own vessels had suffered no little stress, he made his way homewards with the twelve Spanish hostages. But a bad storm scattered his fleet and he alone reached Vigo with one vessel, badly buffeted and suffering for lack of food. He could not have remained three days longer on the water. There he made provision of all that was needful and set sail for England. It is not known where the other ships have remained or what has befallen them."

4. Piracy in South America

Madrid, May 26, 1569.

A recent but unfounded rumour here has it that the inhabitants of Cusco in Peru have revolted. However, I hear nothing so far about this from Seville. On the 21st the Indian Council published the news from Seville that a passenger arrived there from Santo Domingo relates how Don Melendez has captured from the corsairs in Guiana and Porto Rico three ships and a quantity of silver too, looted along the coast. I have been unable to learn whether the pirates were English or French.

5. Treasure Ships reach Spain

Madrid, October 1, 1569.

News has just come from Seville that the fleet of eight sail arrived safely from the Spanish Main at San Lucar on September 28. These eight ships are supposed to be bringing 340,000 ducats for the King, and over one and a half millions in gold for merchants and private individuals. It is hoped that an additional fleet will arrive next April, as many vessels which have made the Indian voyage are still due. The two fleets which came from New Spain and Peru this year brought in more than three millions, and this is good news, for in these times every penny is badly wanted. This is all I have heard up to the present except that Peru is quite quiet. God grant this may be true!

6. The Northumberland Conspiracy

(Original in Italian.)

(No heading, no date.)
Copy of a Manifesto issued by the Earl of Northumberland and other Catholic Lords.

We, Thomas Earl of Northumberland and Charles Earl of Westmorland, most loyal Vassals of Her Majesty, to all true believers in the ancient Catholic Church. All know how that we in common with other people both of the nobility and also of all other ranks who are of the true faith have striven for the prosperity of this good cause, while certain wicked and designing men of the retinue of the Queen by their crafty and malicious wiles have grown great and mighty and have persecuted within this realm the true Catholic religion of God. In this wise have they done injury to the Queen and thrown the realm into disorder. Above all in these latter days have they attempted and encompassed the destruction of the nobility. Therefore we have joined together to resist, not only of our own resources but rather with the help of God and of the people. We will essay to find a remedy against every disorder by restoring for all time the ancient freedom of the Church of God and of the realm. If we do not this of ourselves we risk to be made Protestants by force which would be a sore danger to our State and to our country to which we belong.

The chief demands of these Lords are as follows:

1. The true and ancient religion.
2. The removal of three of the Queen's Councillors.
3. Liberation of those nobles who are in prison.
4. Recall of the former Councillors and a General Amnesty.

7. Hawkins and Drake

Seville, December 7, 1569.

From Cadiz this morning came the following news and immediately after it Don Melendez. He relates how John Hawkins the Englishman, who in New Spain last year had such a fight with the Viceroy and Don Francesco de Luxan, General of the Fleet, recently passed Cape St. Vincent with twenty-five well-found ships, among which are stated to be three of seven hundred tons, thirteen of three hundred, and the rest smaller. There he intercepted a ship trying to make its way to the Netherlands and carried it off together with its entire cargo. The crew he put on land with instructions to inform Don Melendez and Don Luxan that he was proceeding to India and would await them both at Havana. In that place he would call them to account for the damage which, contrary to good faith and despite the sureties given, they had inflicted upon him during the previous year. All those of high degree and all stout-hearted captains were invited to wait upon him there without fail. Every one was utterly horrified at these tidings, than which nothing could be worse for the King and the Indian trade, seeing that with a favourable wind Drake must now be close to the Indian Islands (West Indies). At this juncture the ships from New Spain would certainly be loaded up and on their way, so that the Englishman would have them at his mercy. Don Melendez is neither sufficiently armed, nor has he enough equipment and men to face Drake. But the latter knows how much armament he requires and has made all necessary preparations. And the most annoying part of this affair is that this Hawkins could not have fitted out so numerous and so well equipped a fleet without the aid and secret consent of the Queen. This conflicts with the agreement for the sake of which the King sent an Envoy Extraordinary to the Queen of England. It is the nature and habit of this nation not to keep faith, so the Queen pretends that all has been done without her knowledge and desire. The French write that their King Francis, owing to the tricks played on him during his reign by the English, always had on his lips the following epigram:

> *'Anglicus, Anglicus est cui nunquam credere fas est,*
> *Tum tibi dicit ave, tanquam ab hoste cave.'*

In like fashion she summoned Brederode the Walloon to appear before her and broke faith on this occasion also.

The real reason for this expedition and the further damage it will cause we shall soon learn. May the Almighty protect us from still worse things!

8. *Auto de fé* in Seville

From Seville, the 13th day of May 1569.

The *auto de fé* of which I have already written took place here to-day. Seventy persons were brought forth, of which have been burned two Burgundians, one Frenchman and one Dutchman. The others were for the most part Spanish rabble of poor mien, namely blasphemers of the name of God, and such as had been married twice or more. There were also among them such as did not hold fornication as sin. Likewise were there some of Jewish and Mohammedan faith.

9. The Razing of the Cuilembourg House in Brussels

From the year 1569.

In Brussels, in the middle of the site where formerly there stood the mansion of the Count de Cuilembourg, which has been razed to the ground, there now has been erected

36

a large pillar of grey stones and the following inscription in Spanish, French, Latin and Italian engraved on the four sides thereof: "In the reign of Philip II, the Catholic, King of Spain, it has been decided in his Netherland Provinces, under the regency of Ferdinand Alvarez de Toledo, Duke of Alba, that the palace of the Count de Cuilembourg shall be levelled to the ground, in order to obliterate the very memory of the conspiracies against the Roman Catholic Faith, the King's Majesty, and against the Provinces themselves, which oft have been hatched therein. In the year of Grace 1568 on the 9th day of June."

10. Unrest among the Miners in Schwaz

From Augsburg, the 20th day of December 1569.

In Schwaz it is rumoured that the miners are about to rise on account of the Religion which the Archduke intends to observe in his domain according to his own pleasure. That doth not please the overseers of the mines and they needs must incite the other poor simpletons to rebel. This can, however, soon be prevented by removing the foremen or bidding them follow the customs of the land in matters of religious observance and to keep their mouths tight shut. The others are to work or pray, whether they wish it or not, and therefore may well be kept within bounds.

11. Rebellion in Chile and Peru

Seville, July 29, 1570.

Concerning the Spanish Main, a ship has arrived from Havana and on it a passenger from Cartagena. He brings the unwelcome news that in Peru and Chile, that is to say the more distant settlements, numbers of people have rebelled owing to the severe taxes and imposts inflicted upon them daily. Moreover, they are furious because they are forbidden to plant vines, olives, corn, and the like. Also all that they have been cultivating for some years past has been set on fire and destroyed. It is the King's will that all such articles should be exported from our own country and sold there, in order that his revenue and taxes both within and without the land may flourish exceedingly. The King was not a little put out that they should have thus presumed to be contumacious. This news at the present juncture is very bad, but not surprising, for if the load of a beast of burden is added to daily without regard to his strength but with thought of profit alone, he will lose heart and fall. Certain people who, except for the tribute in gold and silver which they pay to the King, desire to be free of all taxation, and have consequently often taken up arms against the King, walk freely abroad here, their only desire being to enrich themselves by war and disorder.

12. Insolvencies at the Exchange at Antwerp

From Antwerp, the 9th day of December 1570.

Here the Genoese have arranged a competition at the Exchange and because of it two Genoese houses have gone bankrupt this week: they are Giovanni Grimaldi and then Pedro Francesco et Pedro Christophoro Spinola, who have behind them all the Germans here. It has always been regarded as a well-established business, and has long traded in this town. The creditors keep of good cheer. It is, however, to be feared that it may be with this as with other bankruptcies. At first there is ever enough on hand, but in the end no one can obtain anything. The Spinola did show their books to the creditors, but would not deliver them, saying that their agent in Spain is still in a good position. They assert that they are not in difficulties on this account, and also that this came upon them unexpectedly. Therewith the creditors have to be content for the nonce. But they have had the books sealed up and have delivered them to a notary for custody. This bankruptcy has put an end to credit among the Genoese. Within the space of a few years many bankruptcies have taken place, but I have never seen such excitement on the Exchange as there is regarding this. They are owing a large amount, but no one knows how much, for their books have not as yet been balanced. Grimaldi are said to be indebted for 80,000 ducats.

It will probably not end with these two, but they will drag down others of their nation with them.

Herewith your Honour has a list of the Genoese who have become insolvent at Cambray, where these days is held the Besançon payment. This may truly be called a competition. Time will show which of these scoundrels wins the booty, and perhaps the gallows will be their summer dwelling.

The following bankruptcies are reported in letters from Lyons of the 29th day of November: Nicolo Giustiniani & Stefano Rizierola, Tomaso Spinola, fu de Niro, Giovanni Antonio & Girolamo Grimaldi, Jacopo Fiesco & Antonio Lescaro di Messina, Antonio & Tommasso de Franchi di Palermo. Bills have been protested—to Giovanni Francesco & Antonio Fornari di Genova, 11,000 scudi and Gentili di Napoli, for the same amount.

13. War against the Moors

From Madrid, the 31st day of January 1571.

After the Moors have all been driven out of the Kingdom of Granada and distributed over the whole of Spain, it is taken for granted that this war has now been brought to an end. Now, however, in many localities where the Moors have been apportioned, there have appeared maladies, like Modora and Petechia fever. Complaints are made that the Moors, who have suffered so much hunger and destitution, have brought the said diseases with them. In this cold winter, which in December and January has been the severest for many years, these illnesses have taken root and it is to be feared that new ones may develop with the coming of the summer heat.

14. The Battle of Lepanto

Copy of a News-Letter from the Christian Armada, sent on the 8th day of October 1571.

As soon as the Christian Armada arrived at 6 o'clock in the evening in the little channel of Cephalonia, it was at once espied by the crafty Turkish Armada, which lay in the

Gulf of Lepanto. This is not to be wondered at, for the pirate Caragoggia offered the Turkish commander to inspect the Christian Armada and to count its ships, which he achieved with such skill that he suffered no damage thereby. Perhaps he was over hasty in this or prevented by some unknown cause from giving the correct number of our galleys. Thereupon, the wind being very favourable, the Turkish Commander began preparations for battle with great joy, and took on board twelve thousand men over and above the soldiery he had in the Armada. Thus, thanks to divine Providence and Fate, he robbed himself of an advantage, contrary to all usage of sea warfare. Don Juan of Austria also set sail with his Armada and sent ahead several galleys to inspect the enemy. Moreover, he sent forth six galleons from the harbour. These reported that the Turkish Armada was already nearing, and not far from Cephalonia. Thereupon Don Juan attired himself in a light suit of armour and boarded a small ship, called a frigate. Holding a crucifix in his hand, he visited one galley after the other, appointing to each its proper place in the battle and exhorting the crew to fight valiantly against the arch-enemy of the Christian Faith. Not he, but Christ, who had died for us upon the Cross, was the Father of all, and the Patron of this Armada, and he hoped that they would find help and sustenance in His mercy. Thereupon the whole soldiery sent forth great shouts of jubilation and forthwith placed themselves in battle formation. Whereafter the above mentioned Don Juan of Austria again entered his galley and went out to meet the Turkish Armada. Then the sea became quite still and the galleasses, which had sailed ahead, opened with heavy fire which brought great damage and terror to the Turks, causing them to cry: "Maom, Maom!" which means in their language "Big ships, big ships with big cannon!" Thus the Turkish Armada, which had been sailing ship to ship in half-moon formation, fell into disorder and was split into three parts. The first and largest part attacked the left wing of the Christian Armada, the second the centre and the third the right wing, which was led by Don Andrea Doria, who had lost almost all his fighters on ten of his galleys at the outset of the fight, although they had put up a most valiant and brave defence. It would have fared ill with him had not several galleys from the centre squadron come to his rescue, which help instilled fresh courage into his men, so that they forced the enemy again to withdraw. The left wing also put up a brave and gallant fight, but it also would have been in a sorry plight had not the rear, led by the Marques de Santa Cruz, come to relieve it, attacking the enemy in such fashion that the scales of victory turned completely in our favour. There also sprang up a wind to our assistance. In the smoke of battle Uluch Ali escaped. It is unknown whether he has fled to Africa or to the Gulf of Lepanto. Of forty of the principal galleys, of which we captured twenty-nine, one only was he able to save. Our general, Don Juan of Austria—whose achievements I should have reported first of all—rammed with his galley that of the Turkish commander, finally captured it, cut off the head of the Turkish Pasha with his own hand and placed it at the end of a spear of his own galley. The galley of Don Vittorio Colonna was attacked by two Turkish ones, fore and amidships, but he defended himself valiantly and was finally rescued, and thus was victorious. The Venetian Chief, Venier by name, who is seventy years of age, appeared, clad in light armour, on his own galley, at the head of all and fought right valiantly alongside his men, so that he captured Ali Pasha and his vessel. Don Barbarigo also carried himself like a true knight in this battle. An arrow pierced his right eye and he died in great pain and greatly to the sorrow of those near to him.

In this battle Don Quirin and Don Andrea Doria, Don Ascanio della Corina, Signor Fabio Serbelon, Don Pompeo Colonna, Don Prospero Colonna and Orsini with their attendant knights, Spaniards and Italians both, fought with such bravery that it cannot be fittingly recounted in so scant a space. The battle began on the 7th day of this month, two hours after daybreak, and within five hours the Christians had achieved victory with the help of the Lord. Almost all the Turkish nobles and nearly eighteen thousand men were killed, ten thousand taken prisoner, and fifteen thousand Christians, who had been slaves on the Turkish galleys, were set free. These latter caused the Turks much harm when the battle began. On several galleys there were also found a large number of Sultanas and Zechines and on Caragoggia's galley a beautiful young woman, a Christian. She was daintily and richly attired and her neck adorned with large pearls and other precious

41

stones and jewels. She offered to buy her release with 60,000 ducats.

As far as can be gathered in all haste, on our side twenty Venetian noblemen and several thousand men lost their lives. One hundred Turkish galleys are captured, sixty have been sent to the bottom. Plans are being concerted to take the greatest advantage from this victory and to pursue Uluch Ali, who has made his escape. Through God's special grace the generals and colonels are all of one mind and well satisfied with each other.

Praise and glory be to God Almighty and His Blessed Mother in all Eternity. Amen.

15. The Norfolk Conspiracy

Antwerp, October 27, 1571.

London letters state that this Queen has again arrested many gentlemen and continues to do so daily. Amongst them is the Duke of Norfolk. They have been laying a fresh plot to kill the Queen, to proclaim a new King, to set free Her Majesty of Scotland and marry her to the newly proclaimed King. But the plan has failed this time, and several of them will lose their heads. To this nation will happen what befell the Frogs. They would not have the Log for King, and so the Stork was given to them and he ate them all up. What will occur next time will show.

16. Swedes and Muscovites

Danzig, July 20, 1572.

In Moscow the scarcity is so severe that the Grand Duke has been unable to put more than a hundred thousand men into the field. Because of his tyranny the people are unruly. Last winter the King of Sweden treated them pretty roughly with thirty thousand men. Now in summer fighting is impossible, but in winter it can begin again.

On an island near Narva the Swedes with a few thousand men have blocked all traffic and navigation, and quite recently drove back an English ship laden with cloth and salt. It has now arrived here in Danzig, bringing all its papers.

Sweden, Poland and their neighbours have combined to stop all imports into Russia, so the Muscovite has sent the King of Denmark a quantity of money in order that the sea passage through the Sound may not be blocked. In consequence Imperial and Local Councils are to be held in Sweden and Denmark, and at Lübeck as capital of the Hanse Towns, to agree about access to Russia and to select with all due deliberation some suitable spot on the Baltic as market place and repository.

17. Atrocities in Russia

News-Letter from Moscow (undated) 1572.

The only fresh news I have to report at this time is that the Muscovite himself ravages and despoils his own land and nation. The folk are pitilessly and cruelly killed in their thousands in all towns and many villages. They freeze to death and perish by violent means. Corn, cattle, and all else which is needed for man's sustenance is burnt, corn is scattered in the street and the fields and altogether much wanton damage is wrought.

18. St. Bartholomew's Eve

From Amsterdam, the 30th day of August 1572.

Of the extraordinary happenings which took place in Paris a few days ago, Your Honour, without doubt, will already have heard through other channels. If not, then be it made known to you that the Admiral of France was on his way on horseback to court on the 22nd day of this month. As he was reading a letter in the street, a musket was fired at him from a window. He was but hit in the arm, yet stood in danger of his life. Whereupon it is said that the King evinced great zeal to probe into this matter. With this the Admiral did not rest content, but is reported to have said, he well knew who was behind this, and would take revenge, were he to shed royal blood. So when the

King's brother, the Duke of Anjou, and the Guises and others heard of this, they decided to make the first move and speedily to dispose of the whole matter. On the night of the 23rd day of this month they broke into the Admiral's house, murdered him in his bed, and then threw him out of the window. The same day they did likewise unto all his kin, upon whom they could lay their hands. It is said that thirty people were thus murdered, among them the most noble of his following, and also Monsieur de La Rochefoucauld, the Marquis de Retz, the King's bastard brother, and others. This has been likened unto Sicilian Vespers, by which the Huguenots and the Gueux of this country had their wings well trimmed. The Admiral has reaped just payment. We hear that the Prince and his retinue are being watchful that no such fate befall them. Truly, potentates do not permit themselves to be trifled with, and whosoever is so blind that he cannot see this learns it later to his sorrow. Since the Admiral, as has been reported, has now been put out of the way, it is to be supposed that all his scheming plots and secrets will be brought to the light of day. This may in time cause great uproar, as it is more than probable that many a one at present regarded as harmless was party to this game.

19. The Vicissitudes of Trade

Seville, January 17, 1573.

The officials of the Casa de Contractation are despatching with all speed news received last night that a small boat arrived from New Spain announces that the fleet which left here last July bound to that country reached there safe after a rapid voyage. But the harbour on the island of San Juan de Lua has been burnt down and the goods unloaded there, belonging to the merchants, have suffered damage to the value of seventy to eighty thousand pesos. There is always much labour and sorrow in traffic with New Spain.

20. The Driving Forth of the Jews from Vienna

From Vienna, the 15th day of December 1572.

His Imperial Majesty has recently issued here a general
decree, which has also been posted in all parts, that all
Jews who have until this day been domiciled in His
Majesty's lands, greatly to the detriment of the inhabitants
thereof, are to depart with their kith and kin, between now
and the coming Palm Sunday. By this decree also, all and
sundry privileges, even those bestowed before His
Majesty's time, are annulled and withdrawn.

21. Disturbances caused by Students in Paris

From Paris, the 12th day of February 1573.

On the 5th day of February, being the first Sunday in
Lent, the Queen Mother of France drove with her daughter, the Queen of Navarre, and other Princes and Attendants of the Court, about vesper time to the College of
Jesuits to hear the reading of vespers. She was escorted by
M. de Lorraine, M. de Bourbon and three Cardinals driving and on horseback. The students of Paris, who are wont
to indulge in scuffles with the servants of the Court, had
collected in bands outside the College, where they began
quarrelling and brawling with the muleteers. When the
courtiers and the Princes came out of the College and were
about to bestride their horses and enter their coaches, the
students attacked them with rapiers and cudgels, surrounded the carriages with great turbulence, thrust their
hands into the bosom of the Queen of Navarre and mock-
ingly stroked her plumes. The Cardinal de Lorraine they
pushed into the deepest hole in the deepest mud. The aged
Queen they not only assaulted with unsheathed foils, but
also insulted in obscene, foul and lewd terms, which it
would be shameful to repeat. The reason thereof had
not been imparted to me, neither what devilry drove
them unto such disorderly conduct.

The King, with just cause, has been very greatly incensed thereat and has had it announced on the 9th day of February that any student is forbidden, on pain of death, to show his face in the streets. Desiring to see with his own eyes whether the students were obeying his command, he rode on that same day on horseback, clad in armour and his face hidden by a mask, surrounded by a few servants, into that part of the town where the students live, which is known as La Université. Mercifully nothing occurred, for those who instigated the disturbances kept wisely at home. The King has commanded the authorities to investigate the affair and to throw the culprits into the Tower. Many who left their lodgings at night were cast into the common prison. Sentence has not yet been passed on them.

22. Famine in France

From Paris, the 4th day of June 1573.

The land this year has not been tilled in many places and people have been ruined to such an extent by the soldiery that they now perish from hunger and die. One who has seen this with his own eyes in many places, informs me that the people cut the unripe corn from the tilled fields and eat it. Altogether there is said to be great misery and poverty. About three thousand persons thus reduced to destitution came before the King at Fontainebleau, and followed His Majesty so that he might cause bread to be distributed among them. Riots were feared here, for in recent days corn has become dearer by one half. Precautions were therefore taken and those who had corn stored away were compelled to bring part of it to the market. Thus it was brought to pass that what cost in the forenoon twenty-one and twenty-two was offered in the afternoon for seventeen. On the other hand it is reported that the rabble is again preparing to loot and that this time it is to be the turn of the parliament and other noble houses. Therefore it is intended to adopt measures to prevent these things from taking place. Unfortunately those who brought the corn to market are taking it away again. The opinion is held that this poverty and distress will induce the King to conclude a speedy peace with the Huguenots.

23. The Coronation of Rudolf II in Regensburg

From Regensburg, the 4th day of November 1575.

On All Saints' Day there took place in the Cathedral of St. Peter of this town the coronation of the most august Sovereign, Rudolf, Roman Emperor Elect, accompanied by the customary ceremonies. There were present all the Electors and other Princes. The Archbishop of Mayence celebrated High Mass, and as the procession left the church two men on horseback scattered silver coin amongst the people. These bore on one side: "Rudolf II, elected King of Rome on the 22nd day of October 1575," and on the other "Crowned on November 1st, 1575." It also showed a picture of an altar with six balls, over which stood: *"Consentientibus Nobis."* The crowds in the streets and on the square before the Town Hall were enormous. In the Town Hall seven tables were spread for the Electors. In front of the Town Hall a large ox was roasted, stuffed with all sorts of animals. There was also a fountain from the eight spouts of which there flowed red and white wine. The Emperor gave a magnificent banquet, at which each Elector had a table to himself. On the next day the King gave a second banquet for those who came from afar. The Elector of Brandenburg was the first to leave, for he had received news of the dying condition of his Consort.

24. English Money for the Netherlands

Antwerp, January 3, 1578.

This week the Marquis de Havré arrived in Brussels from England. He had a gracious farewell from the Queen and brings good news for the governments of these countries. Her Majesty has granted them a fresh loan of eight hundred thousand florins. This is confirmed in letters from London of the 23rd ult. M. de Havré brings a small amount with him in cash and a Royal Letter Patent or Authorization for the governments to raise the money on Her Majesty's account. She gives her own guarantee, and in addition the Parliament and the City of London consent to pledge themselves as principal sureties to repay the money within a definite period. The general opinion is that there will be no lack of lenders, as investment on such security is safe. Should, however, none be found in this country, it is supposed that the government will send some one to Germany with orders to raise money there. We shall soon see what success the government will meet with. It will be necessary to remind them of their debt to Messrs. Fugger in order either to bring in the money or to get good security for it. God grant they may pay much of it off. We should then endeavour to put things in order for you and make a good profit. If we cannot obtain this security, and war should break out again with Don John of Austria, there will be serious risk of getting nothing back at the moment. May the Almighty deign that things grow better than they seem like to.

They say the Queen is sending the government a regiment of English mercenaries, and has offered three months' pay for them at her own expense. So there will be plenty of men on both sides and the only question is which paymaster will hold out longest.

25. Death of King Sebastian of Portugal

From Lisbon, the 22nd and the 25th days of August 1578.

I cannot hide from you the regrettable and unheard-of disaster which befell our King and his whole army in Africa. On the 3rd day of this month, our King marched forward to encounter the enemy, meaning to arrive at Alcazar on the same day. Now it happened that Mome Malucho was lying in wait for the King's forces outside Alcazar with fourteen thousand men on horseback and on foot, and he sent an advance guard of about four thousand mounted troops in order to skirmish with them. This filled our King with gladness, so that he ordered his whole army to advance. The Captains of the Germans and the Italians did not deem this wise and they came of their own accord to the King to inform him that the soldiery were in no fit condition, and, moreover, tired, because they had had naught to eat for a long while. They craved therefore that

48

they might be allowed to entrench themselves and to wait until provisions and more fighters were brought up from the fleet. The King had in all not more than twenty-three thousand men on foot and sixteen hundred on horseback. The remainder of his forces he had left behind with his fleet or had bidden them to accompany the Sheriff, Mulei Mehemed, who had marched on Masegna, and whose father fell in the ensuing battle. But when the King had listened to the counsel of both Commanders, he shook his head and said: "Let us march, let us march!" He ordered such great haste to be made that the cannon, which had formerly headed the army, was finally left behind and in the end unable to come to their assistance. Thereupon the King in person, with his horsemen, began the skirmish with four thousand men. In the meanwhile more and more Turks joined in, until at last their whole army hastened on the scene in half-moon formation, surrounding our forces and taking the cannon, which fired from behind, but could hit no one but our own men.

The Portuguese nobility withstood the onslaught for an hour, but they almost all fell on the battlefield. Likewise the Germans, Italians and Spaniards sold their lives dearly. But no more than ten or twelve of them came away alive. The rest were slain with their captains. But the Portuguese infantry surrendered at an early hour. Some of them shot first and then ran away, and some let their blunderbusses drop and surrendered.

Our King bore himself right bravely, and, so it is said, killed many Turks with his own hands, but at last, after he had mounted the third horse, he disappeared so that no one has found him either alive or dead until this hour.

Among the noblemen, of whom not more than sixteen are left, there is also the son of the Duke of Braganza, a young Lord, who drove in a gilt coach to meet the enemy. He had a thousand riflemen with him which his father had given him for his protection. But these were all mown down, and the young Lord was taken from the carriage, for he was believed to be the King. The Turks threw him twice into the air for joy, but he cried out that he was not the King, but the son of the Duke of Braganza, and besought them that his life might be spared as his father would ransom him with much money. With this the Turks were well satisfied.

When this sorry news came unto us, you can well imagine how great were the lamentations, the despair and the grief, not only in this city, but in all the land. The men went about as if dazed. The wailing of the women was so loud that it can be compared with that which arose at the taking of Antwerp. It is a woeful matter to lose in one day the King, their husbands, their sons, and all the goods and chattels they had with them. But what is even more terrible is that this kingdom now must fall under Spanish rule, which they can brook the least of all. May God Almighty therefore perform a miracle by our pious old Cardinal, who is a man of sixty-four, and grant him a male heir. It is also said that His Highness is willing to marry for the sake of this kingdom. Although there were others of the royal blood, such as the Infant Antonio, they have all fallen in this battle. Not one is left but our Cardinal, who made his way here at once on receiving the pitiful tidings. As is reported, the pledge of loyalty will be sworn unto him next week.

Otherwise business here continues as though nothing untoward had taken place. The ships that arrived from India are being unloaded, the merchants ply their trade and go to sea; it is the nobility and soldiers alone who have perished. No merchant has suffered thereby since they all stayed behind. The four regents whom the King appointed to rule the kingdom in his absence were ratified in their office by the Cardinal. The Government and officials deal with the people in so friendly a manner that every one is astounded thereat. In spite of these terrible tidings no riots have occurred and if a stranger, who had never been here before came to this city, he would swear by all that is holy that no ill-fortune has befallen this kingdom for one hundred years.

This letter has lain here for lack of news until the 25th. To-day definite information arrived that our King fell in battle and was taken by the Moors to one of their cities, Alcazar by name. His adversary, the Moorish King Malucho, and the other Sheriff have also perished, therefore in one and the same battle three Kings and many noblemen on both sides were slain.

The Cardinal was appointed yesterday Governor of the Kingdom by the Council, and, as decisive news of the

King's death has been received, he is to be elected King to-morrow.

26. Coronation of King Henry of Portugal

Short report on the ceremonies attendant on the bewailing of the late King Don Sebastian and the election of the Cardinal of Portugal, Don Enrique, as King.

On the 27th day of August of the year 1578 a nobleman stepped forth from the Town Hall in Lisbon, clad in black brocade, wearing a long robe closed in front, and trailing behind. Outside the Town Hall he bestrode a horse decked in black. He was given to hold in his hand a large black flag which he let trail on the ground. Three men went before him who were robed in long black cloaks which they also let drag far behind them. Each of them carried a wooden shield. First they went as far as the big church and one of them mounted the highest step and cried out aloud: "Citizens, I give you tidings that your King Don Sebastian is dead!" Thereupon he splintered his buckler against the stone steps. Then they went to the Rua Nova, cried the same news there and broke the second buckler. From there they went to the Hospital where they destroyed the third one. These four men were followed by all the officials of the city, clad in black silken cloaks, also by innumerable crowds who wept pitifully and cried aloud: "Oh! what shall we do?" They kicked one another with their feet and tore their hair. They also ran against the walls with their heads and did other things that were passing strange. The next day, on the morning of the 28th, between eight and nine o'clock, the Cardinal rode from the Palace of the Duke of Braganza, where he had lived, and went on his way to the Hospital. He sat on his mule, which was harnessed in beautiful red cloth, and he was clad in a long red robe. On his head he wore a Cardinal's hat. Three counts led the mule by the halter. All the noblemen present in Lisbon—there were but few of them on account of the African battle—preceded him bareheaded and behind him went all the officials, Alcaldes and such like. Then followed six trumpeters on horseback clad in red and

51

white damask and then three mounted drummers in black. Then came six men on horseback each of whom held a large, heavy silver mace in his hand and thereafter nine heralds in handsome doublets. They had the King's coat of arms on back and front. Behind them rode the Duke of Braganza on a beautiful steed. He carried in his hand an unsheathed gilt sword. On his right walked Don Juan Delo. Near the Hospital there had been erected a high tribune. The Cardinal stepped on to this and took his place on a delicately wrought royal chair. In front of him there stood a table on which lay a book. When the Cardinal was seated a nobleman prostrated himself at his feet and tendered the royal sceptre unto him. Thereupon the Secretary Miguel de Moto took his oath that he would respect the privileges and liberties granted to the country by its former Kings. He then returned again amidst the sound of the trumpets and the kettledrums with unfurled standards to the house of the Duke of Braganza, who with the heralds rode ahead of him with unsheathed sword. The heralds called out in loud tones throughout the city: "Real! Real! Real!" These cries were heard almost all day. May Almighty God give unto this King a long life and make his rule felicitous.

27. Murders in Paris

From Paris, the 5th day of December 1578.

Of news we have none, save that on the last day of November the Secretary of the Duke of Florence, who together with the Ambassador has been here a year or two, was taken into custody by the Court Provost by order of the King. It is supposed that this was done because of several murders which were committed here some time ago, and which the Duke of Florence is said to have instigated. Not long since he caused Don Troilus d'Orsini to be shot at night by his servants between the hours of eight and nine. Suspicion falls upon him because the said Troilus stood in too close a friendship with the Duke's sister. Some fourteen days ago, a Florentine, of the name of Capitano Bernardo, was shot in the suburb of St. Germain. The culprit was caught and put to the rack. After all his members had been broken, he was given water to drink twice as he lay on the wheel. It was only then that much information was gained from him, and it is said he confessed that he had taken money from the said Secretary to commit this and the other crime. The culprit was an Italian who has already done six people to death.

28. *Auto de fé* in Seville

Report of the persons who were brought as penitents to the public auto de fé, held by the Holy Court of the Inquisition upon Sunday the 3rd day of May in the year 1579.

First: Orbrian, a native of Flanders, inhabitant of the city of Xeres de la Frontera, a binder by trade, in his thirtieth year. He had burnt different paintings with the picture of our Lord Jesus Christ and other saints thereon and had put his faith entirely in the teachings of Luther, considering them to be the truth. He had also ventured to teach others. He, showing great stubbornness on account of this, was condemned and handed over to the arm of secular justice, so that he be burnt alive and all his goods and chattels be confiscated.

Second: Juana de Perez, a Portuguese, a woman of forty, domiciled at Riamonto. She was of the Jewish faith and held it through many years, practising its commands and ceremonies and also instructing other persons therein. She has confessed and been reconciled to Holy Church. Will be punished by taking the veil and perpetual seclusion. Her goods and chattels will be confiscated.

Third: Juan de Color, a black, from Rafao, slave of Juan de la Romo, in his thirty-fifth year. He reviled the name of Our dear Lady and other saints when pronounced in his presence. He has, likewise, despised Her miracles. He has been reconciled and punished by taking the habit and two years of imprisonment. Thereafter he is to be restored to his master.

Fourth: Ginos Raros, Englishman, master gunner on the galleon *Granada* in his fortieth year. He has fought with the Catholic Christians in the following of Juan Alquino and has comported himself by land and sea as is the custom among Lutherans. He has been reconciled, and punished with the habit and perpetual prison. The first twelve years he is to serve on the galleys and pull the oars.

Fifth: Fernando Morisco, in his twenty-second year. He has fled from a galleon into Barbary and has disavowed his Holy Faith. He committed robbery on a galliot against God's commandment and was therefore taken prisoner as a corsair. He has been reconciled. He has been punished with the habit and perpetual prison. He is to spend the first year on a galley.

Sixth: Joanna Macozuo, a virgin, domestic and sick-nurse in a nunnery at Seville. She has confessed to having been tempted repeatedly and having visions of the Evil One through which she came to believe various things that are against our Holy Catholic Faith. Whereas she doubted, she has been permitted to return to the Faith. But the habit was taken from her. She is to remain for two years wherever she may be ordered to betake herself, and there fast on Fridays for one year.

Seventh: Luis Morino desired to sail with others to Barbary but has been reconciled. He was punished with the habit and four years' imprisonment. There he is to be instructed in the tenets of the Faith and punished with one hundred strokes of the rod.

Eighth: Alfonso Morisco from the Kingdom of Granada. Like offence, like punishment.

Ninth: Voror Morro, slave of Juan Matthias has incited the aforementioned. Was punished with one hundred strokes of the rod.

Tenth: Thomas Morro. Like offence, like punishment.

Eleventh: Maria, a virgin, daughter of Juana de Perez. She has, in company with others, given herself up to Jewish practices. She was subjected to penance so that she should recant. She has confessed and is to remain six years in prison.

Twelfth: Lorenzo Martin in his thirtieth year. He has said that one should confess to God and not to man. That it is mockery to confess to priests and that the speech and faith of Moors and Christians are alike. He has been subjected to penance and will be kept three months in prison.

Thirteenth: Juan Corineo, a Moor, wanted to sail to Barbary and has said: "Our dear Lady did not conceive as a virgin." Has been punished with one hundred strokes of the rod.

Fourteenth: Fray Juan de Spinosa, of the Order of the Holy Trinity. Has said Mass and heard Confession without having been ordained. Has been subjected to penance, so that he be detained six years in a cloister of the Order. As long as he lives, he will not be ordained.

Fifteenth: Juan de Montis, a Moor, has married twice. One hundred strokes of the rod and ten years on a galley.

Sixteenth: Juan Garcia and Fernando Domos, like offence, like punishment.

Seventeenth: Consalvo de Noguera and Bartholomeo Gonzales for a like offence one hundred strokes of the rod and four years on a galley.

Eighteenth: Pedro Galigo, like offence, like punishment.

Nineteenth: Francis Gonzales, inhabitant of Cadiz, one hundred strokes of the rod and three years on the galley, and Maria de Soto, both on account of marrying twice. She recanted on the pillory and was banished from the district for three years.

Twentieth: Pedro Fernandez, a Portuguese, for bearing false witness in matters of marriage and Rodrigo Fernandez for a like reason one hundred strokes of the rod each.

Twenty-first: Ines de Campo for bearing false witness in matters of faith, three hundred strokes of the rod and banishment for six years from Seville. Her daughter Isabella de Palareos for like reason two hundred strokes of the rod and banishment for six years from Seville.

Twenty-second: Fernando Copos, a Portuguese, and Juana de Ramora have averred that fornication is no sin. Have renounced and disclaimed their crime. They were publicly shamed by being led through the town.

Twenty-third: Isabella Sanchez, Carolona Vandola, Phillippa de Color, a seamstress, Alfonso de Sansiago, Caspar Sanchez, like offence, like punishment.

Twenty-fourth: Francisco Berocano has said that it is no sin if a woman goes to a man and they copulate. Has disavowed his words as frivolous.

Twenty-fifth: Isabella Diaz, a Portuguese, has said that it is no sin to sleep with a strange man. Same punishment.

Twenty-sixth: Diego de Robloz has greatly blasphemed God. Three hundred strokes of the rod and three years on the galleys.

Twenty-seventh: Victorio Rigo has blasphemed God. Two hundred strokes of the rod.

Twenty-eighth: Antonio Martin and Juana Batista, a Moorish woman. Like offence, like punishment.

Twenty-ninth: Sebastian Garcia. For a like reason put into the pillory with a rope round his neck.

Thirtieth: Juan Francis for a like reason put into the pillory with his tongue tied and a rope round his neck. Likewise, Elena Nigra, Juliana Morisca, Anna de Cranco, a Mulatto, and Martha, a Mulatto.

Thirty-first: The Baccalaureate Andreas Perez, priest of San Salvador in Seville, was on account of various misdemeanours, necromancy and invocation of the Devil, subjected to penance and imprisoned for one year, under deprivation of priesthood.

Thirty-second: Andreas Conseno, a peasant, has said that one must not confess one's mortal sins to priests, because they are men. Has recanted in a public *auto de fé* and received one hundred strokes of the rod.

Thirty-third: Fernando Anias, an embroiderer in silks has said: "It is of no account to God whether we fast or not—neither should we worship the pictures." Has forsworn his crime in public *auto de fé*.

Thirty-fourth: Casparo Sanchez has said that God is not present in the Host.

Thirty-fifth: Francisco Roman has said that it is not needful to pray for the souls in purgatory. Both have forsworn their crime.

Thirty-sixth: Juan Francisco has oft-times blasphemed God and said that this was no sin. Has forsworn his crime.

Thirty-seventh: Juan Garcia has uttered divers blasphemies, with regard to Our dear Lady. His tongue was pinioned, a cross was given into his hand and a cord placed round his neck and he was beaten two hundred times with a rod.

Thirty-eighth: Juan Astruez, a locksmith, Juan Lipiotol and Fernando Gil have said that they were relations of the Inquisitors. Since this is not true, they have had a rope placed round their necks and have been exposed to public shame.

Vale! I rejoice that this is at an end.

29. A Christ taken Prisoner

From Seville, the 8th day of June 1579.

Of news we have none of import to give you these days. But a curious occurrence recently took place five miles from here, in a village, St. Ginar by name. An inhabitant thereof took refuge in the church to escape his creditors. But whereas, according to custom, on the day of the Blessed Sacrament, all kinds of entertainment were to take place before the Procession of the Blessed Host, some inhabitants had erected a cart, on which they wished to hold a mystery play showing how our Lord Jesus Christ was captured by the Jews as he was kneeling on the Mount of Olives. But they stood in need of a stately and beauteous man and knowing of none more worthy or better looking, they craved of the man, who had taken refuge in the church because of his debts, that he would play the part of the Lord God in their play. He resisted for a long time as he dared not leave the church on account of those to whom he owed money, but the others gave him the assurance that they would bring the cart, on which the play was to be held, in front of the church; where he could mount and descend and need not harbour fear. Thereupon the latter consented. But when one of his creditors learnt this, he bethought himself of many ways in which he could have his debtor seized and thrust into prison. To that end he held counsel with an Alguazil, who informed him that he had a good friend who would play the part of Judas in the said performance. This man he would present with half a dozen ducats and instruct him that, when they arrived on the Market Place, and Judas gave our dear Lord the kiss, he should likewise give him a strong push, so that he might fall from the cart. Once he touched the ground he would immediately be made prisoner. This proposal pleased the creditor greatly. He thereupon gave the Alguazil some money and promised him more as soon as he had got his debtor into prison. Thus, when the procession reached the market, where the Alguazil and his minions were lying in wait, Judas at once strove to carry out his purpose, and with the Jews pro-

57

ceeded to approach the Lord, whom he took to the tail of the cart, where he gave him so forcible a kiss and a push, that he fell to the ground. The Alguazil captured him then and there; but as the good Lord was looking most woefully at his disciples, St. Peter, who stood next to him with his sword, took pity upon him and almost cleft the Alguazil's head in twain. Thereupon a great turmoil ensued in the whole village, so that the Justice intervened and arrested St. Peter, the Lord, and Judas with all his Jews. Thereupon the Judge proclaimed: sententia, Firstly, Judas to be given the birch for a scoffer of God. Secondly, the Alguazil to have himself physicked at his own cost. Thirdly, St. Peter to be set free, as a pious and faithful apostle, and the Lord likewise. The merchant to forfeit that which the Lord owes unto him and to make no further demands upon him for all eternity.

Of this, for lack of better news, have I wished to give tidings unto you.

30. Tournaments in Prague

From Prague, the 15th day of June 1579.

On the 5th day of this coming month of July, Christopher Popel, the Chamberlain of His Royal and Imperial Majesty, is to hold his nuptials with the daughter of the late Molard, here in Prague, where, at the same time as other frolic, there will be held such like jousts, at which Duke Ferdinand of Bavaria will be Mantenator, as are set forth in the challenge attached hereby. Above all be it known that: whereas the lofty and supreme Pallas, the Goddess of Wisdom and Arms has heard the news that the Knights of the far-famed and illustrious Roman Court exercise themselves in an elegant, yet manly fashion, in all manner of knightly prowess, with assiduity, diligence, zeal and fervour, she has derived therefrom no little joy, being a lover and patron of such arts. To encourage Knights to even greater perseverance and ardour in the exercise of armed skill, and to restrain them from idleness from which spring vice and mischief of all kinds, also to fire them with greater zest in the practice of jousts, she has recalled from the Campis Elysiis, the mighty Knight Philotetus of

58

Greece, who performed such doughty deeds at the siege of Troy and showed himself specially versed in the arts of joust, above all others. Him she sent to the Royal Capital of Prague, in order that he might there promote a new joust with the honourable knighthood. All this she does the more willingly, since she learnt that in the coming month of July there is to take place a notable and stately wedding in the aforementioned city of Prague, at which, doubtless many a good Knight will be present. Therefore, the great Goddess aforenamed wishes one and all of the knighthood to know that they have been asked to attend upon the 6th day of the coming month of July at 12 o'clock at noon, in the square Philocteti, in Prague, in order to essay a new and famous joust under the aforementioned Knight Philotetus as Mantenator. To prove more clearly the pleasure and delight which the mighty Goddess takes in the knighthood and their love of jousts, she has decreed that her own picture or statue be erected on the said square, so that it may serve for this new joust and also act as a fresh incentive, and instil into the whole knighthood even greater joy and enthusiasm. She will also be present at the time stated and at the appointed place. In what guise prizes are to be won or lost at this joust, and how people are to deport themselves follows hereunder: The figure erected will hold in its hand an iron ring or an iron target, at which competitors are to tilt or whereon they are to break their spears. The aforementioned Mantenator will run three carreras with each of the competing Venturiers for a Pretium (prize) of ten to one hundred thalers. Likewise such races are to be run in masques without weapons or armour of any sort, iron gloves or such like privilege. To this end each Venturier is to present himself to the Judge in order that it may be seen and proved that he does not have such advantage or make use of it over the Mantenator.

No one is to run with spears other than those which are handed out by the Judges. Whoever, in the three races breaks several spears on the target, will be deemed to have won the Pretium. Two hits are to count for one broken spear. Whoever tilts the spear lower than the target, either in jumping or in running, ere he arrives thereat, and missing it, again raises the spear and then makes a hit or breaks the spear, is to be held as having won the race. Whoever takes his aim before, or in the act of jumping, is to be disqualified. Whoever breaks the spear after the race or in parrying across the shoulder so that it touches the shoulder, is not to be permitted to win. Whoever grasps (or handles) the spear improperly or is lacking in the elegance required from him, is likewise held to have lost the prize. No one is to be allowed to change his steed during the three carreras. If anyone through soreness of foot or other such legitimate cause be prevented from completing the race, he may be permitted to run in another, but should his horse not run properly and so make it impossible for him to finish the race, he will then be held to have lost it.

Should the Mantenator and a Venturier obtain the same points in the breaking of the spear or hitting the target, they are not to run again; but he has won, who, according to the verdict of the Judge has carried himself through the race in the most elegant and seemly fashion. Since it has occurred at various times that the Pretium was accorded even to those who ran with but little grace, the Mantenator craves of the Judges that they keep a keen eye upon the manner in which the race is run because the Mantenator has much to do with the race, and the Venturier but little. This in case he and the Venturier have scored alike in breaking and hitting. The Judges, in order to award the prize, are not to take into account the number of the runs, but the graceful bearing of the competitors during the race. Should doubts arise, they are to be left to the competence of the Judges.

Herewith and finally the Mantenator craves of the Judges that they adjudicate strictly and solely according to this capitulation. This much will the worthy Knight Philotetus always deserve from the Judges.

Thereupon follow the prizes:

Whosoever breaks the first spear most gracefully and felicitously on the target or the ring, is to win the first prize.

Whosoever in three races, breaks the most spears, or makes the most hits also wins a prize.

Whosoever breaks the most spears in a Folia, is to receive accordingly the Folia prize.

Whosoever is hailed by the eminent Goddess as Mascolo, is to win the Mascolo prize.

60

From these four prizes, the Mantenator, as is customary, will not consider himself to be excluded.

31. Portuguese Fears of Spain

Cologne, July 31, 1579.

The Portuguese here have received letters from Portugal of the last day of June and the eighth of July to the effect that their King is very weak and that great scarcity of grain prevails in their country. Many also have died of plague. A great discussion has resulted among the Portuguese about this, since they do not wish to fall under Spanish dominion. The King has got rid of the Duke of Braganza and Don Antonio out of Lisbon by sending one of them to the Spanish frontier, the other to the opposite frontier. Don Antonio is said to have protested. However, he was obliged to leave Lisbon.

32. The Spanish in Ireland

Antwerp, August 8, 1579.

The affair of the Spanish invasion of Ireland is said not to be so serious as was recently stated. Apparently only three ships with seven hundred men have landed in Ireland, wild reckless folk under a leader who is a rebel out of Ireland. The Queen at once sent five well-equipped ships to the place, so there will not be any trouble.

33. More on the Spanish in Ireland

Antwerp, August 22, 1579.

The latest letters from England confirm the statement that the invaders of savage Ireland have already captured three fortresses and slaughtered the garrisons. The longer the invasion lasts the wider it spreads. Moreover, as the country is situated not far from Spain, perhaps that King will take more interest in it and give up his enterprise against Algiers. The Queen at first sent five ships there, and now another four. Also from the City of London and other towns she has despatched several hundred men. It is reported too that a bishop and some monks from Spain have arrived in Ireland, to convert the people. Many Irish are said to have joined them already.

Yet another report has it that the Duke of Alençon has taken ship for England, and that the Queen has gone some distance from London to meet him. We must await the issue of the negotiations.

34. The Swedes attack and plunder Narva

Danzig, August 28, 1579.

Yesterday an English captain came from Narva. He left his ship in the roadstead, came himself on shore for only a few hours, and then quickly went on board again to sail back to England. He relates that on the twenty-eighth of July the King of Sweden with twenty-three well-equipped ships arrived off Narva. The inhabitants were fairly delighted at this for they thought they were English, French, and Netherlandish merchantmen to whom they could sell their wares at a good profit. So part of the people ran from the town to the water's edge to see who they were and when they would land. Some took boats to row aboard the ships. But when they got there the crews stabbed them and threw them into the water. Then a strong detachment landed. When the inhabitants saw that these were enemies they were terrified and ran towards the town with the Swedes after them. The Swedes then rushed and captured the German portion of Narva and slaughtered most of the inhabitants, although they had been ordered to spare the women and children. Then they crossed the water and took the Russian part of Narva also, except the castle which was within the town. As they had no time to loot, they set the place on fire and returned to German Narva which they cleared out completely. Their booty, amounting to several tons of gold, they quickly got on board. The King of Sweden's Admiral in command summoned the English, French, and Low Countries merchants in Narva and reproached them with having supported the enemies of his King and master. They answered that they were merchants seeking their livelihood, and also that they had permits from the King of Sweden. When the Admiral saw these he said they were no use. He told them further that the goods they had already on board the ships lying in the river could remain their property, but anything in the town was forfeited. And he carried it all off to the great hurt of the Lübeckers. He said too that they must at once declare whether they wished to remain Russian, for if so they must go away at once. But if they were ready to serve his master the King of Sweden, then they could stay. To this they answered that they had come not to serve either the one master or the other but to seek their livelihood. However, when they saw that the Admiral was not satisfied with this, they declared that they would much rather serve the King of Sweden than the Muscovite. Upon this he at once put them into his army, so that they had to serve in the war against their will. Then he looted the town completely and set it on fire. The Englishman above mentioned had to help to set light to it. The town was burnt right down except for one house. The Englishman states that he got away at great risk to his life. He says the King of Sweden has taken so much booty that it will enable him to carry on war against the Muscovite for quite a long time.

35. Henry of Navarre takes Fuenterrabia

Antwerp, September 15, 1579.

The latest letters from London of the fifth of this month state that the Duke of Anjou is expected in October with his entire retinue. The presumption is that something is afoot against Spain, for this very evening we learn during business hours from Lyons and Paris correspondents that the King of Navarre has surprised Fuenterrabia, a fortified town on the Spanish frontier, and occupied it with eight hundred musketeers.

36. French Sympathy with Henry of Navarre

Cologne, September 26, 1579.

The news about Fuenterrabia seems to be true, as the Duke of Terra Nova told Aerschote of it himself. The officer commanding the fortress appears to have fallen under the suspicion of the King of Spain because of the death of Escobedo, and so to have surrendered the place. It is thought here that the Spaniards will leave the Netherlands because they are finding enough to do at home, particularly it seems because the league between France, England and Portugal is making progress, and the Queen of England is fitting out forty ships. The Duke of Alençon is alleged to have promised to come to the assistance of the Portuguese if they should be threatened with war by the King of Spain. His brother, the King of France, is said, however, to be very ill, and if he were to die the Duke would not be able to leave the country easily. Nevertheless, he means to send the help promised and give aid to his brother-in-law, the King of Navarre, as well.

37. Letter from Cochin in India

From Cochin in India, the 10th day of January 1580.

Honourable, most kindly and dear Signor Adelgais!

Before my departure from Lisbon I informed you how I with my companions boarded our ships. Upon the 4th day of April 1579 all five vessels sailed from Lisbon at the same time; but we did not, however, keep together for more than six days, but each soon struck out on its own course, since each captain or pilot believes he knows best how to arrive first at the goal. Although these ships are big and powerful, they strive not to stay together. When we had been on our way for a month and had chanced first on the coast of Guinea and later upon the Linea Aequinoxialis, we realized that we had left Lisbon far too late. We had to sail back and forth along this Linea until we could pass it, and in this wise lost forty-seven days.

Since at this time the sun shines at its strongest and hottest, we had to suffer great heat and torment on this voyage. From thence as far as the thirty-fourth degree in the other half of the globe, towards the South Pole or the Pole Antarctico, as far as the Cape of Good Hope, we had a favourable wind and fair weather, but severe cold. From thence onward we experienced several great storms. To tell the truth, I would have preferred then to be elsewhere than on this voyage. God be praised, we came through. But it is an old experience in seafaring that come or go, one has to meet such storms. This danger lasts for one hundred and fifty miles, which one covers in thirty-four days. We then arrived at the twenty-sixth degree off the height of Mozambique. There the King of Portugal keeps a fort and a garrison. But whereas it was late in the year, we were not permitted to land, but stayed out at sea fifty miles therefrom. If we had gone ashore, we should not have been able to leave again. We then came upon the Linea Aequinoxialis which we passed in three days. Thereupon we passed on again to the other side towards the North Pole.

Here in Cochin we are situate on the ninth degree from this line and on the side of Europe. Lisbon lies thirty-nine degrees off this line. In this place it is rather warm since we are just under the ninth degree. We arrived, thanks and praise be to the Lord Almighty, upon the 10th day of October at the town of Goa, which belongs to the King of Portugal and is the finest capital in this country. Thus we have been on our way here from Lisbon six months and six days, and during that time have seen no land, only the sky and the sea. The Lord God bestows on such journeys His special blessing and mercy, for otherwise it would not be possible to spend half a year between the planks. To sum up, whosoever is well equipped with provisions and a cook, both of which were mine, thanks to the Lord, feels the hardships of such a voyage less than the common people, who suffer great distress from lack of food and drink, especially water, which no money can buy. In such heat one cannot partake of much wine, only water, of which, thanks be to God, I had in sufficient quantity with our food. There were about five hundred persons in our ship of whom not more than twenty-five altogether died on the way from Portugal to India. Some of us, who were well provided with food and drink, extended much help to the poor soldiery. In this half year we have traversed five thousand miles. Although for the direct route from Lisbon to India one counts not more than three thousand miles, one covers at all times for each voyage five thousand miles on account of the head winds.

I have seen many kinds of fish, whereof there would be much to write, especially of those that fly above the sea and have wings. This many will not wish to believe, but I have seen them a thousand times fly as near as the musket will carry. What called forth still greater surprise on my part were other big fishes that are in the ocean and that eat men alive, whereof I have been myself a witness. For when a man fell from our ship into the sea during a strong wind, so that we could not wait for him or come to his rescue in any other fashion, we threw out to him on a rope a wooden block, especially prepared for that purpose, and this he finally managed to grasp and thought he could save himself thereby. But when our crew drew this block with the man toward the ship and had him within half the carrying distance of a musket shot, there appeared from below the surface of the sea a large monster, called Tiburon; it rushed on the man and tore him to pieces before our very eyes. That surely was a grievous death.

There were also many kinds of birds upon the sea, among them many which never see land, but always dwell upon the waters. They eat fish and do not fear the people on the ship. We have with our hands caught several of these birds. They are the size of ducks, but are reputed not to be fit to eat, because they smack so strongly of fish.

I have related our journey day by day, and have made therewith a book, which in good time, if God helps me out of this again, I shall bring with me together with many beauteous things. This voyage is of such nature that he who does not experience it himself, could not believe how arduous it is. Thanks be to God, that myself and my men, four young Germans, have arrived here in India fresh and well; but no sooner did we set foot on land, than four young Portuguese servants of mine expired. On the ship eating and much drinking of water causes havoc, and ashore it is dangerous for some time, because of the many fruits, such as figs and other foods. But also there is a danger on account of the women, of whom there is an abundance. From all the ships a good many men died ashore. Until a man gets acclimatized he has to guard himself wisely. Thanks be to God, I am very well.

Our ships have all five arrived from Lisbon, namely, three in Goa and two here. Now all five ships are here in Cochin. I made a sojourn of four weeks in the town of Goa and built me there a house. From thence I travelled one hundred miles onwards by sea. The voyage can be made in ten to twelve days. The ships are loaded with pepper here in Cochin, twenty miles from Calicut, wherefore they all have to come to this place. I shall maintain two establishments, one in Goa and the other here. I have not yet however, resolved upon which shall fall my choice for remaining definitely. Although Goa is the capital in which the Viceroy of Portugal holds his Court, it is wearisome to journey back and forth every year, as I needs must be present in this our pepper store.

Such a pepper store is a fine business, but it requires great zeal and perseverance. It takes six weeks to receive the pepper from the heathen King of Cochin, who is our friend, and to load it into our ships. After the departure of these ships for Portugal I and my servants have but little to do. The pepper business is profitable indeed; when the Lord God grants by His mercy that none of the ships take damage either in coming or going, then the merchants wax rich. With these sailings, all depends upon the right time to take the journey, to wit, during the month of March from Lisbon to this place, and from here to Portugal during the month of January. Also, when this can be arranged, to leave neither place later than upon the 15th day of these months. Then the risk is slight. But it is dangerous to take one's departure later, for then one comes across heavy storms, and has to go by a circuitous route, and often the ships are destroyed. This happens but rarely, provided the ships do not run aground, founder or otherwise come to grief. Great caution has to be practised in these respects.

This year, in my judgment, we shall not dispatch more than four ships with about twenty loads, although we ought to send thirty. We already possess the money, for so large a sum would not be obtainable by loan. What we are lacking this day can be bought, given a good opportunity, after the sailing of these ships for next year. Of all other spices such as cloves, nutmeg, flour and nuts,[1] cinnamon, maces, and various drugs, this year's supplies are going to Portugal. In precious stones little was dispatched this year on account of the war, which the heathen Kings (of which there are many in this country) waged one upon another. Because of this, precious stones cannot come through from inland into our towns since all of them lie upon the shores of the sea.

All that lieth inland belongs to the Indians, heathens and Moors. We boast of the friendship of two or three of these Kings, but the majority are our enemies. Our fleet is continually fighting them at sea. The King of Portugal despite all his power is too weak for this vast country. The King of Spain, if he but took possession of Portugal, would be the right King for these lands. He should take over the whole of India, all the kingdoms and provinces right into China, where it adjoins Tartary, and unite under his rule his Spanish India with the Portuguese municipalities: this he could accomplish with fifty thousand men. Even though the Indian Kings have a goodly number of warriors, and there are many such Kings, they are not good fighters. One Christian can achieve more than six Indians. Besides, these Kings are continually involved in strife and quarrels amongst themselves.

The land in itself is bad, it produces all the corn, rice and meat that is needed, but no wine and no olive oil: it also lacks five or six kinds of fruit. Wine, oil and Dutch cheese are brought from Portugal. The country is equally warm throughout the year, in winter as in summer. There exists no difference in the seasons. In winter it is as hot as in summer, only that it rains throughout the whole winter, which in summer it does not do. The days are of twelve hours' duration all the year round, they grow neither longer nor shorter. The trees and grass remain verdant throughout the year. We have figs here that are as large as the span of the hand, which figs are picked from the trees the whole year round. One may pick them every day, they are the most important and the staple food for rich and poor alike. Then there is yet another fruit, upon which the people live. It grows on beautiful tall trees, which are

---

[1] It has been suggested that this curious entry is a mistranslation, in the original, for a word unusual to the correspondent. The German *Mehl und Nüsse* could, for example, be something like *Melanos,* and might denote some kind of black pepper.

called palms. These bear a fruit of the size and shape of a melon which contains much water. Whosoever does not know or see it, cannot imagine what manner of things can be made from this fruit. Thou canst however completely trust in me, for my information is good.

From this fruit one maketh wine, which is good to drink, also oil which is good for eating and burning, also milk and fat and a special paper on which one can write. This fruit is kept in store rooms. Its husk is used for making wooden crockery, dishes and other things. Moreover, one makes out of these trees all that is needed for navigation, to wit, the ship, mast, sails, nails, ropes, cables, tow, and likewise wooden bricks for roofing houses. These ships carry provisions in food and drink which are also derived from this tree. I have already seen myself ships thus fashioned. It is a strange thing, and I have desired not to omit to advise thee of this with all the other curiosities here. With God's help, I will write to thee in this coming year more particulars about curious customs and strange happenings; but they are as yet new to me, though I have already been in this country for three months. Every day I see new usages about which one might write a large book. I will endeavour, as time goes on, to collect many strange things and after five years, if I continue in my present purpose, to take them home with me. God willing, I shall employ for my home-coming another route, namely, one by land. From here one goes by sea towards Ormus in Arabia, thence to Persia and there one has good opportunity to travel through the Sophi's land and Turkey. As I learn from those that come and go from Italy, this is a very good road, for it is much used. One finds people in Ormus who assure one that they will bring you safely from Ormus to Italy. It appears quite a common thing. I shall, however, inform myself well beforehand since I have the time to do so. By this route it is not quite two thousand miles from here to Italy or Germany and these one can cover within six months: moreover the Holy Land and Jerusalem and other such like places can be visited on the way, and so I feel much more inclined to see something more of these lands, than to go by sea, where one is in hourly peril of the ship suffering damage or being wrecked.

I ought to recount to thee many other such strange things, which however cannot be done at this moment. In the coming year I will send thee a picture to show how every one is dressed here, to wit, bare or naked, men and women. The King and noblemen as well as the common man, only cover their shame. The Portuguese are clad only in very light garments, linen or silk. On account of the heat, woollens cannot be worn. People here have many beliefs and ceremonies. But as time goes, more and more Indians are converted to Christendom though others remain heathens. The Moors and the Jews retain their Faith. In these lands many creeds exist, but in the towns belonging to the Portuguese, the heathens or Indians are mostly converted to the Christian Faith. I also cannot omit to tell you of another custom of this country. All the Kings have always thirty, forty, yes, even one hundred wives, as many as it pleases them to keep. When such a King dies or perishes in battle, these his wives must throw themselves into the fire and burn to death. In many places outside this town it is the custom also among the common heathen people that the widow of a dead heathen must likewise allow herself to be burnt alive. If she does not, she is mocked and derided. There exists still another custom. When a maiden of a noble house or of reputed ancestry marries, her kinsmen strive to persuade the King to sleep with her the first night. Much money is given to him to that end, otherwise she cannot marry. Of such customs there are many more besides this.

Also, I would tell thee that the five ships from Portugal were sent to our master. Thou shouldst know that from the sale of wine, oil, Dutch cheese, fish, paper and other things, usually the greatest profit is derived; this time no gain at all remains. All this has brought in no more than twelve to fifteen per cent., and on the ready cash brought from Lisbon one makes but a profit of twenty-five per cent. The country is no longer as it was formerly, and apart from this, our Viceroy imposes so many new taxes that all commerce diminishes. If he remains here, no good will come of it. I am of the belief, however, that the King of Portugal will send hither another Viceroy when he hears of the doings of this present one. There is no merchandise now that can be sent with profit from here to Portugal.

In precious stones there is nothing this year; in fact this country is not such as is generally imagined. It takes as much trouble to earn money here as in other places.

Things are no longer what they were twenty years ago. Buying and selling here is more profitable than sending many wares to Portugal. German merchandise has no market here and is useless for this country. Writing tables split in the great heat; clockwork, or anything else made of iron, deteriorates at sea. This year there is nothing to send to Portugal, for pepper, ginger, maces, cocoa-nut fat have all been brought for the contractors, also cinnamon for the King. One really does not know at this time in what to invest one's money.

The fisher has imported Dutch cheese, but is not going to derive great profit from it, since much of it was stolen aboard ship. This likewise happened to our stores. In addition, our sales have been bad. Five ships can bring much into port, and thus everything becomes cheap. The Portuguese here are even more diligent than the people in Lisbon. The Pietras de Bezoar are always very dear and not good. After the ships have departed I will try to obtain privately some of these stones that are good, and to send them to thee next year.

38. Death of the King of Portugal. Don Antonio and the King of Spain

Lisbon, February 3, 1580.

On the thirty-first day of last month God the Lord called to himself from out of this vale of tears our Gracious King Don Henrico. At first this mournful occurrence caused no small panic among the common people, but mercifully there has been no disorder hitherto. God grant that peace may continue. Yesterday Don Antonio was here, but he appeared merely because he wants to be elected King. However, he met with little favour and went on at once to Almeria where most of his supporters are. It is to be feared that he will drag many a worthy man down with him to destruction. We shall soon hear whether the King of Spain is going to try to make himself King of Portugal by force. Up to now no news has come through, not even about what he is after with the army stationed around Seville. If he means to take the throne here he will give the Portuguese no time to get reinforcements or support from the French. There is so much talk that one does not know what to believe. Two envoys are said to be going to the King of Spain to try and get him to swear to recognize the man elected by the Cortes. But, as the King of Spain has hitherto not renounced his own claim, I expect he will not take the oath. He is sure to be unwilling to bear the heavy expense for his army to no purpose. The Portuguese, however, refuse point-blank to become Spanish, though I should like to know what they are going to do about resisting. They have not a single soldier in Portugal who has ever seen any fighting or would know how to lead properly. They have no arms for they lost them all in the African war. They have no money and there is fearful scarcity in the country. Moreover the plague is raging everywhere. Yet, with empty hands, they think themselves strong enough for the Spaniards.

39. Rather Turks than Spaniards

Antwerp, February 13, 1580.

Some of the ships expected from Portugal have arrived and this is the news they bring. The Viceroy at Calicut in Portuguese India writes to Lisbon and other towns that they would rather have a revolution and would submit to Turkish rule more readily than to Castilian. So risings have taken place in three ports, which have declared for Don Antonio, who is in exile.

40. Military Preparations in England

Antwerp, February 20, 1580.

We hear from England that this Queen distrusts the Spanish fleet. She is having sixteen ships fitted out and six thousand men recruited in London. She has ordered also all men in the country to take up arms and make ready in case of need. Sixty thousand men are believed to be under arms already. In March Parliament is to meet, and all nobles who support the Crown are to be present, to consider negotiations about the marriage of the Duke of Alençon. But whether this meets the wishes of many English remains doubtful.

41. The Spanish Fleet, what is its Destination?

Antwerp, February 20, 1580.

It is stated here that His Majesty of Spain has embarked six thousand pikemen for Biscay and that the great fleet is almost ready to sail. But where it is to make for is still unknown. The Queen of England, who perhaps has some information, has commandeered all ships in the country small and large and is fitting out all her warships in the utmost haste. Likewise she is calling up the whole population, so that she is supposed already to have collected eighty thousand foot and four thousand horse. Of these she is to send a portion to Ireland and she will also garrison the ports. Our presumption is that all Spanish naval preparations are intended for the Netherlands.

A caravel from New Spain has reached Seville with six hundred arobas of cochineal on board. Another is to follow with a similar cargo. The Indian fleet is said to be bringing eight thousand arobas which will amount to a large sum of money.

42. Spain will get Portugal

Lisbon, February 26, 1580.

To all appearances we shall not get off in this kingdom without some disorder, for I am credibly informed that Don Antonio is plotting in all directions. However, the struggle cannot last long, for all the best people here are in favour of Spain but dare not let it be seen. But when the King of Spain appears here with his army he will be better received than he expects. And he will rather surrender Flanders than this country. The ordinary man will not take this into account, moreover he believes that one Portuguese is worth ten Spaniards. I fancy the authorities set up in this country have an understanding with the Spaniards. I have no doubt that Spain will take possession of Portugal, as is fitting. I hope that then there will be better government and better business.

43. Philip II named aggressor in Portugal

London, March 19, 1580.

About our matrimonial plans rumour varies. Last week
some nobles of the Duke of Alençon's retinue arrived here.
But we hear of no decision and it is conjectured that the
whole marriage discussion has merely taken place because
of the war in the Netherlands. Paris letters report that the
citizens of La Rochelle have captured a Spanish ship
bound for the Netherlands. The Spanish Ambassador has
applied to the King for its release. In the ship were a hundred thousand Spanish double crowns, and all sorts of
valuable merchandise. But the King has detained this
ship on behalf of his brother the Duke of Alençon, so as
to send the money to the insurgents in Flanders.

We hear from Portugal that the decision about the succession was entrusted to the Pope, to His Majesty the
Emperor, and to other Christian potentates. The Spaniards
are successful in the war, but the war guilt must be laid
to the account of the King of Spain.

44. Huguenots of La Rochelle take some Spanish Treasure

London, March 26, 1580.

Nothing has yet been heard here of the Lisbon ships. But
a ship has come in from San Lucar bringing letters of the
fourth and fifth of this month to the effect that the fleet
and likewise the army are arming and gathering about
Cadiz. The Duke of Alva is in command, and it is believed that Portugal is the object. However, as the Portuguese are arming too and refuse so far to recognize the
King of Spain, it is probable that the Spaniards will still
hesitate to use force.

Recruiting is to be recommenced in this country, no
doubt to show the Spaniards that the Portuguese will not
lack support.

The same letters from San Lucar report that some ships

from La Rochelle have captured the despatch caravel of the Indian fleet with some three hundred thousand ducats worth of gold, silver and pearls. Whether she comes from Peru or America is unknown. La Rochelle letters of the eighth of this month report that this ship came in with two others laden with sugar and other things. No decision can yet be got from the King as to whether these ships are to be regarded as prizes or not, so they are lying off the outside of the harbour and are still being treated as friends. But as the Spaniards in Florida have put Frenchmen to a miserable death, they will no doubt now have to pay for it. Our marriage is going backwards rather than forwards. Four more armed ships are to sally forth to deter the Spaniards from attacking Portugal. A Portuguese envoy is here and is on bad terms with the Spaniards, and it is thought that they are striving for war, in order to annex Portugal.

45. An Earthquake

Antwerp, April 16, 1580.

The earthquake felt here, at Bruges in Flanders and also in Zeeland, was experienced on the same day in London in England as well as in France. Some towers and houses collapsed.

46. Civil War in France

Antwerp, last day of April 1580.

London letters of the twenty-third inform us that open war has broken out in France between the King and the Huguenots. Monsieur Valcour, member of the Council of War of Prince Condé, is said to have arrived in London to ask help from the Queen. Monsieur de Gitri has been sent by this Condé to John Casimir, to get him to prepare for a campaign in France. All those of the religion in Picardy are joining Condé. He already has with him some hundred horse and a strong body of infantry. It is reported that the Duke of Alençon is mortally ill or even dead, and

75

that he was poisoned. At Malines the soldiery has behaved
very badly, and the town has had to promise the English
troops fifty thousand florins to leave the place. Our city is
making itself responsible for this amount, and important
citizens of Malines have come here to give themselves as
surety.

47. The English in the Netherlands

Antwerp, May 7, 1580.

They write from London in England on the last day of
April that the Duke of Alençon's envoy has arrived there
and a second one is due. It is supposed that the marriage
will come off after all. Alençon, too, is said to be less ill.
He appears to have overheated himself playing tennis.

Yesterday the English soldiers left Malines and were
replaced by four hundred citizens from this place to protect the town. Besides them, there are in the place three
companies of Scotch and other troops as well. When the
English moved out of Malines, the inhabitants of the town
fell upon them, wounded some and shot down others.

48. The Spanish in Ireland again

Antwerp, May 14, 1580.

Thirty Spanish warships with troops on board are stated
to have appeared off Ireland. With the help of five of the
Queen's warships the country people seem to be offering
determined resistance and to have sunk three of the largest
Spanish ships. The remainder are surrounded, so that they
cannot get to shore, and it is hoped that not one of the
Spanish warships will get away till English reinforcements
come into Ireland. The English are said to have captured
all the fortresses in Ireland and almost the whole country
and to have killed the fortress garrisons.

49. The Spanish Conquer Lisbon

From Lisbon, the 1st day of September 1580.

My neglect in writing to you for so long a time is due to
the war and strife we have had here. For on the 25th day
of August the Duke of Alba conquered Lisbon at the point
of the sword. The saying goes that nigh upon three thousand persons perished on the side of the Portuguese, part
of whom I myself have seen in the outer town. The dead
lay heap on heap like swine. I went in the company of
the Count of Lodràn, who is quartered in our house, to
the field of battle. All the streets are filled with dead men
and horses, so that we had to walk across them as on a
bridge. Some are still alive, one man lifted a foot, another
a hand, yet another his head. Altogether it was a pitiable
sight. The outer town also which is much larger than the
town proper, was plundered for the duration of three whole
days. Everything was taken away. Not a nail in the wall
was left. But no soldiers came into the town, because the
Duke of Alba sternly forbade it. The army is still encamped without the town. Thanks be to God, no harm has
come to us.

Four days ago five ships arrived here from India. One
more was to have come which had sailed this year for Portuguese India, but it turned back on its way. No one can
say what became of the ships that were sent out to meet
the fleet.

50. The Return of Drake

Cologne, October 20, 1580.

Our Antwerp correspondent assures us of the return of
the English Captain Drake, who is a pirate and has been
away for three years. In India, which belongs to the King
of Spain, he has stolen two millions in cash, has passed
through the Staits of Magellan and come back home. If
this is true many pirates and adventurers will follow after
him.

51. Execution of a Bohemian Nobleman for Street Robbery

From Prague, the 30th day of October 1580.

I know nothing of note whereof to write to you, save that at the last session of the Provincial Law Court the beheading of a stately nobleman, of the name of Vodratsky, who had committed robbery, was ordered to take place, on the 20th day of the month. He was a man of about sixty years of age. His estates were worth over one hundred and fifty thousand thalers, and now they have all fallen to his Imperial Majesty. There was much sorrowing on his account, for after he was sentenced, his wife, with four daughters and two sons all prostrated themselves at the feet of the Emperor, the Empress, and the nobles of the land. This scene took place in public in the Diet Chamber and was most pitiable. His Imperial Majesty granted a reprieve, and Vodratsky might be alive and well now, yet he did not wish this, but said that whatsoever punishment was due to him, he was ready to take. Fourteen days earlier he dined with Herr von Brunnenstein, who in vain attempted to dissuade him from his purpose. As he came out, free and unfettered from the palace, he halted outside the Diet Chamber from whence the officers looked down upon him. With these he held converse for nigh on half an hour until the noble lords were moved to tears, for he entreated them on behalf of his children and commended them to their care, so that they might not be driven from his estates. Thereupon he wrote a letter in the Tower wherein he besought the people to forget him. This the aged Herr von Wartenberg, who has Vodratsky's sister for spouse, communicated to His Majesty. Thereupon Herr von Wartenberg, weeping, brought the following message: "The Clerk is to accept this letter and after the sentence has been carried out and Justice has received its due, it is to be read out in public." Whereupon he, Vodratsky, proceeded to his execution halting a long time before Herr von Dietrichstein and praying for his children. He then went valiantly to his death and was beheaded on a black cloth spread upon the ground. Not far from this spot a carriage waited with a bier thereon. The carriage was drawn by four horses draped in black, and behind it was led his favourite steed. When he had been executed, his servants wrapped him in the black shroud, laid him upon the bier and conveyed him to his domain, where he was buried.

There are still many such fellows in this land, and as rumour has it, the names of one hundred and thirty are registered on a list.

52. Drake's Gifts to the Queen

Antwerp, December 3, 1580.

English letters of the twenty-sixth of last month say that the Spaniards and Italians in conjunction with the Irish rebels built a fort and hoped to get hold of some ships. But these latter were surrounded by the Queen's forces, driven ashore and sunk. So there need be no more anxiety about them. Again the news from London is confirmed that Drake the English pirate has presented the Queen with several horses laden with silver and gold from the booty which he got two years ago off the Peru ships. This Drake is said to be again proposing to make a raid on the Peru ships and to try his luck afresh.

53. Spanish Plots in Scotland

Cologne, February 2, 1581.

They hear at Antwerp that the rising in Scotland has been brought about by Spain to prevent the Queen from helping the Low Countries. It is also stated that the King of Spain wants to arrange a marriage for the Queen of Scots when she is let out of prison. All this is baseless conjecture. It is announced too that six weeks ago Philip Strozzi had assembled four thousand French at Nantes and put them on board thirteen or fourteen ships, giving out that he was going to the aid of Don Antonio in Portugal. It is supposed that he has invaded Scotland with them, though no news has come in since his departure from Nantes. But, if he has sailed for Scotland, the Low Countries government will be suspicious of the Duke of Alençon. The Queen of England has summoned Parliament for January 20. It is said that Parliament is to select a ruler for the country and that the Queen is to make known who will ascend the throne after her death. The next letters will tell us more.

54. Trouble in Scotland and Ireland

Cologne, February 3, 1581.

According to reports from Antwerp the Irish rising is far from being as completely quelled as the English say. Besides in Scotland a fresh collision has occurred between Catholics and Protestants. The Catholics demand that the English Queen should release the Queen of Scots from her long imprisonment and freely allow her return to her own country. The English declare that no one but the young King of Scotland shall ascend their throne. Thus considerable discord may arise between the two kingdoms. It is also reported that the Scotch have captured and beheaded their English Viceroy and that Strozzi and his troops have entered Scotland from France, in spite of his having said that he was taking them to Portugal.

55. Religious Feuds in Antwerp

From Cologne, the 20th day of April 1581.

Those of the Reformed Faith in Antwerp now covet the Church of St. Michael, which has been previously refused to the adherents of the Augsburg tenets. It is supposed however, that those aforementioned will obtain not only this church, but finally all the churches. On the 13th day of this month Burgomaster Junius arrived in Antwerp at the Convent of St. Claire with the renegade Abbot of St. Bernard. They urged upon the nuns that it was not good to live so secluded a life, and exhorted them to leave the cloister and to be married. The spouse of the said Abbot is especially reported to have spoken many lewd words.

This is the beginning of an attempt to entice all the clerics from the monasteries and the town of Antwerp.

From Antwerp, the 2nd day of May 1581.

Eight days ago the soldiery and the Calvinists mutilated all the pictures and altars in the churches and cloisters of Belgium. The clergy and near on five hundred Catholic citizens were driven out and several among them cast into prison. Thus an end has been made of the Catholic Faith in Brussels, and Calvinism has been installed in its stead. Since then, the masters of the guilds or brotherhoods, and the artisans, whose ancestors had founded several beautiful chapels and altars in the Church of our Dear Lady, have demanded that they themselves should be allowed to remove from the church the painted pictures and other ornaments. Upon the evening of the Feast of the Ascension they began to pull down the altars, occupied the churches and kept them locked until this day. . . . It is not known whether they will destroy everything within the church, but it is believed that it will come to pass here as it did in Brussels. . . . But as Catholics and Calvinists cannot keep peace with the Lutherans and Anabaptists it will ill serve the promotion of commerce and many persons will leave this town.

From Antwerp, the 6th day of May 1581.

Four ships lie here laden with sculptured and carved statues, bells, brass and stone effigies of saints, brass candlesticks and other such like ornaments from the churches. All these are to be dispatched to Narva and Moscow. The consigners hope to do good business with them.

From Antwerp, the 5th day of July 1581.

In the past days the Calvinists here have wrought much havoc. On the day of St. Jacques they ravaged the Church of Our Lady, the Church of St. Jacques, and the Palace Chapel, as well as the Convent of St. Michel, where up to now the Catholics held their religious exercises and ceremonies, in such fashion that they have wrecked everything therein, with the exception of the organ and a few pictures. They spared nothing and destroyed everything completely. On the 27th day in broad daylight, a Captain of the burghers, a painter with sundry artisans went with large hammers and other iron instruments into all the monasteries, chapels, hospitals and other houses of God, in short to every place where there still existed pictures and altars and destroyed them. Many of the wooden effigies were burned in the streets, where the burghers kept guard. Not one person did protest against this, since the rule of the clergy is completely destroyed and at an end here.

56. Entry of His Imperial Majesty into Augsburg on the 27th day of June 1582

When His Imperial Majesty arrived in Augsburg on the 27th day of June all the Electors and other Princes present betook themselves across the stone bridge. The burghers with pipes and trumpets occupied their usual places. From three o'clock until five the entry took place in the following order:

First came the Imperial Provost, then the horsemen of the Hereditary Marshal of State, Baron von Pappenheim, and of the Duke of Saxe-Coburg. Thereupon followed the trumpeters of the Elector of Mayence, of Treves and of the Duke Maximilian of Bavaria. Then the arquebusiers and the Bavarian pages. These were followed by the Bavarian gentlemen-in-waiting, the Salzburg trumpeters, the Salzburg nobles and horsemen. Then came the Würzburg trumpeters and horsemen and after them the halberdier lieutenant and the court officers of His Imperial Majesty. Behind them rode the troop of the Palatine of Nuenburg and of the Landgrave of Leuchtenberg and the twelve Imperial grooms, leading His Majesty's horses, then twenty trumpeters with golden banners and the Roman Eagle. Thereupon followed the Imperial pages with His Majesty's helmet and body armour and then came the mounted groom of His Majesty and the gentlemen-in-waiting of His Majesty and the Princes. Then rode the equerries, dapifers, chamberlains, and other officers and Councillors of His Majesty, behind them the heralds of Bohemia and Hungary. Then followed the Lord Marshal and the Master of the Horse, and the two sons of the Count

Palatine Philip Ludwig. Then came Duke Maximilian of Bavaria, Count Palatine, Philip Ludwig, Duke Johann Casimir of Saxony and then the Landgrave of Leuchtenberg. Preceding His Imperial Majesty came two heralds of the Holy Roman Empire in their official garb, thereafter His Majesty on a beautiful Spanish steed under a canopy of yellow silk. The canopy was carried by Augsburg Councillors of the highest rank. Joachim, Baron von Pappenheim carried His Majesty's naked sword in front of him. His Majesty's lackeys walked in front of the canopy and one hundred of the bodyguard in the Imperial livery walked at each side. Behind them rode the two ecclesiastical Electors, the Princes of Mayence and Treves and the Bishops of Salzburg and Würzburg. Then came the two marshals of His Majesty's household, the Baron Wolf Rumpf and Herr Christoph Poppel. Behind them rode two pages with the Sword of State and the musket of His Majesty. Then came the archer Captain with three noblemen who wore beautiful morions, ornamented with gold, and behind them a hundred archers in German costume with morions and wearing armour under their coats. His Majesty's Household and State coaches concluded the procession.

When His Majesty had reached the market square before the cathedral and dismounted from his horse, he stepped beneath a canopy which had been prepared by the Bishop of Augsburg and the clergy. Under this he entered the cathedral. There he remained for a brief space and thereafter passed through the cathedral into the Bishop's Palace.

57. Ban on the Catholic Faith at Antwerp

From Antwerp, the 15th day of July 1581.

This afternoon at 1 o'clock, the Town Council issued an announcement whereby it is no longer permitted to practise the Catholic Religion. It is still, however, permissible for Catholics to baptize their children in their own fashion and have their marriages blessed by their priests. The adherents of the Reformed Faith wish to have it all their own way, but this kind of rule will not endure as time goes on, and evil will arise from it, for too much rope is being given to the community.

58. Drake laying in Stores

Cologne, July 20, 1581.

From Antwerp a quantity of munitions of war is being taken over to England and bought there. They say that within a few days over 300,000 feet of fuse was sent there, also that besides the ten first ships yet another ten are to be equipped. With these the pirate Drake is to sail to India to loot. It is stated too that some ships have arrived off the Azores from Brazil to take in water, and they have been held up there. This is Antwerp news; if there should be anything in it we shall soon learn from Lisbon and Spain. On the 13th inst. letters came to Antwerp from England with tidings that nothing yet is known for certain about Don Antonio.

59. Persecution of Jesuits in England

From Antwerp, the 16th day of September 1581.

Several English Jesuits, who had come from Rouen to London, and, at the behest of the Pope, were trying to convert the people to their Faith, were taken prisoner in London. Three were hanged and two were quartered. They are said to have committed all manner of treachery and to have denounced the Queen shamefully. A further sixteen are to be executed.

60. Marriage of Archduke Ferdinand with the Princess of Mantua

A short and simple account of what happened at the marriage of His Serene Highness Archduke Ferdinand of Austria with the Archduchess of Mantua. (Undated.)

On Wednesday, the 9th day of May 1582, the gilt sword and the Archducal hat, which were sent to him by His

Holiness the Pope through Franciscus, Bishop of Sebaste, were presented to His Serene Highness by the said Bishop after Mass had been said and the written message of His Holiness had been publicly read before the altar in the new cathedral at Innsbruck.

On Friday, the 11th day of May, Duke William of Bavaria as the accredited Envoy to these nuptials of His Roman Imperial Majesty arrived at Innsbruck in time for the morning meal with his beloved spouse, Maximiliana, sister of his princely grace, the Landgrave of Leuchtenberg, the two Landgravines of Baden, as well as a considerable number of Court attendants, counts, squires and noblemen, with four hundred horses in all. On the same evening the Archduke Charles of Austria arrived with his beloved Consort and the three princely offspring with a magnificent suite of attendants consisting of privy and trusted Councillors, counts, squires and noblemen, together with five hundred horses. His Serene Highness Archduke Ferdinand with his sons and Duke William of Bavaria came to meet them as far as Hall and accompanied them to Innsbruck. On the following Monday, the 14th day of May, the date of the nuptial ceremony and the entry, Archduke Ferdinand rode beyond the cloister of Wilten, alongside the mountain Isel, with Duke Wilhelm of Bavaria as Imperial Envoy, Archduke Charles of Austria, Cardinal Andreas of Austria and their stately and impressive retinue. Among the courtiers were Count Wilhelm von Zimbern, who entered Innsbruck with forty-one horses, Count Hannibal von Hohenembs, the Counts von Thurn, Schwarzenberg, Liechtenstein, Ortenburg and many other counts, squires and noblemen. From Innsbruck as far as the mountain Isel there lined up five thousand lansquenets and arquebusiers, clad in armour. Several tents had been erected on this spot, among them two which were particularly large. There their Serene Highnesses dismounted and awaited the royal bride, who presently arrived with her mother, the Duchess of Mantua, Duke Ferdinand of Bavaria and the Margrave of Baden. These two Princes had been dispatched on a mission to Mantua with eighty horses to accompany the plighted bride. The members of the Court and the squires of Tyrol had been sent to meet her as far as the frontier below Rovereto. They remained in the other tent opposite that of His Serene Highness until the ninety pieces of heavy ordinance, which had been brought from the armoury, and the arquebusiers had fired. After this was done, Archduke Ferdinand with the above-mentioned princely personages went on foot half way between the two tents in order to greet his beloved promised bride by word of mouth as well as the royal personages who had accompanied her. The Count von Hohenembs welcomed the mother of the bride in the Italian language and Herr Caspar Baron von Wolkenstein made reply and gave thanks.

Thereupon the entry began. At the head were the whole of the mounted troops and the servitors together with the trumpeters and the army drummers, then followed the counts, squires and nobility, the Landgrave of Leuchten-berg, both Margraves of Baden and Burgau, Duke Ferdi-nand of Bavaria, the Prince of Mantua, the Cardinal of Austria, then Archduke Ferdinand. On his right rode the Imperial Envoy, Duke Wilhelm of Bavaria, on his left Archduke Carl of Austria. Then followed the betrothed Princess with her mother, and a stately retinue of ladies-in-waiting in elegant gilt litters, and carriages on springs. On either side stood the aforesaid soldiery. They rode through three large triumphal arches, fashioned of woodwork and cloth. The first was in front of the Gateway of St. George, where stood eight men holding the coat of arms of the hereditary lands of His Serene Highness, and Latin verses, celebrating the country's joy at the arrival of their future mistress. The second arch was near the Gate of the Outer City: it was ornamented with an artificial weir and four springing fountains. The third was in the town in the square in front of the Tyrol Chamber with the golden roof. Hereon stood four heroes, and above them twenty-eight boys in gilt clothing with silver bells, and yet above these a band. As soon as the procession had dismounted from the horses, litters and coaches, it wended its way towards the new Imperial Cathedral. There in front of the open church door the Archduke was united with the promised bride by the aforesaid Bishop in canonical robes. The trumpeters blew a joyous blast and vespers were said. The upper church in which stood all the princely wedding guests, was hung with golden ornaments and the whole building with beauteous Dutch tapestries. Hereafter, the sixteen royal wedding guests partook of the evening meal at a table in the golden room. The counts, squires and noblemen, and all the Court and ordinary attendants were served in the inns.

After the feast, followed dances which were first led by the Archduke Ferdinand, then by the Imperial Envoy and so on according to precedence. Archduke Carl and the Prince of Mantua led the bride as ushers. His Serene Highness and both Margraves danced ahead with torches in their hands. On the 15th day of May an elegant and princely joust took place in the lists. All the royal personages, with the exception of the Cardinal appeared in brave raiment and broke their spears on a figure in the presentment of a stag. Archduke Ferdinand received the first prize because he broke the most spears. Although Duke Wilhelm of Bavaria had a fall from his horse, it all passed without mishap, thanks be to God.

On the 16th day of May, there was held a magnificent tourney on foot in which once more the royal personages and others of eminence took part. They brought into the lists a huge Trojan horse and a castle, together with a fortress made of wood; this which they called the town of Louvain, they attacked and stormed.

On the 17th day of May, there was a splendid chamois hunt above Innsbruck near Zirl on the St. Martin's Rock to which came all the royal personages. On the same evening there was held in the Court Garden an exceeding fine artificial display of fireworks with the firing of several large pieces and shooting muskets and fire bullets.

On the 18th day of May, Archduke Carl, the Duke of Bavaria, the Margrave of Baden, the Landgrave of Leuchtenberg, together with their princely spouses, ladies-in-waiting and other members of the Court of Innsbruck went by water on their way to Munich.

So this princely bridal home-coming and nuptials, thanks be to God, passed in beautiful weather, with goodly peace, unity and concord.

The old Duchess of Mantua with her son, the Prince, are still in Innsbruck.

61. Festival of the Circumcision in Constantinople

Festivities in Constantinople on the Circumcision of Mehemed, son of the Sultan Murad. (Undated.) Presumably in August 1582.

The festivities were fixed for the 2nd day of June 1582, on which day the ceremony in Seraglio which had lasted eight days, came to an end. There the gifts of the Sultanas and other great ladies of the kingdom were presented to the Prince. These gifts consisted of horses, richly-adorned slaves, jewels, garments, and such like. In addition to this, fireworks were burnt day and night for a whole week.

On the day named, the 2nd day of June, at the Sultan's command, there assembled in the great Hippodrome all the Pashas, Viziers and the *Beglerbeghs* of Greece and Anatolia, the *Aga* of the Janissaries, the *Capudan* Pasha and other great men of the Realm, together with all the Janissaries. The wax torches destined for the ceremony were about two and a half yards in height and of most unusual thickness. These torches were richly decorated with flowers, gold and silver, and are therefore very heavy. From the Hippodrome the whole gathering proceeded to the Sultan's Palace. First strode the Khan and other great personages of the Sublime Porte in robes richly embroidered in gold. Then there appeared Mehemed, the son of the great Sultan, on a horse beautifully caparisoned with jewels. The head harness was set with diamonds and a double row of pearls of immense value.

The youth, who was about sixteen years old, was clad in a richly embroidered coat of green satin. He has an elongated face, pale of colour, his eyes are black and have a serious expression. He greeted the people with lofty gesture. Behind the Prince came six horses, led with halters, with silken saddle clothes, richly embroidered with gold. The ceremonial procession arrived in the Seraglio about the hour of midday. There in accordance with the customs of the country, was made loudly resounding music, on kettledrums, trumpets and other instruments. Then the actual festivities began. There appeared one hundred men with staves, at the end of which were bladders filled with air. They were led by a man who rode a small donkey.

With these bladders they struck at the inquisitive assembly in order to drive them off. Then came one hundred Janissaries who had been chosen to guard the seats in the Hippodrome which were destined for the foreign ambassadors. On the first day of the festivities, tight-rope dancers showed their tricks, which they performed with quite amazing skill. Others, again, turned somersaults, which it is impossible either to comprehend or to describe. Also several very skilled spear throwers exhibited their accomplishments for admiration. At nightfall an illumination was arranged and this lasted until morning. Four castles filled with fireworks were lighted on the square of the Hippodrome and presented a truly entertaining sight. On the second day there were shown some other clever feats by the tight-rope dancers. There appeared among others a man who allowed a heavy block of marble, on which six men rained blows with hammers, to be placed across his naked belly. Another climbed a very high column placed on a pyramid and performed daring tricks thereon. This man was granted his freedom by His Majesty, and received moreover a gold embroidered robe and a gift of twenty piastres daily for his lifetime. Other jugglers allowed horseshoes to be nailed to their heads. On this day began also the presentation of the gifts from the Great of the Realm and the foreign Ambassadors, which continued day by day. Particularly to be mentioned is the Persian Ambassador, who altogether made a brave show. He had arrived with a retinue of two hundred sumptuously clad followers and witnessed the display in the circus from a box which had been specially erected for him. From behind the grille on their stand, the Chief Sultanas were also able to enjoy the spectacle. In the evening two wooden castles filled with fireworks were set ablaze.

On the third day various artificially prepared objects were exhibited, among them about three hundred large figures of animals, made of sugar. This lasted until midday, thereafter gifts were presented to all the Ambassadors who had been invited by His Majesty. The Hippodrome was sprinkled by twenty water waggons. A juggler performed there, he hit himself in the face with a stone with all his strength without any harm resulting therefrom. Another executed bold somersaults and was masked. Both were presented with gifts from His Majesty. The Sultan ordered seven thousand flat cakes made out of cooked rice to be brought, also six thousand large loaves of bread and great quantities of mutton. When all this was spread upon the ground, all the poor came rushing in the greatest haste to get hold of the food, and this proved a very entertaining sight. Thereafter was held a hunt of Hungarian boars. In the evening there were once more illuminations and fireworks.

On the fourth day, other jugglers disported themselves on the aforementioned pyramid, on which they performed tricks. On this day the different craftsmen paid homage to the Sultan, among them the weavers of golden shawls worn by the women here on their heads. Then followed three hundred youths from twelve to sixteen in age, in robes worked with gold, who sang songs in praise of the Sultan and his son. This performance pleased the Sultan so much that he gave them a bag with one thousand sequins and ordered them to come to him again the next day. Then there was shown in the Hippodrome a carriage which moved by itself, whilst another to which there were harnessed a horse and a donkey, went up in the air on a tight rope. After this once more gifts of great value were presented. In the evening there took place a feeding of the populace, and four thousand rice cakes, six thousand loaves of bread, and twenty roasted oxen were served on large tables.

On the fifth day the workers of the Arsenal were entertained. They were given six hundred oxen, a thousand sheep and an immense amount of rice soup. Each worker loaded himself with his portion and betook himself home with it. In the evening there took place the feeding of the populace with bread, mutton and rice. Then came yet another boar hunt and finally illuminations and fireworks.

On the sixth day there were only entertainments for the people, illuminations and fireworks.

On the seventh day five thousand Janissaries were regaled in the Hippodrome, together with their *Aga*. They ate off carpets in six great large galley tents. In the evening there was a feeding of the people and fireworks.

On the eighth day there were games in the Hippodrome with monkeys, cats, pigs, goats, and such like animals, who performed wondrous tricks. Then came sixty riders in sumptuously ornamented yellow satin robes with breastplates and morions, who held combat with a hundred and fifty richly attired foot soldiers armed with staves. Then two wooden castles were brought in, in one of which were Christian slaves, who were armed with arquebuses and morions. They also had drums, such as we use. These two castles were stormed the while numerous shots were fired. After this there was a combat between Turkish and Persian warriors and at the finish many riders were thrown out of the saddle with halberd strokes. The Emperor and Ali Pasha were pleased with this spectacle. In the evening the populace was fed again and fireworks were burned.

On the ninth day the Venetian Ambassador handed over to the Grand Seignior a hundred and fifty gifts from the Venetian Rulers. Among them were four gold embroidered robes and many silken ones. A race with riderless horses was arranged. A juggler danced on a very high platform. He fell from it and was killed. Then a fox, boar and hare hunt took place. In the evening the people again received victuals and splendid fireworks were burnt which lasted until daylight. The earlier displays were shorter.

On the tenth day four thousand Spahis with their *Aga* were entertained. Everything proceeded as at the feast given to the Janissaries, and the Spahis made music. In the evening: feasting of the populace and fireworks.

On the eleventh day came all their singers, who may be described as mad. They ranged themselves in the market place where the Sultan was, and it was said that they were praying to God for the life of the Sultan. But their method of praying is peculiar and laughable. In the evening fireworks. On this day was seen in the Hippodrome a circus rider, who stood on a horse that was in full gallop. He also sprang from the ground to the galloping horse with great skill. Then the horse stood still and the man sprang on to its back and remained standing there. The horse stood as motionless as though carved in wood. In the evening there was again food for the populace, likewise fireworks. Many loaves of bread were flung among the people from the windows of the palace. The Sultan's son threw sequins, aspri, and other coins, six thousand sequins' worth in all, from a window and sixty silver dishes besides. Until 4 o'clock of the morning gorgeous fireworks were burned.

On the twelfth day the Grand Master of the Artillery was

entertained with three thousand gunners. This was carried out in a way like unto that used for the Janissaries and the Spahis. Then there appeared in the Hippodrome a hundred richly dressed horsemen, who fought in Spanish armour. Later they shot with arrows at a disk fastened to a very high pole. They showed great prowess. In the evening the populace was regaled and two galleys and three castles which had been filled with fireworks were burned.

On the thirteenth day one hundred and seventy richly robed men of the Spinners' Guild rendered homage to the Sultan. Then fifty mounted archers gave an exhibition. After the feeding of the populace an artificial mountain, erected by the slaves of the Capudan Pasha, in which fireworks were hidden, was set alight. This was not successful. On the other hand, other pieces, such as a giant dressed as a Jew, a dragon, four castles and a ruin made a pleasing spectacle.

On the fifteenth day their Capudan Pasha was entertained with eight thousand of his sailors.

On the sixteenth day the guilds paid homage to the Grand Seignior. In the evening there were fireworks and a meal for the populace.

On the seventeenth day four thousand shield bearers and their Pashas were entertained.

In the Hippodrome, the Greeks held a peculiar vaulting contest. In the evening six thousand sequins and silver coins were thrown among the populace.

On the eighteenth day the fruit sellers brought magnificent offerings of fruit to the Sultan.

On the nineteenth day there came all the Christians of the town of Pera. There were about two hundred and fifty of them and each one was more handsomely attired than the other. They wore robes of cloth with black velvet caps, and were richly adorned with jewels of great price. First came one hundred exquisitely dressed men with glittering spears on their shoulders. Then followed the remaining Periotes and twelve youths who executed dances to the accompaniment of loud music. His Majesty sent them embroidered kerchiefs and four thousand aspri. Then one hundred and fifty armourers did homage, followed by the goldsmiths, then one hundred and fifty cutlers and two hundred tinsmiths. And then followed one after another various guilds of the town with their beautiful and rare handiwork. The master remembered them all with presents of gold. As the populace was being fed that day, the onrush of the poor was so great that more than a half of the food was mangled, and the rest so badly spoiled that not even the dogs would touch it. Nevertheless His Majesty had it proclaimed that he found great pleasure in this, and that the festivities would be prolonged for forty days.

On the twentieth day the guilds appeared once again. Moreover, there was shown a rare and beautiful animal called a giraffe.

On the twenty-first day a thousand very rich merchants adorned with immensely valuable jewels did homage to the Grand Seignior.

On the twenty-second day there were once more circus riders, feasts for the people and fireworks.

On the twenty-third day I saw a man who stood on his head on the back of a galloping horse.

On the twenty-fourth day the wrestlers of the Sultan gave a performance. They achieved the most dangerous jumps with surpassing skill. In the evening the Sultan and his son threw fifty silver dishes, eight thousand sequins, aspri, and other coins among the populace. At night fireworks and feeding of the people.

On the twenty-fifth day there were equestrian tricks. Within a circle of six hundred paces a disc was shot at, and besides this many other warlike riding feats were displayed.

On the twenty-sixth day a fifteen-year-old stripling gave an exhibition of tight-rope dancing.

On the twenty-seventh day the Sultan threw six-and-sixty silver dishes and six thousand sequins to the people. The fireworks lasted the whole night.

On the twenty-eighth day the guilds brought as gifts to the Sultan the most beautiful products of their craft.

On the twenty-ninth day numerous inhabitants of Zara gave a performance and there was a great feast. In the evening the Sultan threw sixty silver dishes to the populace and likewise eight thousand sequins. The Sultan and his son watched the fireworks until morning.

On the thirtieth day the guilds once more appeared. In the evening feeding of the populace and fireworks.

On the thirty-first day two elephants were shown who

bowed before His Majesty. Four trained lions were also exhibited.

On the thirty-second day very costly gifts were presented to the Sultan, who once more threw from a window sixty silver dishes and six thousand sequins to the people.

On the thirty-third day fifteen guilds brought wonderful gifts for the Sultan.

On the thirty-fourth day a tight-rope dancer danced with his feet shod, and his coat put on hind part before, so that his arms were crossed and unmoveable.

On the thirty-fifth day fifty horsemen shot with arrows at a golden apple, which was placed on a pole about ten yards high. The victorious marksmen were presented to the Sultan, who gave them gifts. In the evening he threw sixty silver dishes and five thousand sequins among the populace.

On the thirty-sixth day a man allowed six men to break a great block of stone on his belly without his taking any harm therefrom. Then others threw large stone blocks at a target. Another had a large beam laid across his naked belly and pushed the wood, which six men had pulled along with difficulty away from his belly, without making use of his hands. In the evening the Sultan threw silver dishes and sequins in larger quantities than usual among the people, because on the following night the Vesier Mehemed Pasha performed the circumcision of the Prince. For this service he received from the Grand Seignior ten thousand golden sequins, two large silver dishes, and many gold embroidered garments. Also the other Pashas and Sultanas and the first wife of the Vizier, who is a sister of His Majesty, were liberally presented with gifts.

On the thirty-seventh day a horse race was arranged.

On the thirty-eighth day fifty horsemen held a tourney.

On the thirty-ninth day there were performances by Zariotes and by fifty riders clad in yellow satin.

On the fortieth day there paid homage to the Grand Seignior one thousand Muezzins who made a terrible din with their music. In the evening money was again thrown to the people. At the order of the Sultan the festival was prolonged for a further fourteen days.

On the forty-first and forty-second days there were banquets for the foreign Ambassadors, rope dancing, equestrian entertainments, feeding of the populace and fireworks.

On the forty-third day His Majesty went to the baths. He was attended by four Viziers and Mehemed Pasha, who unrobed him. To the latter he presented a dagger set all over with jewels also everything that he wore. His son, whom the Sultan loaded with presents, did likewise.

On the forty-fourth day there were more festivities but no more great fireworks. From the fortieth day onwards the Ambassadors did not attend the displays, the feeding of the populace was discontinued, and the people began to disperse.

On the forty-fifth, forty-sixth and forty-seventh days there were tight-rope dancing and fireworks.

On the forty-eighth day, a tight-rope dancer who carried a man on his back, gave a performance; another man was bound to his legs. The Sultan presented him with a big bag of sequins and a gold embroidered robe. Besides this he assured him of a life-long pension of twenty-five aspri daily, but forbade him in future to risk his life in such a manner.

On the forty-ninth day, the Zariotes displayed their accomplishments once more.

On the fiftieth day there were fireworks the whole night long. It was the most beautiful display of all and lasted until the morning.

On the fifty-first day His Majesty returned to the Seraglio of Ibrahim Pasha, and from there to the new Seraglio. And thus ended the festivities.

62. Tribulations of Spanish Ships in Distant Seas

Lisbon, September 10, 1582.

Nine days ago an Indian ship which sailed last March to India with our own ships returned here. She lost her way off the coast of Brazil and met such rough weather that for a long time she could not cross the Line. Finally she had to come home. Four days since we got news from San Miguel that two ships from Portuguese India have come in there. They are bringing Don Christoval de Erasso here in company with six warships. Of the four ships expected from India this year there is no news. Some maintain that this is because the ships have not arrived in India from Malacca and cargoes are short, so they will not sail at present. But nothing is yet known, and the uncertainty makes business slack. In foodstuffs there is nothing doing.

63. Warring Religions in Scotland

Paris, November 10, 1582.

It is fairly well known what changes Monsieur d'Aubigny, otherwise Earl Lennox, wanted to make at the Court of the King of Scots. The King removed him from Court thinking thereby to appease his adversaries. But they are not content with this, keep the King under restraint and want him to allow them to force this d'Aubigny into exile, and to confiscate his property. The King is said now to be at Littlebury, d'Aubigny at Dumbarton, a strong fortress on the coast, where with a few men he can hold out for a year against all Scotland. The good understanding long existing between the King and the captive Queen his Mother has caused the King to withdraw his favour from the Huguenots. Monsieur de la Mothe Fénelon, long since Ambassador-in-ordinary to England, has been sent away from here. The Queen of England has despatched two Commissioners to Scotland and offered that King a safe-conduct to come to her. So this fire will probably spread in England too.

64. Attempts to bring Turkey against Spain

Madrid, Spain, May 5, 1583.

The Queen Dowager of France has sent a ship from Marseilles to Constantinople, to try and persuade the Grand Turk to send a fleet out this year to stir up trouble in the Levant. Certain galleys have already turned up, but it is hoped they will not do much harm. Six more large galleys are being got ready at Marseilles, on pretence of being sent to the Grand Master of Malta. Some think the French would like to make an attempt to catch Spinola's Genoese galleys, which often sail to and fro with money.

65. Elizabeth ready to help the Northern Netherlands

Cologne, August 1, 1583.

The English Captain Norris, who has long been in the service of the States General, came from England to the Prince of Orange in Zeeland on the 4th inst. He reports that fifteen thousand English soldiers are ready now. These the Queen is to send to the States General. It is known what security she requires for payment. On hearing her demands the Prince of Orange seems to have summoned the States General to see what security could be given to the English. We hear also that Duke John Casimir wrote to the States General that, if they would pay off a portion of their old debt to His Highness, and would give security for the fresh payment, he would bring with him efficient troops, both horse and foot. But as it is notorious that the States cannot pay the men already recruited, still less will they have the means to pay His Highness and to furnish security to the English. It would appear that to put off the unhappy government in this way simply means prolongation of the war and greater ruin for the country.

66. Driving out of Devils in Vienna

(Copy of a letter of the Arbogast Nachtrube.)

From Vienna, the 3rd day of September 1583 of the old calendar.

The Jesuits here, two weeks ago, in company of the Bishop drove out a devil from a poor maid. Her mother is a witch and lies still in jail. First it was all of no avail, but finally she was given a drink of holy water. She had not long partaken of this before Satan left her.

As I had completed this letter, there arrives a courier from Constantinople and reports that Herr Frederick Breuner, the Ambassador of His Imperial Majesty, has died there.

67. Arrival of an American Treasure Fleet

From Madrid, the 26th day of September 1583.

The fleet from Spanish India, praise be to God, arrived upon the 13th day of this month without mishap. It carries a shipment of about fifteen millions. It is said that they unloaded and left a million in Havana, because the ships were too heavily laden. This is a pretty penny, which will give new life to commerce.

68. The Plague in Prague

From Vienna, the 15th day of October 1583.

Rumour has it that His Imperial Majesty will again shortly come here, because the plague has spread, not only in Prague itself, but also on the outskirts, so that His Majesty knows of no safe place for his Court. The aforementioned contagious disease is on the increase here also, and up to four-and-twenty persons succumb daily of the plague, wherefore amongst other measures it was ordered to close the public baths.

Concerning the Papal Calendar, practically no one takes any heed of it. Neither has His Majesty decreed that it should be observed, but he has merely announced that this should be done because, in fulfilling the Pope's injunction and request, His Majesty was but rendering a service unto him.

69. Plots against the Queen

Antwerp, January 21, 1584.

Letters from London in England report that the Queen has had sentence passed upon the persons who tried to assassinate her. One of the oldest women of the bed-chamber has been burnt alive, a gentleman of the Court was first hanged and then quartered, another nobleman who killed himself in prison was burnt. Two other gentlemen of high birth are being closely watched in their houses as they have fallen under suspicion. The conspiracy against the Queen is said to have originated in Rome and Spain.

70. Vengeance

Antwerp, February 4, 1584.

We have received no letters from England this week, but learn through a courtier of the Queen of England that the country is entirely shut off, and that no one can get away from it without a pass and without great danger. This English courtier has gone to the Prince of Orange and confirms the news of the great conspiracy against the Queen of England. At the castle of Greenwich, six miles from London, the Queen's chamber was to have been blown up with powder. By a lucky accident the secret was revealed, and the Queen had some important people arrested. The French and Spanish ambassadors, likewise all Frenchmen and Spaniards, are to be removed from the country, and the Spanish ambassador is said to have left already.

71. Jesuits executed

Cologne, March 8, 1584.

Letters have reached Antwerp from England to say that that Queen has executed five Jesuits accused of having a part in the conspiracy against her. There is also an unfounded rumour of the discovery of a plot against the King of Scots. A shot is said to have been fired at him but to have missed. If there should be anything in this we are sure to hear soon.

72. Warlike Preparations in the Northern Netherlands

Antwerp, April 7, 1584.

The inhabitants of Zeeland, Holland and Antwerp are fitting out several powerful warships. It is thought they will sail from here to Spain and Portugal. The Queen of England is also said to be about to equip powerful ships against Spain.

73. Antwerp Sea Trade in Difficulties

Antwerp, June 30, 1584.

Warships are being kept at sea to stop supplies to the English, and likewise to those coming from Lisbon, Spain and France. Three ships have been intercepted, two English laden with wheat, one from Spain with molasses. If the embargo is strictly kept, it will cause want and distress in many ways.

74. The Murder of William of Orange

From Antwerp, the 16th day of July 1584.

In the evening—the 12th of this month—we received the news, the truth of which was later confirmed, that on the 10th day of this month, the Prince of Orange was murdered in Delft, by a Burgundian, one named Bartholomew Gerard. The latter had on the day previous been dispatched from France as messenger to the Diet, and to the Prince of Orange, to report on the death of the Duke of Alençon. And a quarter of an hour after his arrival, the Prince no longer lived. As I write this, there comes the news that the said Bartholomew Gerard has been tortured at Delft, and has confessed that he was persuaded in Italy by a Jesuit, in the name of the King of Spain, to kill the Prince of Orange. The Jesuit had promised him thirty thousand pounds for the deed. Should he, however, be discovered in the act and lose his life, his friends were to receive the money. Thereupon he was sent by the said Jesuit to Paris to the Ambassador of the King of Spain there, one named Taxis. The latter sent him to the Queen Mother of France, who gave him letters to the Prince of Orange and the Diet in Holland, to announce that her son, the Duke of Alençon, had departed this life. Before he came to Holland, he went to the Prince of

Parma, to whom he communicated his plan. Not until after this did he appear before the Prince of Orange.

75. Prospect of an English-French Alliance

Paris, August 15, 1584.

As the Queen of England greatly fears Spain and Scotland, she wishes to conclude a defensive alliance with the Crown of France, but whether this will come about we do not know.

76. France at last joins in the Alliance

Antwerp, February 21, 1585.

A few days ago letters came from Cambrai, England and Middelburg, announcing that the negotiations with the King of France to obtain his support for these countries have ended in his deciding to send help. The English write to their representative here to instruct English people, who for the moment are in small numbers, not to leave the place. At Middelburg also where they are to be found with their goods, this nation has been informed that in a few days a change will take place in this country.

77. The Derby Embassy to Paris

Paris, February 21, 1585.

Yesterday Earl Derby reached St. Denis, not three miles from here. He has with him a great retinue of nobles.

The permanent English ambassador at this Court went out to meet him, and the King caused the Duc de Montpensier to escort him on his way. Great preparations are being made to entertain him with banquets, masques and other amusements. The King is putting him up free in the same way as the Dutch Envoy, and much money will be spent. The English here announce that their Queen expelled all Jesuits a month ago. They were first given

101

a gratuity, and then taken to the frontier to go wherever they wished.

78. The Garter conferred upon the King of France

Paris, March 5, 1585.

The English Envoy, the Earl of Derby, entered this city in the afternoon of the 23rd ult., and the Duc de Montpensier representing the King rode out to meet him. On his entry he was escorted by four hundred horse. On the very next day he had an audience of His Majesty, and on the following Thursday, which was the 28th of February, on behalf of his Queen he conferred the Order of the Garter upon the King in the Church of the Austin Friars. His Majesty wore the usual dress of a Knight of the Order. In addition to the Knights of the Order here, there were present at this ceremony the Papal Nuncio and the Spanish and Venetian ambassadors. The Garter is valued at fifty thousand crowns. In return the King is said to have prepared a magnificent coach with all fittings to still greater value for presentation to the Queen of England. The Envoy was most honourably feasted at banquets, especially by the King. Next week he is to return to England, and we are not told what other subjects he may have negotiated about here on behalf of his Queen.

79. Nuptials at the Court of Philip II

From Saragossa, the 12th day of March 1585.

Yesterday, at 4 o'clock, the Duke of Savoy arrived here. The King rode out beyond the river to meet him and received him in most gracious fashion. He allowed him to make his entry on horseback at his right hand. This the Duke would not have at first, but he was forced to consent for His Majesty so wished it. The Spaniards were not a little astonished at this. To-day at 12 o'clock the Church Ceremony took place, whereafter the King dined in public with the Duke, the bride and the eldest Infanta. This evening a dance will be held, and thereafter the marriage will be consummated. The bride looked on this day mightily morose. I know not, whether perhaps she is dissatisfied with the appearance of the Duke, who is small and ugly. If this be the case, she may, after the dance of this night, conceive a better liking for the bridegroom to-morrow.

The Duke of Savoy arrived in such state that the inhabitants were astonished thereat. First there came riding in front one hundred postilions, all attired in yellow cloth, then came the aposentadores in beautiful liveries, and then the servants of the postmaster also in livery. Then there rode over two hundred Savoyard followers, clad in yellow velvet. Then with the Duke there came a hundred stately gentlemen and cavaliers, all robed alike in violet coloured velvet. The velvet of the cavaliers was nearly covered with gold and silver lace. Among the many gentlemen of high rank there are the eldest son of the Duke of Nemours from France, stately and opulent marquises, earls and knights, so that the Duke has won a great reputation among the Spaniards.

As this letter has been delayed for a day, there is something else I should like to add that has taken place meanwhile. This is that yesternight we looked on at the dance which lasted until 11 o'clock. What happened later at the consummation of the marriage, the bride will know. To-day neither the bride nor the bridegroom have been seen. On the 21st day of this month a tourney will be held, that we must await, though our stay is burdened with heavy expense. This evening the cavaliers from Arragon will hold a hunt and break lances.

More from Saragossa, the 18th day of March.

From my last writings you will know what has happened here. Since then naught of particular interest has come to pass. The Duke of Savoy wished to play the Pelota with the people he had brought with him against the local gentry. But this the King refused to allow. Although there has fallen a fair amount of rain during these days, His Majesty has twice or thrice ridden to various churches. The Gentlemen of the Court, and the grandees, and the arragonesque cavaliers of this town wish to hold jousts on horseback on the coming Thursday. Three or four days later the Castilians want to hold a similar tourney on foot, and a hunt as well.

103

The King is to leave here on the 27th or 28th, some say for Barcelona, others for Montserrat in order to pass Holy Week there with the Duke and his retinue. Where and when the Cortes will be held, no one knows for certain. There are so many surmises and opinions that there is nothing to write about. Time will show.

80. The Spanish Besiege Antwerp

From Antwerp, the 15th day of March 1585.

On the 12th day of this month the Corporation called together all the guilds and desired that the burghers should advance money in cash for the sustenance of the troops here and should state how much food, wine and beer each company consumes. The money is not to be returned until our river has been freed from the enemy's occupation and our district is opened up once more. Thereupon they determined to deliberate upon this. With regard to our waterway, it remains as before. Means are lacking for reopening it, athough various preparations to free it are being made. This, however, is held by many to be nothing but mockery and procrastination.

81. Death of Pope Gregory XIII

From Venice, the 14th day of April 1585, through the Antwerp courier.

Well born and gracious Sir,

Up to the evening of the day before yesterday, everything that was needful had been reported to you, but as to-day we have an opportunity to send this to you, we would inform you that His Holiness the Pope died in the Lord, on the 10th day of this month at 12 o'clock. May the Almighty be merciful to his soul. Within the space of ten hours he was first in good health, then ill, then dead, suffocated by a catarrh. Farnese shows no elation and all those who were sick abed were made to rise through this shock. One lays twenty-five per cent. on Farnese being chosen Pope, thirteen on Savelli, on Sancto Severina eight, on Fachinetti six, and on Mondovi five. One lays thirty per cent. on the Pope's election taking place before the last of May.

82. Persecution of the Huguenots in Marseilles

From Marseilles, the 16th day of April 1585.

This town has been in sore tribulation and was to have been plundered on Palm Sunday, moreover the throats of all the Huguenots were to be cut. But from this God Almighty preserved us. The second Consul wished to carry out with the Captain the plan to make themselves masters of the town. They thrust many of the Reformed Religion into prison and gave the people to understand that this was done at the King's command. Thereby they embittered the commoners and made them rebellious. On the 10th day of this month at 10 o'clock at night the Consul together with the Captain went to the house of General Cabané, who belongs to the Reformed Religion, presented him with a letter in which nothing was written and immediately thereon massacred him in his house. Thereafter they went to other Huguenots, dragged them from their beds and led them out to the Tower of St. Felician. Others they bound by one thigh and dragged alive through the town up a certain mountain. There they inflicted upon them divers stabs and threw them naked into the sea. On this account the most noble houses here have armed themselves and insisted that the Consul should show them the King's commands in the Town Hall. But he made answer that his instructions were not to be shown to all and sundry. The Captain who was the brother of the aforesaid Cabané was taken prisoner. He himself did kill his brother because Cabané had no children. The Grand Prior from Aix was promptly sent for and arrived in the night with one hundred well-equipped horsemen. He went immediately to the prisons and freed the poor prisoners who fell at his feet and thanked him profusely. Then he examined the imprisoned Consul and the Captain and had them hanged on the gallows at night between the eleventh and twelfth hour. Yesterday their heads were severed from their bodies, which were cut in four pieces and displayed in the streets. The Consul's head was

impaled on a high staff in front of the Porte Royale and
that of the Captain in front of his brother's house.

83. Attempt to Relieve the Siege of Antwerp

From Cologne, the 6th day of June 1585.

On the 21st day of May in the night those of Antwerp
made fast, one to another, sixteen large and small shallow
ships, which were equipped with large, strong-wrought
grappling irons in front and underneath. These they sent
with full sails and with a mighty wind against the rafts
in front of the Palisade. They rammed them so hard that
all the anchors broke and that the ships, together with the
rafts, came near unto the Palisade. There they stopped.
Thereupon four other ships, which were loaded with powder, iron chains, large grave-stones, and millstones followed, in order to burst up the Palisade completely. The
first of these blew up into the air a short distance from the
Palisade, without causing any damage. The second was
driven ashore and left lying in the sand. She also blew up
but caused much havoc. The third ship came near to the
Palisade with a strong wind and at full speed. The Spaniards immediately loosened two ships from the Palisade
and let her through. She also exploded at pistol range without any harm being done. But the fourth and largest
ship on which those of Antwerp had built all their hopes,
was boarded by four sailors who were supposed to be willing to sacrifice their lives for the welfare of their King
and Country. They, however, threw away the quickmatch,
cut down the sails and steered the ship ashore, afterwards
unloading her. They took therefrom a hundred small barrels of gunpowder. Of these the Prince of Parma made
them a gift, as well as of the ship and all that was therein,
together with his commendation. Thereupon the Armada
left Holland and Zeeland for the dikes, but upon seeing
that the Spaniards were holding them strongly garrisoned,
went back below Lillo.

84. English troops at Middelburg. Drake at Sea

Cologne, August 9, 1585.

From Holland on the 2nd inst. comes news that six thousand English soldiers are daily expected in Zeeland, and that the Queen of England has declared war against Spain because English ships and English subjects and property are being detained in Spain, and some property has already been sold. The Queen has done the same in England. It is also announced that the Queen will actively support the Hollanders and Zeelanders, and will call upon Denmark and Sweden to help. From Middelburg under date the last of July, comes the statement that Colonel Norris, the Earl of Leicester and Lord Pelham are to be in command of the English troops sent by the Queen in aid of the Hollanders and Zeelanders, and already arrived at Middelburg. Without the Queen's consent no ship or letter may leave the country in future. The offices of the Spaniards and Portuguese in London have been closed and their trade records removed. Those who refused to submit their books were imprisoned. It is confirmed that Drake the pirate and his fleet are at sea not only to lie in wait for a fleet from Peru, but that he has actually taken an island from the King of Spain and held up some fishing-boats off Terra Nova.

85. Trade slack at Lisbon

Lisbon, August 17, 1585.

Since my last letter no ship has come in from India, though the *Buen Viage* is awaited with special anxiety. As no Hamburg ships have put in either, trade is almost entirely quiet. Three days ago twenty-four ships came in from Brazil, and sixteen have gone on to Oporto. They bring much sugar and three thousand quintals of Brazilwood. It is to be hoped this will revive business here, for, as the Dutch ships are still detained, there is no trade. The night before last there was a heavy wind and two of the largest Dutch ships used it to get away. When this was seen they were pursued, but the wind fell again, so they had to be left. The next morning by order of the Marquis de Santa Cruz, all troops were put on the galleys. During the same night of storm eighteen detained ships sailed away, though they had previously been deprived of their sails. It is not known what they could make fresh sails of, so soon and so secretly. The ships still remaining will have to be punished for the fugitives. But the country too is suffering from the detention of the ships, for the prices of corn and provisions have risen greatly all round, and there is a shortage already. To-morrow four galleys are to sail to the islands and elsewhere along the Spanish coast to intercept the English and French pirates. God grant they may soon bring in the overdue Indian fleet!

86. Trade diminishing at Cologne

Cologne, August 29, 1585.

They write from Zeeland that the Queen of England is putting off the States General with fair words, and that she does not mean to help them, for she would be taking too heavy a burden upon herself.

Many Netherlanders are leaving here for Antwerp, Malines, Louvain and Brussels. This is already noticeable on Change.

87. The Taking of Antwerp

From Antwerp, the 21st day of August 1585.

On the 17th day of this month the treaty of the handing over of this city was concluded and on the 20th day of this month it was read and made public. No particular joy nor jubilation on account thereof was manifested by the populace; only the Italians and some Catholics burnt bonfires. The Town Council made but little ado about the reading. Everything is quiet here. The troops display inexpressible home-sickness; the reformed preachers will these days travel by ship to Holland and Zeeland. Nothing has as yet been seen of the waggons with provisions, wine, and beer, which, according to rumour, are said to be in the camp. In the Parma's camp wine costs half a thaler the pint. According to information given out here, the Prince of Parma is not to enter until the 1st day of September, which is his birthday. It is said that he has kept for this occasion a special favour not included in the treaty, which he will bestow upon the town. It will then be seen with what affection he regards it.

88. The Expulsion of the Huguenots

From Paris, the 18th day of October 1585.

The day before yesterday a new edict was proclaimed which threatens all Huguenots in France with pain of death and the loss of their goods and chattels if they do not leave the country within fifteen days. But women and children are allowed to remain until six months have elapsed from the first *édit de réunion*. This edict is particularly directed against those who are fighting. Their goods will be sold from the very hour it appeared and the proceeds employed for the maintenance of the royal troops.

89. The Sea unsafe for Trade

Antwerp, November 9, 1585.

As the sea remains so blockaded and shut off, commerce is quite at a standstill, and, although those who trade with Spain and Portugal would like to use Flemish ports, they dare not put out even from there because of the freebooters, of whom there are quantities at sea. They have latterly captured Spanish fishermen and carried them off to England, and other ships of considerable importance they have taken to France and stripped completely. God console the losers! The Zeelanders now have English garrisons in Flushing, Briel and other places, and it is thought that English are to go to Enkuisen as well. Leicester, Essex and Cumberland, all three of them distinguished Earls, are expected in Holland, besides Lord Grey, who is Colonel in

Ireland and has lately suppressed great disorder there. Mr. Sidney is expected too, with many other nobles, all of whom will strive to defend Holland.

90. A Sorry Week in Augsburg

From Augsburg, the 2nd day of December 1585.

The week just passed has been an unhappy one, for on Monday a carman hanged himself, kneeling. On Tuesday a goldsmith of the name of Ostwald, sprang into the Lech in the Sachsengässlein, wishing to drown himself on account of debts. But his neighbours saved him. On the night of Thursday, a cloth-shearer of the name of Huber who was drunk, fell into the Lech and was drowned. His body was found on the next day. On the same day a peasant woman of Pfersen killed a young male child—her own flesh and blood. On Friday a fisherman, who is also a gardener in Pfersen, persuaded his betrothed to accompany him to another village, because there would be holiday there two days running. When she had agreed to this and they were a little way from the town, he stabbed her seven times with a crooked blade and sorely wounded her. As several persons saw this murder from afar and raised a great clamour, the malefactor took flight towards the city. The keeper of the gate caught the miscreant and by order of the authorities he has been thrown into prison. The wounded girl was carried to the Pilgrim's House, where she yet lies in a hopeless state. Last night a weaver of the town was stabbed to death, on account of which the small gates have remained closed this day. In the past night also, a miller in the upper town threw his wife into the river and tried to drown her. But people came to her assistance.

91. The Murder of the Signora Accaramboni

New tidings of a pitiful act of murder that took place on the 22nd day of December of the new calendar in the year 1585, at Padua in Italy, a town belonging to the Venetian rulers.

The Duke Paolo Giordano Orsini, Duke of Bracciano, scion of one of the noblest Roman families, had for wife the sister

110

of the now reigning Grand Duke of Florence, with whom he had as issue of the marriage-bed a young Prince of the name of Giovanni. But as the said Duke had but little sexual intercourse with the former Duchess of Florence, he was induced by fleshly desire to break his marriage vows.

He conceived a burning passion for the wife of the nephew of the now reigning Pope Sixtus. But she did not wish to turn unfaithful to her husband, and therefore told him that she was married and that no other man should approach her. Thereupon the said Duke forgot himself and had the husband of the lady (the nephew of the Pope) horribly murdered. He then once more approached the widow of the murdered man. But she curtly refused him because he was married and she a widow and not wishful to do such a thing. Thereupon the Duke Paolo Giordano forgot himself still further and had his own spouse, sister of the present Duke of Florence, put out of the way, in order to still his concupiscence for the above-named widow. Then, for the third time he paid his addresses to her. This time she made subjection to him but only on condition that he married her, which he did.

Meanwhile the Cardinal, the present Pope, did not rest in his desire to avenge the innocent blood of his nephew. But as he was not of much consideration, he has been placated. However, when he became Pope, the Duke wished to be reconciled with him. He knelt before him and begged for his blessing. Thereupon the Pope said: "Duke Paolo Giordano, you insulted the Cardinal Montalto: but Pope Sixtus pardons you. Do not come again, however, of that we warn you." The Duke was greatly alarmed at this speech and removed himself with his spouse to Padua, in Venetian territory, where he kept Court and had up to five hundred persons at his board. Nevertheless, before two months had passed, he died at Salo. Foul play was suspected. He left his spouse, who belonged to the noble Roman house of Accaramboni, a large property. The Grand Duke of Florence was by no means pleased with this testament, and took charge of the young forsaken Prince Giovanni, calling upon the widow at the same time to put aside the will. Should she marry again, he would deal handsomely by her: but he urged upon her to enter a convent or to remain a widow. Then also would he make handsome provision for her. But to this she

111

would not agree, and wished to abide by the testament and to keep a retinue of one hundred persons. On the 22nd day of this month, at 2 o'clock at night, according to Italian time, her palace in Padua was found open. Fifty well-armed men thereupon entered and cruelly shot the brother of the Signora Accaramboni, a certain Duke Flaminio; as to the lady, they stabbed her where they found her at prayer. Although she pitifully entreated that she might be permitted first to conclude her orisons, the murderers fulfilled their deed. The most distinguished among them is Ludovico Orsini, the first chief of the Government here, cousin of the dead Paolo Giordano. Thereafter he entrenched himself with his assassins in his house. In the meanwhile the news was brought here and the Government has dispatched one of its Senators to Padua with authority to destroy the house of Orsini and to take the murderers alive or dead. The said Orsini surrendered himself with a dagger in his hand, and his house was fired upon from several large cannon. Thereby a number of his retainers perished, the remainder being taken prisoner.

From Venice, the 27th day of December 1585.

Yesternight the Government here decided that the Colonel Ludovico Orsini was to be strangled three hours after the delivery of their letter. His accomplices were to be dealt with according to their deserts. Without doubt they will be hanged and quartered.

The chief culprit Orsini confessed that he had perpetrated this murderous deed at the command of great personages. The students in Padua have armed themselves and cried out "Justice, Justice!"

From Venice, the 1st day of January 1586.

It has been recently reported that the Colonel of this Government, Ludovico Orsini, acted murderously and with his own hand slew in gruesome fashion the wife of the late Duke Paolo Giordano, Duke of Bracciano, and her brother, Duke Flaminio.

When the decision that he must die within three hours was made known to Ludovico Orsini, he confessed that although his years numbered but four-and-thirty, he had put to death with his own hands forty persons, believing that Justice would never lay hands upon him because he

112

belonged to so illustrious a house. He had hoped likewise that he would not be publicly executed. But when he was informed that he was not to be strangled in a public place but in a chamber, he gave thanks for this judgment and penned two letters, one to his spouse and the other to the Government here. He commended to the latter's care his spouse and child, as well as his estate, so that they might not suffer on his account. He also made a will by which he bequeathed to the Government his armour, worth over and above six thousand crowns. The remainder of his property he left to his wife, who was at the time with child.

He gave fifty crowns to his executioner, in order that he might be dispatched quickly.

The brother of this Ludovico Orsini, Don Latino Orsini, is Governor of Candia under the Venetian rule. But shortly afterwards the Government sent a frigate to divest him of the command because they no longer put faith in him. And just as high as the house of Orsini had stood in esteem, as deep is now its fall.

After Ludovico Orsini had been strangled, his body was borne to the cathedral, the coffin decorated with tapestries and left lying there through the whole of this the 27th day of December. Then it was brought hither and interred in the Church of the Madonna dell' Orto, where Don Giordano and Don Valerio Orsini, the forbears of Ludovico, also lie buried.

The murdered Signora Accaramboni was a woman of great eloquence for as Ludovico Orsini was about to murder her, she was at prayer, and when the murderer said to her:

"Do you recognize me?" she made answer "Yea, now it is time to prepare my soul. I beg of you by the Mercy of our Lord Jesus Christ, to let me make my confession and then do with me as you please." "Nay," answered the enemy, "now is not the time for confession."

In Padua near on six hundred burghers paraded in arms and cried "Justice, Justice!" Now follows the list of those who were publicly executed: Count Paganello Ubaldi and Captain Splandiano da Fermo. These two were the servants of the murdered lady, who did open her dwelling—the palace—and who were accomplices in the bloody deed. They were riven asunder with red-hot tongs, and

113

killed with a hammer and then quartered. Buglion and Furio Savognano, two noblemen and secret advisers of Ludovico Orsini, have been secretly strangled.

Agrippa Tartaro de Monte Falco, the Comte de Camerion and thirteen more, some of them nobles, others arrant scoundrels, were all hanged.

Colonel Lorenzo Nobile del Borgo, Liverotto, and da Fermo were torn to pieces by the mob as they were firing upon the house. Twenty of the people lie imprisoned. They also will probably be hanged.

92. Leicester in Zeeland

Antwerp, December 28, 1585.

It looks as though in future there would be different news to report and more of it than hitherto. On the 20th inst. my Lord or the Earl of Leicester made a brilliant entry into Zeeland with four thousand men, six hundred horses, and many well-armed and well-found warships and others. He was received with great rejoicing and enthusiasm. It is said everywhere that in the name of Holland Duke Maurice, son of the Prince of Orange, has renounced the Provinces of Holland, and handed them over to Leicester, so that Holland and Zeeland will become quite English. About this there is much pondering among people here. God grant that things may be so disposed that real agreement and sound peace may result. It is said that the Earl of Leicester will hold his Court at Utrecht. With this exception, as almost the whole week was a holiday, we have heard hardly anything from outside, and all wonder what to think about this arrival of the English. The Catholics firmly believe we shall reach a satisfactory peace, but others fear a big war again. Time will show all this in the end. Some days ago it was announced that the King of Spain had sent some emissaries to the Queen of England, and that she had sent some in return, but this is thought to be mere talk.

93. The Plundering of Santo Domingo

Report of the 11th day of January 1586 on which Santo Domingo on the island of Spagnola was captured and was pillaged by the English pirate, Francis Drake. This report was forwarded to the Royal Council for India.

On the 11th day of January of this year, a mighty Armada, belonging to the Queen of England was to be seen lying before this town and harbour, composed of thirty large and seventeen small ships, which had already been sighted from afar on the previous day towards noon. Their Commander was Francis Drake. The fleet took its course to the south. Thereupon there arose much disquiet in the town, and forthwith the President and the Councillors foregathered with the burghers and the citizens, in great concern, in order to decide upon measures for self-defence. These they have taken on the coast at the place where a landing of the enemy was to be feared. They sank many barrels filled with sand into the river and behind them ranged four hundred men so that they could shoot at the enemy with their muskets. On land they erected earth works. They supplied the first with a parapet and cannon. In Cabia, half a mile from the town, troops were stationed in order that they should keep watch and check the enemy, should this become necessary. The President and the Councillors also called together the most experienced burghers, to ask them whether in their opinion the enemy could land at any other spot and do damage.

They were assured with one accord that, with the exception of Cabia, there was no landing-place on the whole coast. As now there was no longer fear on that score, all resistance was directed towards the river, as many mighty ships had been seen sailing towards it. Besides those mentioned heretofore, three others came quite near, seeking a favourable opportunity of attack. Meanwhile the other ships sailed hither and thither, keeping themselves well out of range of the cannon shot from the fort. They were recognized as enemies and fired upon, but the powder was worthless and the projectiles failed to reach them. It can be imagined that disquiet arose through the menace of the enemy. The authorities rested not a moment

115

throughout the night, but were continually on the alert, so as to keep all in good order. They noticed that the populace had begun to leave the town, in order to flee from the designs and wrath of the enemy, and to save their wives, children and goods. This they did, although it was forbidden on pain of death. Thereupon came the news that a great number of the enemy were approaching the town, and were about half a mile from it. They had landed three miles from here at a place where to do so was thought to be quite impossible. All in all there were only about one hundred and twenty men on horse and on foot left to take into battle, in order to make as good a stand as possible against the enemy. The chief Captains of this handful were: the Licentiate Juan Fernandes de Mercado, the Licentiate Balthasar de Villa Fane, the local Auditor of the Royal Council and with them was the Fiscal Licentiate Aliago. The President, as General, accompanied by these gentlemen, and also the Licentiate Arero, who belonged to the Council, marched out at the head of the above-mentioned troop. They went close on quarter of a mile to meet the enemy. The President and also the other gentlemen were on horseback, armed with spears and shields, with them was also Don Diego Orsinio, the Captain of the galley, which His Majesty had here. This galley at the time was on shore for repairs, so that she was useless. As they drew near to the enemy, the President and his horse sank into the bog, so that steed and man were covered with mud, in full view of the troops. This was held to be of ill-omen. Thereupon the President betook himself back to his dwelling. He was urged to do this, for owing to his age and infirmities his ability to wage war had departed. He was accompanied by the venerable Licentiate Arero. The remainder of those heretofore mentioned took the leadership and are highly to be honoured for their bravery and stout-heartedness. They are worthy of great favours to be bestowed upon them by His Majesty. All the more so if victory had been granted to our side. With courageous spirit they offered their lives to the enemy although they were well aware of his great strength, nigh on seven hundred.

These were well armed. They were mostly musketeers, archers, and arquebusiers, also spearmen and halberdiers. Furthermore, there were another six thousand men in the ships. The enemy had divided into three groups and waited for our troops. But when the latter perceived the power and strength of their opponents they were filled with fear. Therefore the Licentiate Balthasar, who showed a brave spirit during this expedition and wished to do credit to his office, gave the soldiers a Christian admonition, exhorted them to be brave and stout of heart, challenged them to the fray and approached the enemy within bullet range.

The Licentiate Mercado also showed that his spirit was no whit less ardent or brave. These two and others of the nobility took up front positions and went into danger in order to induce the rest to follow them, but instead of so doing they broke into flight, heedless of all admonitions and penalities with which the Licentiate Balthasar was threatening them. He called out to them to turn back and to attack and face at least two discharges of bullets, taking no heed of who fell. He wished that God and the whole world should see that they had done their duty. But this was of no avail and they all retreated. The nobles and the Councillors remained behind exposed to all the danger of the shots which were fired from the ships, whose prows were directed against the rear-guard. They re-entered the town through the Gate of Zemba, through which they had passed out. From there they fired three cannon at the enemy and laid low two or three of their men. Now that there was no longer any resistance, the town and harbour were given over to the enemy, who took possession thereof. The fort, too, had no chance of defending itself. They plundered the town from one end to another and took all the private property including that of the nobility, in order to avoid giving cause for offence to the ordinary citizens. The Licentiate Villa Fane is worthy of great compassion, for nothing remained to him. When he was told that he ought to save his belongings as the others had done, he refused to do this, and said that as his property remained here, here would he also die.

Then the enemy set fire to the town. When a goodly portion of it was burnt, a remedy was found to save at least the churches and what remained. Five-and-twenty thousand thalers were then given to the enemy. When they had received this sum they withdrew on the 10th day this month of February after they had been five weeks in the town, which they left without guns and defenceless.

117

Those galleys and ships which they did not take with them, they burned. Their vessels were loaded with the bells from all the churches and cloisters. Of these have been destroyed and burned: St. Domingo, St. Francisco, the Church of the Mother of God, Santa Clara, Regina Angelorum. These are left in such a state that neither monk nor nun can abide in them. Without the grace of God and help and assistance from the King they will not be able to hold this land under discipline. They also so burned the Church of St. Barbara, that it is now a sorry sight. They then destroyed, burnt and barbarously profaned the pictures of God and His saints. Nothing remains but life itself, which has to be spent in great poverty. The distress is great, and the worst of all that the island is in such bad condition that only a very feeble resistance will be offered to enemy ships. The populace is affrighted and in a dangerous temper. Would that His Majesty took pity on us and showed his authority, for it was for his sake in the first place that this new world was discovered. To keep two galleys for the protection of this island is not enough. It has pleased God, our Lord, thus to confuse the enemy's brains that they did not press further onwards and destroy the land and its inhabitants.

All this time the Councillors have kept round the town some two hundred men who troubled the enemy by day and night, killing some of their people without loss on our side, and making it impossible for them to press further.

The enemy brought with them a parson of the Lutheran Faith in order that he should proselytize. When two preaching monks opposed this, they were imprisoned, hanged and died martyrs. Given in Santo Domingo on the 20th day of February 1586.

94. Bad Times in Mexico

News-letter of the 15th day of March 1586 from Mexico.

Yesterday the ship from New Spain, which left there upon the 1st day of March, arrived here. On the 25th day of February a ship with three hundred men and all manner of munitions sailed for Havana to render assistance. Those who have landed here previously from Havana, report that the country is ruined and that there is no demand for merchandise. They were obliged to take off twenty per cent. and to give long credit for the little that was sold. A ship brings nine hundred arobas of cochineal as counter cargo. Different reports are current about the arrival of the fleet. Some say yea, the others nay. Whether it comes or not, it will bring but little money back, for no one will wish to spend because the goods are worth more in Spain than here. What is sold here will have to be given on credit. He who has sailed for Havana with the said three hundred men, writes that he has learnt for certain that the English pirates have gone to Honduras and there taken possession of the Porto Canaros, which is the most important port there. They have also taken away the ships among which was one containing three hundred loads of cargo. It is held for a certainty that the pirates will also go to Campeche and visit the whole coast. They will also make a stay in order to see whether it is possible to capture the fleet from New Spain. On this account it is feared that it will not be able to venture forth. This is all that is known. It is the most deplorable tidings for commerce that can be imagined. Our Armada, likewise, does not hurry. It is written to us that our Viceroy of Peru lies in Truxillo near unto death.

95. The Spanish on the Red Sea

From Constantinople, the 15th day of June 1586.

On the 14th day of this month two galleys arrived here from Alexandria, bringing news that the Armada of the King of Spain of about seventy large and small ships, has arrived from India, through the Persian Gulf, near Aden, a three days' journey from Suez. They have diligently examined everything there and appear desirous to build a large fortress near Aden, on African soil, and thereby to cut off the Turks from Indian navigation.

96. Drake in Santiago, Porto Rico, and San Domingo

Madrid, April 5, 1586.

You have already learnt what the English did on the island of Santiago, and how they pillaged and set fire to everything and got clear away. But this unfortunately is not the end of it, for on the 27th March, news dated the 24th came here from Seville, that the English pirate, Drake, after all the damage he did at Santiago, took and plundered Porto Rico and the island of San Domingo. They say he has carried off and done damage to the tune of over two millions. He killed or ill-treated all priests and monks he could get hold of, and is fortifying himself in San Domingo too. They fear he has also taken Havana. If His Majesty does not soon provide assistance, no fleet will be able to sail from India or to come from there this year. This is of course a grievous loss and a great danger for all India, and one which hits trade especially hard. His Majesty had information about the plans of this Drake in good time, but paid no attention. Also he gave no orders to the Indian Council or any one else to intercept Drake. Nobody will believe this till we have to bear the shame and loss of it. Now we must expend much money, labour and trouble, and shall be unable to do any good at first. What is more, this will put a check on the success we hoped for in the Netherlands. They say His Majesty has given orders to get ready and equip the fifteen galliots lying at Seville and Lisbon, but not yet quite completed and insufficiently provided with soldiers, and thirty more ships too. But it is to be feared that, as is their custom, they will go about it so slowly that the enemy will manage to carry his plan through first, will fortify himself and do still more damage. May God Almighty grant in His mercy that all may soon be changed, and that this piracy may be withstood. As is also stated, His Majesty has ordered the six hundred thousand ducats sent three weeks ago to Barcelona for shipment to Italy to be brought back, as the cash will probably be wanted for the fresh war. If things had only been looked to earlier, we could have managed with a smaller sum.

97. A French Consular Report from Egypt

Copy of a Report of Paolo Mariano, French Consul in Egypt, July 20, 1586. (Mariano is very well informed about affairs in those countries and speaks their languages like a native.)

(Original in Italian.)

I have received a letter of the 15th of May from Cairo, in which my friends inform me of the occurrence of events of the greatest importance. Pepper at Cairo has risen to 26 ducats. Thirty-six galleons and four Spanish galleys have come into the Straits of Suez. They have been to the port of Mecca, the approach to the Yemen, and have done much damage, and taken many prisoners and a lot of booty, for this district is very populous. They were accompanied by Mahomet Bey, Captain of Alexandria. This man is undoubtedly of Neapolitan birth, and used to be Captain of Mecca. The fleet sent out a pinnace to pillage near Aden. The boat was captured and the Spanish crew confessed that an additional fleet of forty galleys and twenty-five others was expected to construct a fortress in sight of Aden, in a place which formerly belonged to the Portuguese. But I am unaware that the Portuguese ever possessed anything except Aden. When the second fleet arrives, the other fort is to be put up. This is a very important and astonishing affair. And it is certain that they have evil designs upon this country. The people there are greatly alarmed and demand help from the Great Lord. This must be already on its way. Plague is said to have broken out at Mecca, but no report of it has reached me. I tell you this because it is possible that your business requires a knowledge of these occurrences, as trade to India might be the sufferer. Shippers in the Arabian Sea know about the circumstances, and so hesitate to entrust foodstuffs to the merchants of Aden. What they, and especially their representatives at Cairo, will do about it I do not know, as I have no news from that quarter. I desired to inform you of this for my own peace of mind and to your profit, all the more as the Bailo of Venice assure me they have not received the news yet. So I am the only one to pass it on. I beg your Magnificence not

to doubt this special information, for I have received it
from my friend in Arabic. I have this day visited all the
government officials of Cairo, staying here with the excellent Ibrahim Pasha, and he assures me that the Cherif
of Mecca has not yet transmitted the news to the Grand
Turk. All were amazed and almost beside themselves at the
importance of these matters. Given at Pera on the 15th
June 1586.

98. Drake at Havana
Is there to be an Armada?

Madrid, July 26, 1586.

About that Drake or English pirate we have no news since
he took the port of Havana and despoiled the inhabitants
of fourteen hundred ducats. But Havana letters of May 4
report that Drake is on the island of San Antonio not far
from Havana, to await the fleet there. Havana, however,
was garrisoned with two thousand fighting men and had
no fear of him. What the twenty galleys which sailed from
Seville on the last day of May have accomplished we shall
soon hear. God grant they may get in safe and bring out
the fleet, so that it does not fall into the hands of Drake.
A few days ago they declared here quite positively that
some of his Captains had sailed away home from him,
ships and all, because he had broken his word over the
partition of the booty. There is constant talk of a mighty
fleet which our King is to fit out next year, and send against
England. But it does not look much like it at present, and
as the custom is here they will go to work slowly, just as in
everything else, and wait till the loss has grown very great.

99. Drake in London with Great Wealth:
The Queen shot at

Antwerp, September 6, 1586.

London letters of the 2th ult. recently received announce
that Drake the pirate has arrived in London from India
with fifty to sixty ships. He is said to have brought great

122

wealth with him, but the ships are not yet unloaded. They also write of an important case of treason against the Queen's life. Monsieur de Guise had arranged with certain nobles to come to England, but the conspiracy was discovered, and some sixty persons, many of high birth, have been imprisoned. A man who came here from England recently says that this plot took place before his departure from London, and that an Englishman shot at the Queen. But before he fired, the bullet, without his noticing it, fell out of the pistol, so he missed her. Nevertheless the Queen's hair seems to have been singed. The Earl of Leicester is stated to have pitched his camp between Utrecht and Amersfoort.

100. The Wild Irish

Cologne, September 15, 1586.

The Earl of Leicester seems to be assembling his army. There are about fifty-five companies of foot, and twenty-four troops of horse and fifteen hundred Irish as well. These Irishmen are almost all naked and have their bows and arrows with them. They are very quick runners, and there are also some hundreds of them who go on stilts the height of a man. They are to walk through the moats surrounding the towns and climb the walls.

101. Wrecks off Ostend and Savage Executions in London

Middelburg, October 23, 1586.

Two days ago a couple of ships came over here from England, and though some thirty ships were lying at anchor over there, so that they might make the crossing in concert, the wind did not suit them, as it was blowing a gale, so they sailed back to London. One of the ships, which was sailing in company with the two above mentioned, was wrecked and all three were so driven by the gale that they got ashore on the Ostend sandbanks. There they lost all their sails and had to drift at the mercy of God. Finally the two ships reached here safely on the flood. On the one ship all the passengers and the German mail are said to have been lost. Those who came over on the two ships which were saved report that fourteen of the conspirators against the Queen of England have been executed. Some were quartered alive, among them a Jesuit, others executed with the axe, others again with the halter. One among them was dragged at the horse's tail from prison to scaffold through the streets. His mother had offered to give as much money as the horse could carry from the prison to the place of execution. This mother had also offered to maintain at her own cost a company of mercenaries for so long as the war should last in Holland and Zeeland, if only her son might be kept in prison for life. All she desired was to save his life and shield him from so shameful a death. But this was quite useless, and the course of justice was not interfered with. Those executed implicated the Queen of Scots in the conspiracy in order to destroy her. Parliament is assembled to judge whether this Queen has not forfeited her life. After the execution of these fourteen persons a new plan was discovered, to shoot the Queen out hunting. So five people, all of English birth, nobles and courtiers of the Queen of England, were at once imprisoned and a few days later quartered alive.

102. Incrimination of Mary Queen of Scots

Antwerp, November 1, 1586.

The announcement comes from Zeeland that the Earl of Leicester has given permission by licence, which has to be purchased, for ships to sail to Spain, Portugal, France and other places and to export merchandise, but with the exception of munitions and food-stuffs. On September 20th and 21st, O.S., fourteen of the conspirators against the Queen of England were executed. They confessed that the Queen of Scots was the instigator of this conspiracy, wherefore Commissioners have been despatched to examine her.

103. Arrival of part of a Fleet from New Spain

Madrid, November 6, 1586.

God be praised, the fleet from New Spain has arrived safe at San Lucar. What gold, silver and merchandise it brings for the King and for private individuals I will report later, also how eight of these ships were lost, though the crews and cargoes were saved. It is thought that the continental fleet which is to bring seven millions in gold and silver has not yet assembled, and will not come out till next spring. May the Almighty in His loving-kindness protect and guard from harm and woe the fleet which sailed from Seville on October 23, and is to bring back twelve millions. Further news that I hear is as follows. With the arming of the so-called Armada against England progress is small and slow. It is true that in the last few days some Spaniards have agreed to make a loan to His Majesty amounting to one hundred and fifty thousand ducats, the money to be delivered at Lisbon in one month. And with it some soldiers, brought there from Andalusia, are to be paid. Then some new warships are to be completed. But what will finally come of the thing next spring will allow us to see.

104. Trial of Mary Queen of Scots

Cologne, November 13, 1586.

It is announced here from Middelburg that the English Captain Drake arrived there on October 30, and proceeded to the English camp. He has brought over £50,000 in cash, and as much more in bills as the Queen of England could raise through English merchants. At Rouen in France English ships and property have been detained because a pirate stole to the value of £4000. So about £6000 in costs will be entailed. Letters dated the 8th have reached Middelburg from London. In them it is confirmed that many members of the nobility and of the Council, with two thousand horses, have ridden sixty miles away from the city to conduct a trial of the Queen of Scots. It is thought she would not be indicted in this manner if she alone had caused the conspiracy against the Crown, but, as so many lives have been lost because of it, further proceedings are to be taken against her.

105. Sentence of Death against Mary Stuart

On the 27th day of December 1586.

In letters from London it is written that Parliament has condemned the Queen of Scotland to be executed by the sword. But the Queen of England will not suffer this. The King of France has dispatched Monsieur de Bellièvre to the Queen of England, earnestly to beseech her to spare the life of the Queen of Scotland. How this matter will further develop is awaited with anxiety.

106. A Wedding Feast in Prague

From Prague, the 22nd day of January 1587.

A list of all the meat and poultry which were consumed on the occasion of the wedding festivities of His Honour William of Rosenberg held in Prague from the 11th to the 14th day of January anno '87, during three meals: deer 36, venison 12 tons, boars 36, sucking pigs 9 tons, roes 49, hares 1290, turkeys 27, pheasants 272, partridges 1910, field hares 11,560, Westphalian cocks 50, oxen 75, sheep 764, calves 173, lambs 221, fattened pigs 32, young sows 160, Indian cocks 200, fattened capons 500, fattened hens 5560, young hens 900, fattened geese 1350, eggs 20,620, lard 17 hundredweight, cheese 2 tons. Skate fish 960, char fish in pasties 70, large pike 300, small pike 420, carps 5800, a very large she-pike. Rhine wine 70 pails, Hungarian wine 100 pails, Moravian wine 40 pails, Austrian wine 17 barrels, Bohemian wine 47 barrels, sweet wine 10 kegs, pale ale 150 barrels, Rakonitz beer 8 barrels, barley beer 18 barrels.

Spices, marzipan and sweetmeats, wheat for rolls and corn for rye bread—a goodly amount.

In all estates, towns and villages, a goodly number of

poor people were likewise fed and it is not yet known how much has been consumed.

107. A fresh Plot traced to the Queen of Scots and the Guises

Antwerp, February 14, 1587.

In letters of the 24th ult. from London it is reported that more treason against the Queen of England has been discovered. Some French are said to be in prison because of this, and the French ambassador has been confined to his lodgings. Some English gentlemen are said to be in prison too. It is stated that this treason originated with the Queen of Scots and the Duke of Guise. From Brussels it is announced that the citizens at Haarlem and in Guelderland have expelled the English soldiers quartered there and submitted to the King of Spain.

108. Execution of Mary Stuart

Exhaustive report of the way in which Queen Mary Stuart of Scotland and Douairière of France was beheaded on the 18th day of February of the new calendar, in the castle of Fotheringhay in England.

After there had been revealed to the Queen of England, Elizabeth, several plots, hatched at the instigation of the Pope and the heads of the neighbouring states, enemies of the Crown of England, the said Queen found that she had not only to fear for her throne, but also for her life. She then realized that their aim was to release the Queen Mary of Scotland from her durance and to establish her as the next heir, although she was a Catholic and had been detained in prison in England for many years. In this prison she was persecuted for a long time by the Parliament and the States of the Scottish Kingdom, in order that she might be condemned to death, for she had murdered a king, and had set fire to a house with gunpowder, because she was in love with Bothwell, a Scottish baron. Thereupon she abdicated in favour of her son James, the present King of Scotland. But when she again escaped from prison, she assem-

127

bled troops, so as to rob the said son of his crown. However, she was put to flight and returned again to England. In spite of these charges Queen Elizabeth yet desired to spare her life, not wishing to be her judge, on account of her being such a near blood relation.

But as the Scottish Queen now presumed to covet the Crown of England, the English Queen could not let her go free and scathless, because her life, her country and religion were imperilled. Also she did not wish to create any suspicion in the minds of the Scots. Although the Scottish Queen was kept in such lax and pleasurable confinement that she could even go hunting and enjoy all the pleasures of the chase, she, nevertheless, did not rest content with the pastimes that were allowed to her. She tried many and various devices to become free again, namely through encompassing the death of the Queen of England. To this end she enticed many persons of the nobility, among them the Duke of Norfolk, as well as other earls and gentlemen, so that the Queen of England was to have lost her life at her Court in the previous summer. On that account the above-named lords met a miserable end. Also England was to have been attacked by foreign troops, the Scottish Queen set upon the thrones of Scotland and England, and the Romish faith established in both kingdoms. All of this the Queen of England gathered from various informants, and the Queen of Scotland was proved guilty in the presence of the nobility, the knighthood and the officials.

It was discussed in Parliament and by the States, how the person of the Queen and the religion of the country could be guarded in future against such dangers. As, however, the Scottish Queen was a close blood relation, her life was to be spared. Since also she was not in the free enjoyment of her liberty and rights, a sentence of death would make a rare and amazing departure.

Thereupon Parliament decided thus:—the life of the Scottish Queen would mean the death of the English Queen and the ruin and destruction of England and of her religion. Therefore it is admitted that she, the Scottish Queen, has to be put to death. Shortly thereafter, a conspiracy was discovered against the person of Her Majesty, wherein her ambassador and others of her retinue were involved. Thereupon, latterly, the Queen of England has resolved to abolish the cause of such evil and of the above-mentioned danger, although she agreed to the execution with but a heavy heart. She therefore dispatched several persons to carry out the sentence upon the Queen of Scotland. The officials who received this command hastened forward the execution, but this against the repeated injunction of the English Queen. Because of this, the secretary of Her Majesty, Davison, was thrown into the Tower and several others fell into disgrace.

And the execution therefore took place in this wise:

At the command of the Queen of England (through the secretary, Beale) the Earls of Shrewsbury and Kent, who were at the time in the neighbourhood of the castle of Fotheringhay, together with other gentlemen, knights and noble persons, with Sir Amias Paulet and Sir Drury, who had order to guard the Queen of Scotland, had on the previous day, namely the 17th day of February, made known to the imprisoned Queen the will of Her Majesty of England. Thereupon she made reply that she was prepared and had long awaited this. She inquired when the execution would take place. Although this was left to her own choice, she asked that it might take place at once, on the very next day, namely on the 18th day of February of the new calendar, on a Wednesday. She besought God's help thereto. At the same time as this notification there were laid before the Queen various apologies, namely that the kingdom of England and its Queen had been compelled to make such a decision.

Hence on the 18th day of February, at 7 o'clock of the morning, the aforementioned earls, knights and noblemen forgathered in the castle of Fotheringhay. Two followers were allocated to each knight, but only one to the others present, so that about eighty to a hundred persons entered the castle, beside the guard and the officials of the court.

There, in the large hall, in front of the fireplace, in which burnt a great fire, a dais had been set up, which was twelve feet wide and eight feet high. It was completely covered with black cloth, and thereon stood a chair with a cushion. As now all was ready, and the gentlemen had collected there between the hours of eight and nine, a message was sent to the imprisoned Queen that the gentlemen had come on the errand of which she had been forewarned in the afternoon of yesterday, and wished to know whether she were ready.

129

The messenger, however, found the door of her chamber locked and bolted. All her people were with her in the chamber. When the gentlemen heard this, they sent a messenger once more commanding him to knock at the door, should he not find it open and to deliver the former message.

But he found the door unlocked. He sent one of the Queen's servants to her in order to acquaint her with his command. The servant brought answer that the Queen was not yet ready. After half an hour, the gentlemen sent to her once more, and thereto she made answer that she would be ready in half an hour.

After this time the chief official went to the Queen. He found her on her knees with her ladies-in-waiting, praying, and told her that her time was now come. Thereupon she stood up and said that she was ready. She was led between two men of her retinue into the antechamber. There she found all her people assembled. She exhorted them all to fear God and to live in humility of spirit. She took leave of them all, kissed the women and held out her hand to the men to kiss. She begged them not to grieve on her account but to be of good cheer and to pray for her. Then she was led to the stairway. There all the gentlemen advanced from the hall towards her, and the Earl of Shrewsbury said to the sorrowing Queen: "Madame, we are here to carry out the behest of our most gracious Queen of England, which was communicated unto you yesterday." The warrant and sentence the Earl of Kent held in his hand. The Great Seal of the Crown of England was thereon. Then the Queen replied that she would as lief die as live any longer. As she turned round she perceived her most distinguished servitor, Melville, and said to him: "My faithful servant Melville, though thou art a Protestant and I a Catholic, there is nevertheless but one Christendom and I am thy Queen, born and anointed, of the lineage of Henry VII. And so I adjure thee before God that thou give this command to my son: I beg him to serve God, and the Catholic Church, and to rule and keep his country in peace and to submit (as I have done) to no other Master, although I had the right good will to unite the kingdoms of this island. I renounce this, may he do likewise, and do not let him put overmuch trust in the presumption of the world. Let him trust God and then he will be blessed by Him. Let him speak no evil of the Queen of England, and thou, Melville, art my witness that I die like a true Scotswoman, Frenchwoman and Catholic, which belief has ever been mine." These words and such like did she repeat.

Thereupon Melville made answer: "Most venerable and most august Princess, as I have been at all times your Majesty's faithful servant, so will I now with the help of God, faithfully and honestly transmit to the King, your Son, your Majesty's words and message."

Thereupon she turned to the above-mentioned gentlemen and desired to have her priest with her on the dais, so that he might bear witness for her to the King of France and in other places, that she had died righteously and a good Catholic. To this the gentlemen made reply that it had been ordained otherwise.

She then demanded that her servants might remain with her. This was refused, in order to curb her impatience and to free her mind from certain superstitions. Nevertheless five of her servants and two tiring-women were permitted to come to her, because she complained that she was being poorly served. She promised that she would cause no hindrance, either by cries or by tears. Further she demanded for her servants and her maids liberty to depart, with good escort, and free of cost to their own countries without let or hindrance. This the gentlemen promised her. Also that they should be permitted to retain everything that the Queen of Scotland had presented to them. But she repeated once more: "I desire that this take place." Thereupon she was led by two servants of the Governor to the dais. There she seated herself upon a chair, for she could stand but with difficulty. The two earls seated themselves beside her. Then the Secretary Beale read the warrant and the sentence of execution in an over loud voice.

The gown in which the Queen was attired was of exquisite black velvet, which she had likewise worn when she appeared before the gentlemen. In her hand she held a small cross of wood or of ivory with the picture of Christ thereon, and a book. On her neck hung a golden crucifix, and from her girdle a rosary.

Near her stood a doctor of theology, Dean of Peterborough, who, at the command of the gentlemen spoke words of Christian comfort to her, exhorting her to die as a Christian with a repentant heart. She at once interrupted him and begged him to keep his peace, for she was fully prepared for death. The Dean answered that he had been commanded to speak the truth to her. But she said for the second time: "I will not listen to you, Mr. Dean. You have naught to do with me. You disturb me." Thereupon he was bidden to be silent by the gentlemen.

The Earl of Kent said to her: "Madame, I am grieved on your account to hear of this superstition from you and to see that which is in your hand." She said it was seemly that she should hold the figure of Christ in her hand thereby to think of Him. Thereupon he answered that she must have Christ in her heart, and further said that though she made demur in paying heed to the mercies vouchsafed to her by God All-Highest, they would nevertheless plead for her with God Almighty, that He would forgive her sins and receive her into His Kingdom. Thereto the Queen made reply: "Pray, then will I also pray." Then the aforesaid Doctor fell on his knees on the steps of the dais and read in an over loud voice a fervent and godly prayer for her, most suitable to such an occasion, also for the Queen of England and the welfare of the Kingdom. All those standing round repeated the prayer. But as long as it lasted the Queen was praying in Latin and fairly audibly, holding the crucifix in her hand.

When this prayer was now ended on both sides, the executioner knelt in front of the Queen. Him she forgave his deed, as also all those who lusted after her blood, or desired her death. She further forgave all and sundry and craved from God that He might also forgive her own trespasses. Thereafter she fell on her knees in ardent supplication and besought the remission of her sins. She said that she trusted to be saved through the death of Christ and His Blood and that she was ready to have her own blood spilt at His feet, wherefore she held His picture and the crucifix in her hands. Further she prayed for a happy, long and prosperous reign for the Queen of England, for the prosperity of the British Isles, for the afflicted Christian Church and the end of all misery. She also prayed for her son, the King of Scots, for his upright and honourable Government and of his conversion to the Catholic Faith. At the last she prayed that all the saints in heaven might intercede for her on this day, and that God of His great goodness might avert great

132

plagues from this Island, forgive her her sins and receive her soul into His heavenly hand.

Thereupon she stood up and prepared herself for death. She doffed her jewels and her gown, with the help of two women. When the executioner wished to assist her, she said to him that it was not her wont to be disrobed in the presence of such a crowd, nor with the help of such hand-maidens. She herself took off her robe and pushed it down as far as the waist. The bodice of the underskirt was cut low and tied together at the back. She hastened to undo this.

Thereafter she kissed her ladies, commended them to God, and because one of them was weeping too loudly, she said to her: "Have I not told you that you should not weep? Be comforted." To her she gave her hand, and bade her leave the dais. When she was thus prepared, she turned to her servitors, who were kneeling not far off, blessed them and made them all witnesses that she died a Catholic and begged them to pray for her. Afterwards she fell on her knees with great courage, did not change colour, and like-wise gave no sign of fear. One of her tirewomen bound a kerchief before her eyes. As she knelt down she repeated the 70th Psalm: "*In te, Domine, speravi. . . .*" When she had said this to the end, she, full of courage, bent down with her body and laid her head on the block, exclaiming: "*In manuas tuas, Domine, commendo spiritum meum.*" Then one of the executioners held down her hands, and the other cut off her head with two strokes of the chopper. Thus ended her life.

The executioner took the head and showed it to the people, who cried: "God spare our Queen of England!"

When the executioner held up the head, it fell in dis-array so that it could be seen that her hair was quite grey and had been closely cropped.

Her raiment and other belongings were by command taken from the executioner, but he was promised their equivalent in money. Everything that had been sprinkled with her blood, also the garments of the executioner and other objects, were promptly taken away and washed. The planks of the dais, the black cloth and all else were thrown into the fire, at once, so that no superstitious practices could be carried on therewith.

Her body was carried out, embalmed and made ready for burial. Where this will take place is as yet unknown. Her servants and courtiers were instructed to abide there until her remains had been honourably laid to rest. She was four-and-forty years of age, and was the most beautiful princess of her time.

She had as first spouse, Francis II, King of France, after him Henry Stuart, the son of the Earl of Lennox, her cousin, a truly handsome young man, by whom she had issue James V, King of Scotland. But after she had caused Henry Stuart to be murdered, she took in marriage the Earl of Bothwell, who was imprisoned in Denmark, lost his senses and there died.

After this execution had taken place, the portals of the castle remained shut, until Henry Talbot, son of the Earl of Shrewsbury, had been dispatched to the English Court. When, the other day, he brought the tidings to London, the citizens of this town lit bonfires on all sides and rang the bells, because they were rid of the danger in which they had lived so long. It looks as if the populace believed that a new era had begun in which they hope that all will remain at peace.

Described by Emanuel Tomascon, who was present at the happenings.

(On the report is a note in old handwriting: From a Calvinist source.)

109. The Guises will fight England

Antwerp, March 25, 1587.

This week we had news from France that the King of that country will not consent to war with England. So the Guises and their adherents will carry on the war on their own account. With this object they have already assembled a large number of horse and foot in Picardy. They had meant to filch Boulogne from the King, but as the Governor heard in time he was able to frustrate their attempt.

110. Drake takes Cadiz

Madrid, May 30, 1587.

On the 24th inst. they wrote from Cadiz how Francis
Drake, the English pirate, made a surprise landing there
with forty-eight ships great and small, not all warships.
He pillaged and stripped about fourteen ships laden with
all sorts of merchandise and lying in the roads, and stayed
there for some days. Those ships which he could not take
with him he afterwards burnt or sank. Thereupon the
chief citizens with women and property fled to Seville
and elsewhere, although the King at once sent five hundred men to the fort as garrison, together with some galleys. On the 25th inst. news again came from His Serene
Highness the Cardinal Archduke Albert of Austria to the
effect that this Drake, after sailing away from Cadiz, first
proceeded to Cape St. Vincent and remained there ten
days with his fleet, and after the 15th went to the province
of Algarvia situated in Portugal, not far from the town of
Lagos. There he landed some two thousand men and drew
them up in order of battle, as though the enemy were in
sight and forced to fight him. With his troops he advanced
in battle order to within half a mile of the town of Lagos,
whereupon the citizens in great haste ran up on the walls,
and the Governor made a sally with three hundred horse.
On this Drake slowly retired. Now, although the Governor
pursued the marauders with his troopers, neither side attacked or harmed the other. On the following day, that is
the 16th, Drake landed again with some troops and appeared before a fortress named Sagres, situated near the
town of Lagos. He took it after two assaults, as he had
brought with him scaling ladders and other apparatus for
attack. Although one hundred and fifty Portuguese soldiers
were in the fortress, they offered no resistance. Drake burnt
the fortress with the monastery and the altars and pictures
in the church. The monks fled to safety. Then he came to
two castles, from which the garrisons had likewise fled.
These also he burnt down and razed. All the cannons,
armour and weapons, as also all the wood which he found
there, he carried off to his ships. On the 18th he arrived

with his fleet off the port of Lisbon, and on the morning of the 19th he passed between the two harbour forts. And although Don Alonzo de Bazan, brother of the Marquis de Santa Cruz, sailed out with the seven galleasses which he commands at Lisbon, he began to skirmish with his cannon, and the firing and skirmishing lasted till six o'clock in the evening. But the firing of the big guns from the enemy's ships was so severe that the galleasses were ultimately forced to retire, without producing any effect on the English. When the English fleet had also withdrawn a little way in its turn, a few soldiers were sent out to prevent the English from landing. But early on the 20th inst. the English fleet left the river and went out to sea, in what direction is unknown. Thus far the Lisbon letters of May 25. His Sacred Majesty of Spain has slept long enough, and from pride, preoccupation or parsimony has paid no attention to such visitors. But now he has been roused afresh and must hurriedly protect himself with money and troops. The Marquis de Santa Cruz is already arming, and money and troops are being sent him in great haste. He is to sail from Lisbon as soon as possible with thirty-two well-armed galleasses and pursue the enemy. As news has been received that Don Antonio of Portugal is to sail from England with another fleet, and it is likewise impossible to know whether he too will not come to Portugal and join Drake and whether one of the fleets or even both may not again make for India, His Sacred Majesty has ordered the Duke of Medina Sidonia to sail out as quickly as possible and pursue the enemy with 32 galleys which are already fitted, and 32 big warships also which are being prepared. With the utmost despatch His Majesty is sending money to Seville in Andalusia and to Biscay, where some large ships are likewise being constructed for war, and to all places where it is required. Troops are being raised all over Spain. Recently also fifteen hundred soldiers, all trusty Spaniards, arrived in Cartagena from Sicily. Another two thousand are expected from Italy. It is said too that men are to be transferred from Germany to Italy as garrisons in place of those who have been brought to Spain.

There is moreover some fear that the Portuguese might have an understanding with Drake or Don Antonio. Now what will happen over all this time will show. A large sum of money was recently sent for the King from here to Barcelona through some Genoese and Messrs. Fugger of this city. It should have gone to Italy and the Netherlands, but whether much of it will reach the Netherlands and the unhappy troops there we shall hear shortly.

P.S.—Just this moment His Majesty is sending a Knight of Malta, who is a famous Italian architect, with some workmen to Cadiz, to pull down the old fortress and build up a new one.

111. The Peru Fleet arrives safely

Antwerp, September 16, 1587.

Urgent letters from Spain of the 4th inst. report that the Marquis de Santa Cruz has arrived with the entire Peru fleet, one hundred and seventeen vessels in all. Moreover two ships from Calicut have reached the Azores in safety. It is hoped that he has by now reached Seville and Lisbon unharmed. The Peru fleet is said to be bringing fourteen millions in gold and silver and over three millions in merchandise. This is indeed a great sum.

112. Judgment on the Witch Walpurga Hausmännin

Confessions of Walpurga Hausmännin, formerly licensed midwife at Dillingen, who, for almost thirty years, practised witchcraft and was in league with the Evil One. She was burnt at the stake at Dillingen on the 20th day of September anno Domini 1587.

The herein mentioned, malefic and miserable woman, Walpurga Hausmännin, now imprisoned and in chains, has, upon kindly questioning and also torture, following on persistent and fully justified accusations, confessed her witchcraft and admitted the following. When one-and-thirty years ago, she had become a widow, she cut corn for Hans Schlumperger, of this place, together with his former servant, Bis im Pfarrhof, by name. Him she enticed with lewd speeches and gestures and they convened that they should, on an appointed night, meet in her, Walpurga's, dwelling, there to indulge in lustful intercourse.

137

So when Walpurga in expectation of this, sat awaiting him at night in her chamber, meditating upon evil and fleshly thoughts, it was not the said bondsman who appeared unto her, but the Evil One in the latter's guise and raiment and indulged in fornication with her. Thereupon he presented her with a piece of money, in the semblance of half a thaler, but no one could take it from her, for it was a bad coin and like lead. For this reason she had thrown it away. After the act of fornication she saw and felt the cloven foot of her whoremonger, and that his hand was not natural, but as if made of wood. She was greatly affrighted thereat and called upon the name of Jesus, whereupon the Devil left her and vanished.

On the ensuing night, the Evil Spirit visited her again in the same shape and whored with her. He made her many promises to help her in her poverty and need, wherefore she surrendered herself to him body and soul. Thereafter the Evil One inflicted upon her a scratch below the left shoulder, demanding that she should sell her soul to him with the blood that had flown therefrom. To this end he gave her a quill and, whereas she could not write, the Evil One guided her hand. She believes that nothing offensive was written, for the Evil One only swept with her hand across the paper. This script the Devil took with him and whenever she piously thought of God Almighty, or wished to go to church, the Devil reminded her of it.

Further, the above-mentioned Walpurga confesses that she oft and much rode on a pitchfork by night with her paramour, but not far, on account of her duties. At such devilish trysts she met a big man with a grey beard, who sat in a chair, like a great prince and was richly attired. That was the Great Devil to whom she had once more dedicated and promised herself body and soul. Him she worshipped and before him she knelt, and unto him she rendered other such-like honours. But she pretends not to know with what words and in which fashion she prayed. She only knows that once she heedlessly pronounced the name of Jesus. Then the above-mentioned Great Devil struck her in the face and Walpurga had to disown (which is terrible to relate) God in heaven, the Christian name and belief, the blessed Saints and the Holy Sacraments, also to renounce the heavenly hosts and the whole of Christendom. Thereupon the Great Devil baptized her afresh, naming her Höfelin, but her paramour-devil, Federlin.

At those devilish meetings, she ate, drank and fornicated with her paramour. Because she would not allow him to drag her along everywhere he had beaten her harshly and cruelly. For food she often had a good roast or an innocent child, which was also roasted, or a sucking pig, and red and white wine, but no salt.

Since her surrender to the Devil, she had seemingly oft received the Blessed Sacrament of the true Body and Blood of Jesus Christ, apparently by the mouth, but had not partaken of it, but (which once more is terrible to relate) had always taken it out of her mouth again and delivered it up to Federlin, her paramour. At their nightly gatherings she had oft with her other playfellows trodden under foot the Holy and Blessed Sacrament and the image of the Holy Cross. The said Walpurga states that during such-like frightful and loathsome blasphemies she at times truly did espy drops of blood upon the said Holy Sacrament, whereat she herself was greatly horrified.

At the command and threat of her whoremonger she had oft dishonoured the consecrated font, emptied it before her house or even destroyed the same. This she was made to do only a few days before she was cast into prison, when she was in the parish church from which she took a holy water stoup and carried it home. Then her devil paramour arrayed in handsome garments encountered her in the little street between the great cloister and the stable of Martin Müller. He desired to take the holy water stoup out of her hand and forced her to hurl it against the wall. She had also been obliged sorely to dishonour the blessed Mother of God, the Holy Virgin Mary, to spit out in front of her and say: "Shame, thou ugly hussy!" Her paramour, Federlin, came to her in many divers places in order to fornicate with her, even in the street by night and while she lay in durance. She confesses, also, that her paramour gave her a salve in a little box with which to injure people and animals, and even the precious fruit of the field.

He also compelled her to do away with and to kill young infants at birth, even before they had been taken to Holy Baptism. This she did, whenever possible. These as follows:

1 and 2. About ten years ago, she had rubbed Anna Hämännin, who dwelt not far from Durstigel, with her salve

on the occasion of her first childbirth and also otherwise damaged her so that mother and child remained together and died.

3. Dorothea, the stepdaughter of Christian Wachter, bore her first child ten years before; at its birth she made press on its little brain so that it died. The Devil had specially bidden her destroy the first-born.

4. Ten years ago she had poisoned with her salve the second child of Anna Kromt, who dwelt by the Altheim Gate, so that it died.

5. When, four years ago, the organist's wife was awaiting her confinement, she touched her naked body with her salve whereby the child promptly died and came stillborn.

6. Ten years ago she destroyed and killed at birth the girl child of the wife of the present tollman.

7. Twelve years ago she had killed at birth, with her salve and by strangulation, a girl child of the Pallingerin, who dwelt in a little house near the Danube baths.

8. Three years ago when she was called to a mill to the miller's wife there she had let the child fall into the water and drown.

9. Six years ago she was called to Eislingen to a poor woman who dwelt near the church. She killed the child by pressing on its brain at the time of delivery.

10. Eight or ten years ago she was called to Steinheim to a poor woman who lived on the other side of the river on the left bank. There also she killed the child by a special manipulation.

11. When six years ago, she partook of food with Magdalena Seilerin, called *Kammerschreiberin* (wife of the chamber scribe), she had put a salve in her drink, so that she was delivered prematurely. This child she, Walpurga, secretly buried under the doorway of the said wife of the scribe on the pretext that then she would have no other miscarriage. The same she also did with many others. When she was questioned under torture for the reasons of this burial, she admitted that it was done in order to cause disunion between two spouses. This her Devil-Paramour had taught her.

12. A child of Stoffel Schmidt she had, four years ago, put to death and after dug out of the grave.

13 and 14. She confessed that, when, eleven years earlier, the spouse of the late Chancellor, Dr. Peuter, lay a

long while in travail, she had rubbed a Devil's salve on the placenta, whereby she became so weak that she had to be given Extreme Unction. Three hours later, mother and child remained together and died.

15. She had also rubbed a salve on a beautiful son of the late Chancellor, Jacob by name: this child had lovely fair hair and she had given him a hobby-horse so that he might ride on it till he lost his senses. He died likewise.

16. Eight years ago she gave the rightfully wedded wife of Otto Vischer, when she was big with child, a drink, whereafter the child was born dead.

17, 18, 19, 20, 21, 22, 23 and 24. She did slay a child of each of the following: George Gopen, Sybilla Turnerin, the wife of Jäglein, Anna Seirin, Girg Gärtner, Klinger, the coppersmith Simon Leberwurst, the groom Hans Durst.

25. A child of the Governor here, Wilhelm Schenk von Stauffenberg, named Werner, she had so infected with her salve that he died within three days.

26 and 27. She had smeared and killed yet two other children of the Governor with her salve.

28 and 29. She had killed a boy child of both Master Niklas Brügelmaier and publican Kunz.

30. Three years ago she had sucked out the blood of publican Kunz's child, a twin, so that it died.

She confesses likewise, that the blood which she sucked from the child, she had to spit out again before the devil, as he had need of it to concoct a salve. She could work the children no harm if they were protected by holy water. But if she herself gave the child holy water, she was able to do it damage, as she had previously passed water into it.

31, 32, 33, 34, 35, 36, 37, 38, 39, 40, 41, 42 and 43. She confesses that she killed a child of each of the following: Venedigerin, Hefelinin, Landstrasslerin, Fischerin, Eva auf der Bleiche, Weberin, the wife of the town scribe, Kautzin, Mechin, Weinzieherin, Berlerin and Martin Kautzin, but two of the Berlerin.

Only a short time since she had wished to smear with a salve the small boy of Georg Klinger, but she was encountered by people and was not able to achieve this.

She also rubbed the wife of the Governor with a salve, but as she wore a neck ornament with blessed medals on it the salve did not work.

In the foregone winter at eventide she had rubbed the

housewife of the town scribe on the arm with her salve, shortly after she suffered great pain and to this day suffers day and night in spite of all the remedies she has tried.

When eight years ago she was helping Michel Klingler to push a cart, and Klingler wanted to lift the shafts with his head, she touched it with her salve. Since then, Klingler is fading away and death is the only thing before him.

To the daughter of Hans Striegel, who is now in the little cloister, she gave a drink in her youth, since when she languishes and is in bad health.

She rubbed with her salve and brought about the death of Lienhart Geilen's three cows, of Bruchbauer's horse, two years ago of Max Petzel's cow, three years ago of Duri Striegel's cow, two years ago of Hans Striegel's cow, of the cow of the Governor's wife, of a cow of Frau Schötterin, and two years ago of a cow of Michel Klingler, on the village green. In short, she confesses that she destroyed a large number of cattle over and above this. A year ago she found bleached linen on the common and rubbed it with her salve, so that the pigs and geese ran over it and perished shortly thereafter. Walpurga confesses further that every year since she has sold herself to the Devil, she has on St. Leonard's Day exhumed at least one or two innocent children. With her Devil-Paramour and other play-fellows she has eaten these and used their hair and their little bones for witchcraft.

She was unable to exhume the other children she had slain at birth, although she attempted it, because they had been baptized before God.

She had used the said little bones to manufacture hail; this she was wont to do once or twice a year. Once this spring, from Siechenhausen, downwards across the fields. She likewise manufactured hail last Whitsun, and when she and others were accused of having held a witches' revel, she had actually held one near the upper gate by the garden of Peter Schmidt. At that time her play-fellows began to quarrel and struck one another, because some wanted to cause it to hail over Dillingen Meadows, others below it. At last the hail was sent over the marsh towards Weissingen, doing great damage. She admits that she would have caused still more and greater evils and damage if the Almighty had not graciously prevented and turned them away.

142

After all this, the Judges and Jury of the Court of this Town of Dillingen, by virtue of the Imperial and Royal Prerogative and Rights of His Right Reverence, Herr Marquard, Bishop of Augsburg, and Provost of the Cathedral, our most gracious Prince and Lord, at last unanimously gave the verdict that the aforesaid Walpurga Hausmännin be punished and dispatched from life to death by burning at the stake as being a maleficent and well-known witch and sorceress, convicted according to the context of Common Law and the Criminal Code of the Emperor Charles V and the Holy Roman Empire. All her goods and chattels and estate left after her to go to the Treasury of our Most High Prince and Lord. The aforesaid Walpurga to be led, seated on a cart, to which she is tied, to the place of her execution, and her body first to be torn five times with red-hot irons. The first time outside the town hall in the left breast and the right arm, the second time at the lower gate in the right breast, the third time at the mill brook outside the hospital gate in the left arm, the fourth time at the place of execution in the left hand. But since for nineteen years she was a licensed and pledged midwife of the city of Dillingen, yet has acted so vilely, her right hand with which she did such knavish tricks is to be cut off at the place of execution. Neither are her ashes after the burning to remain lying on the ground, but are thereafter to be carried to the nearest flowing water and thrown thereinto. Thus a venerable jury have entrusted the executioner of this city with the actual execution and all connected therewith.

113. Inducements to be held out to the Turks to join in the War

Constantinople, November 26, 1587.

The English ambassador has received instructions from His Gracious Queen that he is recalled unexpectedly and, as some asseverate, in disfavour. But the ambassador declares he has himself requested His Gracious Queen's permission to return home, in order that he may explain the exact state of affairs here by word of mouth, and persuade the Queen to induce the Sultan to support her against the King of Spain with all his power.

114. Turkish Preparations for War

Constantinople, December 9, 1587.

Ibrahim Pasha is having heavy work executed here in the Arsenal on the pretext that he is to take the sea in person with a large fleet. But those who know, especially those who hold important positions in the Arsenal, consider this impossible. But since the Sultan receives much injury from Christian pirates every day, and the Venetian ambassador and other good Christians encourage him daily, it is rather thought some fifty galleys will move out from here and cruise in the Archipelago and along the Barbary coast. One hundred and fifty small vessels are to sail out and devastate the territory of the King of Spain. But it is thought more likely they will sail merely wherever they can find the most plunder and will try to prevent the King of Spain's fleet from getting out.

115. Armada Preparations

Cologne, December 24, 1587.

The presumption in Brussels is that the vessels being pressed forward at Antwerp and other places are to sail next year against England. Four regiments of German mercenaries are to be put on board them. So next spring there will be strange doings enough, since the King of Scots has declared himself the enemy of the Queen of England and probably has an understanding with the King of Spain.

116. The Great Armada is Made Ready to put to Sea

From Madrid, the 18th day of May 1588.

The last courier from Lisbon brings news of there having arrived a letter from London. Therefrom one learns of the preparations which are being made here. The people are reported to be unwilling to embark, and it is presumed that the Catholics will join forces when the Armada arrives. It is also suspected that various lords will be their leaders.

There were many women on board the Armada. The Duke ordered the captains to make a list of how many of them each had in his ship, and he requested them to bring the list to him in three or four days. It was found that there were somewhat more than six hundred. They were then not only put ashore again, but also removed from Lisbon. This was done after the soldiery had already come on board the ships. They were far from pleased on this account, but were comforted with the report that there were comely wenches in England.

117. English Trade in the Elbe

Hamburg, June 13, 1588.

To-day comes news that the English have arrived on the Elbe with over thirty ships. But they have anchored at Freiburg, a large village on the Holstein side twelve miles from here. It seems as though they wished to ascertain what arrangement they can make with Hamburg before approaching nearer. Before closing this letter I happen to meet one of the eight chamberlains, who informs me of the circumstances regarding these English vessels. There are twenty-nine merchantmen and seven warships. The Admiral had orders from the Queen to suggest to the Hamburgers that they should permit the unloading of these ships at Staden, and if they would not do this in friendship and of good will then he was to carry it through by force and stake his existence upon it. The Queen would then attack the Hamburgers by land and water wherever and however she could get at them. The Queen writes herself to the authorities, and the despatch has this day been read out to the Council. She insists on the vessels remaining this time at Staden. If the Hamburgers could subsequently arrange with the English to grant them the same privileges as the inhabitants of Staden, she would, if the latter do not object, make no difficulties. But the city of Hamburg will suffer, and it must again leave all its ships at home. This is really a very high-handed action on the part of the English in a river belonging to the Empire.

118. Hans Limburger sees the Armada at Sea

Hamburg, June 23, 1588 (O.S.).

I simply must tell you that the skipper, Hans Limburger, has arrived here with his vessel from Cadiz. He broke through the embargo, and has a cargo of salt, wine, raisins, cinnamon, and a little sugar. He put out from there on the 20th ult., O.S., and passed Lisbon on the 24th. In the distance he saw the Spanish Armada and sailed abreast of it all day. The next day it was blowing rather hard and he could not see it. He is of opinion that the Armada put out on the 23rd of May Old Style or the 2nd of June New Style and was shaping a course for the Channel. The skipper met an English warship on his way and this brought him into Plymouth, to Drake's Armada. He was entertained by Drake for three days and the English were rejoicing that the Spanish Armada was at sea. Afterwards Captain Drake gave the skipper a permit, so that he might be allowed to pass, and quickly formed in order and put to sea in spite of a contrary wind. If an action is fought, there will be terrible loss of life. On two consecutive days here the sun and moon have been quite bloody. What this signifies the merciful God alone knows. May he defend the Right!

Postscript.

Letters have just come from Cologne reporting that the Prince of Parma has news that the Armada sailed from Lisbon on the 30th May. God grant it all prosperity!

119. The Pope is in alliance with Spain

Rome, June 25, 1588.

The Pope recently signified to one of the Cardinals that he was in alliance with the King of Spain. He intended to grant him a million crowns in aid, so soon as news reached him that the Spanish Armada had disembarked its men in England.

120. Rumoured Defeat of the Armada

Antwerp, July 2, 1588.

This afternoon news came from Bruges that His Highness the Prince of Parma has received information from Calais that the Spanish and English Armadas have met on the English coast and the Spanish Armada has been beaten. No details are reported.

121. Perhaps the Armada will not sail

Antwerp, July 11, 1588.

Letters from England of the 28th ult. have announced that the Queen of England's fleet put out under Captain Drake one hundred and forty sail strong, as it had been learnt that the Spanish Armada had also sailed and had been seen at sea. But in London letters of the 4th inst. this does not appear. It is thought that the Spanish Armada is near Lisbon. Therefore the Queen has commanded the Admiral, who is in port at Boulogne, not to put out with the fleet but to await further orders. From this some conclude there will be peace in the Netherlands. From Morocco it is reported that the King there has a strong force in the field to help the Turks in their siege of the fortress of Oran. If this should be the case it would ill suit Spain and there would be grave doubts about the sailing of the Armada.

Besides this we hear from England that Martin Schenk is still there asking for money. He hopes to get some.

122. Excommunication of the Queen of England

From Salzburg, the 14th day of July 1588.

There is war against England in the air, and nothing will come of attempts for peace, for His Holiness the Pope has

147

had a Bull read publicly in the Chapel of the Vatican in the presence of my most gracious Lord of Salzburg. Therein the Queen of England is declared to be dispossessed of her kingdom, her lands and her subjects, being long since a condemned heretic. Her subjects, of whatever rank they be, are released from the vow whereby heretofore they had sworn her allegiance.

The Pope also deprives her of all the titles she had held up to now, divests her of all honours and transfers them all to the King of Spain. On this account the latter is now to declare himself to be rightfully chosen and appointed King of England and Ireland, and Protector of the Catholic Faith in that country. He is to wage war upon the Queen and to endeavour to bring her lands and her people under his sway. His Holiness has publicly proclaimed His Majesty King of Spain, England and Ireland, and will bestow this title upon him for all time, on condition, however, that His Majesty when he obtain possession of these provinces pay tribute to the Holy Roman See with a certain yearly pension as is done on behalf of the Kingdom of Naples.

In order that His Majesty should be able to do this with the greater ease, His Holiness is granting him a million crowns for his assistance: half of it for the present putting to sea of the Armada, and the other half whenever His Majesty's forces have set foot in England and captured an important harbour.

123. The Armada has been destroyed in a Storm

Middelburg, July 22, 1588.

Five ships from Lisbon have reached Calais bringing salt and spices. I got this news after closing my last letter, and the rumour was then circulating that these ships had brought tidings that the Armada of the King of Spain had been utterly destroyed and annihilated. These ships would seem to have met a portion of the Armada which had got back to Lisbon. But, as the news reached here so quickly and unexpectedly, little credence was placed in it, and I did not care to write anything to you about it. Since then, however, the English mail has come in bringing many letters, and in them it is stated that a vessel has arrived from Lisbon announcing that it twice met ships of the King's Armada. The first time twelve, the second time seventeen very badly mauled. And when this vessel asked the Spaniards what had become of the rest of the Armada, it received the answer that they did not know, as they had parted company in a storm. The storm had come on so quickly and so unexpectedly that they had had no time to anchor. But what really happened is unknown. The storm seems not to have lasted more than an hour.

Drake and the Admiral of England are still at sea; how they have fared we know not, but we hope to hear from them soon, as the wind from England is favourable now. This news only reached here yesterday and more is eagerly awaited. Some suppose that Drake too was in this storm.

124. It has sailed home because of Plague

Prague, July 26, 1588.

It is rumoured here that the Spanish Armada has sailed back to Lisbon because plague has broken out on board. The English are said to have sailed after them. But where this news comes from I cannot find out.

125. Anxiety to hear of the Success of the Armada

Constantinople, July 28, 1588.

Despatches arrived here recently from the Queen of England touching the recall of her embassy, and they were delivered to all Viziers a week ago. At present it is supposed that this embassy will not be allowed to depart before there is some definite news about the Spanish Armada and its accomplishments. People here are inclined to wonder what the Sultan thinks about the new friendship with this Queen and about her offers. It is to be hoped that the will of God is no other than that justice should take its course, and that she should meet the fate she deserves from the King of Spain when his plan has succeeded. We are waiting for this here every day. The embassy is ready

149

to start and proposes to go home from here through Poland and by Danzig. The English embassy received the required permission through the Hoja of the Sultan, and, as is customary, took leave of the Sultan on the 24th inst. From now on it may, as announced, start for Danzig through Poland any day.

On the 25th inst. the French ambassador despatched his cousin to France with all speed, no doubt on account of the news which had come about occurrences in Paris between the King and the Guises. There is much talk here on the subject, and it is asserted that the Guise is already virtually King of France and the other is totally deprived of power.

126. The Pope to raise Money for Spain

Rome, July 30, 1588.

The Council of the Roman people assembled on Tuesday and debated how to raise the money to enable the Pope to meet his engagement to make a contribution to the King of Spain for his expedition against England.

127. Hans Buttber's Account of the Armada

Hamburg, August 3 *and* 4, 1588.

Hans Buttber has arrived off the town in a big ship. He comes through the Channel from San Lucar. He was with Captain Drake for four or five days and joined the Englishman on the 21st, O.S., of last month, just after the latter had had an engagement with the Spanish Armada. From the 21st to the 26th they had skirmished and fired heavily at each other, but they could not board, and the English with their little ships sailed so well and manœuvred so skilfully, firing meanwhile, that the galleasses could not get at them. Drake captured Don Pedro de Valdez, Admiral of fourteen vessels, and had him and ten other nobles brought on to his own ship. He gave them a banquet and treated them very handsomely and entertained them besides with trumpets and music. On this ship he took sixty guns and made four hundred and fifty men prisoners. Moreover, he got yet another ship which caught fire of itself. All this happened in presence of the skipper. On the 26th he received a pass, but only on condition of carrying a letter to another English port. There 28 Queen's ships were lying. As soon as their Admiral read the document he got ready for sea to join Drake, but sent two yachts to Holland and Zeeland to tell them to keep a sharp look-out there and prevent the Dunkirk people from coming out.

This noon there comes from Holland a vessel which was at Enkhuizen actually on the last day of July. It brings news that eighteen ships of the Spanish Armada were sunk by gunfire, and eight taken and brought to England. The rest of the Spanish Armada has fled to the French coast. If this is true it will somewhat abate Spanish insolence and give the English fresh courage, though they have no lack of insolence either.

128. Armada beaten, English in pursuit

Hamburg, August 5, 1588.

It is reported that the English Armada has beaten the Spanish and taken twenty-two ships and sunk eighteen by gunfire. Many vessels have been burnt. Some two hundred Counts, or Dons as they call them, together with the young Santa Cruz, have been taken prisoners to England. Moreover, the Admiral and Vice-Admiral with two other large ships, each of almost six hundred tons, have been brought in to Zeeland. Two galleasses seem to have been destroyed, the remainder are still at sea.

At Dunkirk a great dispute over the Armada has arisen between the Marquis de Renti, Governor of Hainault and Admiral-at-sea, and an Italian Marquis. They quarrelled so furiously that the Italian called Renti a traitor. So they had recourse to their weapons, and the Marquis received four bad wounds and the Italian is gravely injured and will hardly escape with his life. Captain Drake seems also to have been shot and badly injured. The English are pursuing the remains of the Spanish Armada. The Duke of Parma was unable to get out of Dunkirk with his fleet, and cut down four or five Captains with his own hand because they would not support him at the right moment. The upshot is that the activities of the Holy League are greatly limited and the English will do great damage at sea by rapine and theft. God dispose all for the best!

129. The Armada back at Corunna. No great damage

Venice, August 12, 1588.

Letters from Spain and Madrid of the 20th ult. report that all the ships of the Spanish Armada which had been dispersed by gales at sea returned to Corunna on the 13th ult. without having suffered any particular damage, but some vessels which, owing to storms, had to go as far as England were pillaged by fisher-boats. A very malignant sickness prevails on the Armada. So the General, Duke Medina Sidonia, is disembarking the sick and replacing them with healthy men. Consequently there has been a great concourse of people from all directions, as the intention is to renew the expedition against England as soon as possible.

130. Wholesale Destruction in the North Sea

Middelburg, August 12, 1588.

The Spanish Armada so long talked about has now at last appeared, but seemingly to its undoing. Firstly, on the 5th inst. a despatch pinnace arrived from England with orders that the Zeelanders and Hollanders should keep themselves in readiness on all coasts and particularly not let the Duke of Parma and his Armada get out of Dunkirk. The English meant to do their best against the Spanish Armada. This pinnace also brought the report that the Armada had been seen off the English coast and that it intended to invade England in force. At that time the English Armada was assembled in one place, and the Spaniards could not sail in because the English always had the wind in their favour, and the Spaniards perpetually got the powder smoke from the English ships in their eyes. On the 6th inst. came two more pinnaces from England with orders to keep firm hold of the Prince of Parma and his fleet. They also brought news that twenty-two Spanish ships had been sunk, and the Vice-Admiral, together with all the distinguished nobles who had taken refuge from other ships, had been brought to England. So they have driven the Spanish Armada between Dover and Calais and in the meanwhile examined the Vice-Admiral. He is said to have admitted that the object was England. The intention was to get as far as Dover and Calais and occupy the English there, while the Prince of Parma was to have invaded England at some other point. He was supposed to be supporting the Spaniards with his force of 70,000 men. On the 11th inst. another pinnace came from England with orders that the Prince of Parma was on no account to be let out and all ships ready for sea were to be sent to England. The pinnace also reported that both fleets had fought bravely for eight hours between Dover and Calais and that at the end the English had given chase to ten Spanish ships. Of these some were driven ashore and promptly wrecked, but most of them were brought to England. So, having fared thus badly, the majority of the Spanish Armada assembled in the Straits of Dover and hoped for aid from the Prince of Parma. On the 10th inst. the English again attacked the Spaniards afresh with all their forces and damaged them severely. The Spaniards were obliged to flee into the North Sea, but the English continued their pursuit. This night the Prince of Parma tried to put out from Dunkirk, as the Spanish Armada had been seen to flee from there. Four large well-found ships came out first, but, bless your heart, our ships played with them as a cat with a mouse, caught them at once and sank all four. The Spanish ships are lying up and down the coast like birds without wings. The English fire without intermission and shoot away sails, masts, stays and all rigging off the ships, so that they are unmanageable. Whenever they drive the Spanish ships ashore they are lost. On the 11th inst. our boats' crews got two big ships, one called the *San Philippo* of more than 1200 tons, the other the *San Matheo* of the same size, both galliots. The one they got off Blankenberghe, the other near Dunkirk. Off one ship most of the nobles seem to have escaped to Nieuport, not far from Dunkirk. Our men hope to get hold of more of these ships. The sea is driving ashore near Flushing much artillery and wreckage from the burnt ships as well as burnt corpses, so that it is a horrible sight. In Flushing there are heaps of captured Spaniards. They say the Prince of Parma has betrayed them, for the Spanish Armada went thus far up the country relying on his promises, and hoping to receive great assistance from him. Indeed they were of opinion that he would accomplish more than the Armada, for he had always promised them to come out with 500 sail and be a match for the English alone. He was going to make the invasion with 70,000 men, but now he is bringing woe and misery on all the splendid Spanish ships. They curse him horribly, and it is to be feared he will fall into complete disfavour with the King and be recalled from the Netherlands. Altogether the wretched devils here do nothing but complain. Our sailors wanted to kill all the Spaniards because they would not surrender. Their ships are built as high as churches. But we took pity upon them. The seamen who brought in the ships above mentioned numbered 150 in all. They marched through the town at noon in procession two abreast with all the Spaniards' best clothes on. In costume one looked like a Portuguese, another like a Spaniard, a third like a Biscayan, a fourth like an Italian. People here thought they were prisoners from the Armada, because of the many expensive costumes. In the two ships there was plenty of booty, about 120 brass guns, many of iron, and a quantity of provisions.

A vessel has also arrived at Flushing from Calais with the report that Duke Medina Sidonia and de San Lucar, in command of the Spanish Armada, has been brought in there. Half his head seems to have been shot off. They say he was the most powerful man in all Spain. The Spanish Armada has had a terrible time of it. A Scotchman has come in here also. He saw the Spanish Armada in the distance on the North Sea and says it is barely over 80 vessels strong and the English are after it with 250 and firing heavily with a favourable wind. The Spaniards have had no rest day or night for sixteen to eighteen days.

We shall hear more yet. So much has happened in the last four weeks that very little has been said about trade. At every place in the country men have been standing to arms in case they should be wanted. It is hoped the Prince of Parma will at length be wearied out, although the commissioners are still sitting so that one might expect some very wonderful result. I leave it at that. Time will perhaps bring more strange events, and the war may move to yet other places. The English will not quiet down all at once, for they now have 500 to 600 well-found ships at disposal and might do wonders with them. Perhaps they will pay a visit to Spain and Portugal, as these two countries are very bare of ships and guns. The Spanish Armada brought with it many galleys too, among them two quite big ones from Italy. They had hoped to get them over here, but they hung in the sea and were swamped. So with them also the Spaniards had no luck. Many things have occurred also that I do not know about. The English actually lost three or four large ships. The biggest, the *Elizabeth,* was burnt in the fight, and it is said that with all these fires the sea was as bright and clear by night as by day. The glare could be plainly seen from the land here, along the coast where the wrecked ships and dead men lie driven hither by the wind. It would be well were God's will done and an end made, but I fear that the war will go on still longer.

131. The Pope regrets the Armada is back at Corunna

Rome, August 13, 1588.

Last Sunday the Spanish ambassador in residence here informed the Pope that owing to storms at sea the Spanish Armada had reassembled and on the 16th ult. was still lying in the harbour of Corunna. It has lost eleven vessels, large and small, and this the Pope was evidently very sorry to hear.

132. No Papal Favours till the Armada succeeds

Rome, August 20, 1588.

The Pope has signified that Don Eduardo Farnese, whose elevation to the Cardinalate is so strongly urged by the King of Spain, shall be made a Cardinal so soon as the Pope receives news that the Spanish Armada has landed troops in England.

133. No Audiences at the Escorial

Venice, August 23, 1588.

The Spaniards have received letters from Madrid of the
28th ult. and announce that His Majesty of Spain is at the
Escorial, and is giving no audiences, as is His Majesty's
custom when he has important matters to consider.

134. Rome hears the Armada has beaten the English

Rome, August 27, 1588.

Last Monday a printed sheet was published here, describ-
ing how the English fleet was beaten by the Spaniards.
This is confirmed by a messenger from the Duke of Savoy
also, and Cardinal Morosini writes to the same effect. But
the Pope and some Cardinals are still doubtful, and the
Pope has said that he will not hand over the promised
million to the King of Spain and make Eduard Farnese a
Cardinal until the Spanish Armada has disembarked troops
in England.

135. Prague rejoices over the Success of the Armada

Prague, August 30, 1588.

Yesterday evening a messenger came here from Milan with
the announcement that the Spanish Armada has fought the
English and the English have succumbed. At this the rejoicing here is universal. But whether it is correct we shall
not know for certain till the regular mail comes.

136. A Circus Rider at the Imperial Court

From Prague, the 31st day of August 1588.

A few days ago an Italian showed especial skill before His
Imperial Majesty and the Archdukes. First, he shot with a

156

Persian arrow behind and in front of him in full gallop, thereupon he stood in such wise that he put one foot to the ground and then again bestrode his horse. Thirdly, he stood on his saddle in full gallop. Fourthly, he unsheathed and again sheathed a sword in full gallop. Fifthly, when his horse was running fast, he stood with his head upon the saddle and had his feet up in the air. Sixthly, he turned back in his saddle and to the front again in full gallop. Seventhly, he trotted his horse in a circle, stood upright in his saddle and placed a long pole upon his head. This pole he guided with his head and shoulders and brandished like a fencer with his two hands. The horse which he had worked so hard, did not sweat and was to all appearances a Turkish horse. This skill pleased His Majesty and the Archdukes full well, and the rider received a large gift as a reward.

137. Persecution of the Protestants in Salzburg

Copy of the Princely Mandate of Salzburg concerning the exercise of the Religion, on the 3rd day of September 1588.

We, Wolf Dietrich, Archbishop of Salzburg by the Grace of God, Legate of the Holy Roman See, hereby declare and make known: In our Capital of Salzburg, we have found several of our citizens and inhabitants opposed to our old and true Catholic Faith, who after loyal and fatherly exhortation, information and instruction, in spite of the several weeks' respite granted, have stubbornly persisted in their pre-conceived and antagonistic opinions. On this account we bid them to leave the town and the Archbishopric, for the sake of preventing further trouble and embarrassment. So that they may know how it stands with their real and movable property and their merchandise, we have publicly announced the following articles:

Firstly: It is our earnest will that those who leave our town of Salzburg make a statement of all their real estate and property before their departure and omit nothing nor leave it unregistered. This also applies to those who have already left. This statement is to be handed to us in writing. Should any one show disobedience herein or hide anything, his property is to become forfeit to us as fiscal prop-

157

erty and subject to our domain. So that those who are no longer here should not remain in ignorance, they are to be advised of this by our Civic Authorities, through their tenants, or their own messengers, otherwise we shall proceed against the recalcitrant with heavy fines.

Secondly: They are to sell their houses and property, in and around our town, within one month, to such persons as shall find favour in our eyes, or, after this time has lapsed, make them over to them for a reasonable sum until the latter can dispose of them. Since we shall not permit that the houses be closed or that we see bad servants and citizens within them, we shall let such houses and gardens through our Civic Authorities to others for a low rent. For as Prince and Ruler of these lands we are not willing to have our capital stand partly empty, but wish that it should be fully inhabited.

Thirdly: Those who leave this town for the sake of their faith are not to hold any civic rights or honours in our Archbishopric. They are to be treated here as foreigners and strangers, but if any one of them should again return to the Catholic Faith, and tender the customary allegiance, we will reinstate him fully in all things. In the meantime, however, they are to be allowed to take their goods and chattels through our Archbishopric, unhampered, as do other strangers and foreigners.

Fourthly: They are not to venture to trade in the outer town of Salzburg or any other town in our Archbishopric. But should they resort to smuggling or carry on their calling with their own servants or other citizens and inhabitants of this town in any other name, their wares are to be considered our fiscal property.

Fifthly: They are to be permitted, as need arises, to travel through our Archbishopric. But they must not cause any offence and must frequent only the open inns. Neither are they allowed to sojourn longer than three days without our Councillor's knowledge, especially within our town of Salzburg.

Sixthly: Whatever they have need to transact in our Archbishopric, this may they do, but only through Catholic proxies, and not through sectarian servants.

Seventhly: Those who hold guardianships and have foster-children are to make over their trust-moneys and render proper account of them. In their place are to be appointed Catholic guardians who will bring up the wards in the Catholic Faith.

Eighthly: Wards, who are not here, but live in sectarian places are to be cited and brought hither by our Town Council. They are to be sent to strange places only with our foreknowledge.

Ninthly: All those who have already put their property in order or do not hold any and are ready to depart, are to leave our town of Salzburg and our Archbishopric within fourteen days of this date and see to it that they are not encountered here any more.

All this is our Will, Wish and Command.

In true Testimony of this our Mandate we have signed and written it by our own hand.

Issued in our town of Salzburg on the 3rd day of September in the year 1588 after Christ our Lord and Redeemer's birth.

WOLF DIETRICH m.p.

138. Lack of Powder prevents Pursuit

Staden, September 22, 1588.

We recently informed you that the Spanish Armada had invaded Scotland. This was incorrect. They did indeed land in order to procure fresh water and then sailed back to Lisbon. From lack of powder and munitions the English were unable to pursue the Spaniards further, but sailed back to England. Else they would have been able to do the Spanish Armada much harm, because the wind was foul for it. About the losses of the two fleets nothing is yet known. It is thought certain that the Admiral with Drake as Vice-Admiral and 80 of the largest and best ships will sail to Lisbon and Spain in order to intercept the remainder of the Armada before it gets home. But they might have their trip for nothing. Some Jesuits and women found among the Armada prisoners have been hanged in London. In addition they have hanged an Englishman sent as a spy by the Prince of Parma. We are also told that there is an old gentleman of 84 among the prisoners. He was apparently among those sent by the Prince of Parma to negotiate peace, and is said to have written to the Queen not to fit out a navy for fear of endangering the peace. He is imprisoned as a traitor, but what will be done with him is unknown. Several more such people may be found yet.

139. Return of the Circumnavigator Cavendish

From Middelburg, the 6th day of October 1588.

Mestre Candis, a nobleman, who on his own venture, had set sail twenty-five months before with two ships and one pinnace, has arrived in England. He sailed round the world along the route of Magellan and robbed, burnt and sank nineteen ships in the Pacific. On land he burnt ten towns and inflicted great damage upon the Spaniards. Among other things he conquered a big galleon which was on her way from China to the Indies or Peru. She was richly laden with silks and other wares. According to the inventory found, her cargo was worth 350,000 ducats. He took what was best, loaded it into his ships, and burnt the rest with the galleon. He returned home by way of the Cape of Good Hope, richer by almost one million. The two hundred men he had with him have all grown wealthy. The English Earl of Cumberland is also said to have the intention of setting out upon such an expedition.

140. Contraband of War

From Antwerp, the 12th day of November 1588.

The Queen of England has requested the Eastern Ports to allow no pitch, resin, masts and other shipbuilding material to go to Spain and Portugal. In case of noncompliance she has decided to confiscate these goods, should they fall into English hands.

141. The End of the "Great Armada"

Report from England about the Spanish Armada, received in Augsburg from Hamburg on the 19th day of November 1588.

The Armada of the King of Spain set sail from Portugal with one hundred and thirty-five ships, to wit: four galleasses from Naples, four galleons from Portugal, ten vessels with victuals, fourteen Venetian ships, among them several galleons. The remainder was made up of other large and small craft. The Armada arrived in Corunna on the 5th day of July, from whence it intended to sail for Flanders, there to join forces with the Duke of Parma and invade England. At that time the English Armada was in Plymouth Port.

After they had been under sail from Corunna eight days they arrived in Ostend and thereupon lay south of the shores of England, where for four or five days they had various skirmishes with the English Armada. On that occasion the English took two ships. On one of these there was Don Pedro di Mendoza, whom they took prisoner and so to England. Storms south of England caused them the loss of four Portuguese galleons which remained stranded on the French coast. They then proceeded and cast anchor off Calais, since they could no longer get as far as Dunkirk. They wished to wait for the Duke of Parma in Calais, but he sent word that he could not be ready under eight days. Thereupon the admiral sent reply that he would again set sail for Spain. Meanwhile the English sent forth against the Spanish Armada several burning ships, so that they were forced to cut their moorings and to retire hastily. Each ship left two anchors behind and four of the largest galleasses were stranded and wrecked off Calais. The following day at eight o'clock, the two Armadas had a further encounter, heavily bombarding each other for eight hours. In this battle the Spanish lost four ships, namely two Portuguese galleasses, a vessel from Biscay and one other. All four went to the bottom of the sea. Three large Venetian craft remained behind off the coast of Flanders and were in great peril of going under. The inhabitants of Flushing took two of these ships, and the third was shipwrecked. One of them had on board the Colonel commanding the garrison of Seville. According to the prisoners' report the Spaniards lost four thousand men in the battle off Calais, amongst them the Commander-in-Chief of the cavalry at Naples and Seville. The Spaniards are said to have left one hundred and twenty ships, although others could count only one hundred and ten. The big galleon, which the Duke of Florence had sent, was not to be seen anywhere after the battle.

Hereafter the Armada made off and was pursued by the English for five days as far as Scotland. When they counted their men there they found that they had already lost eight thousand, most of whom had been killed or died of disease. From thence they set sail for Ireland without taking provisions on board. Off Ireland they lost two ships, the *San Sebastian* and the *San Mathias,* which had four hundred and fifty-six men on board. Lacking fresh water, the fleet threw many horses and mules overboard off Ireland. When they sailed away from Ireland, the Commander-in-Chief, the Duke of Medina Sidonia, ordered each one of his captains to set his course for Corunna or the first Spanish port. They thus sailed together throughout ten days. Then the storm separated the Duke of Medina Sidonia with twenty-seven of his ships from them and no one knew where they had gone. The last time the Armada was assembled it counted no more than seventy-eight ships. Of the big galleasses not one was left. Two of the Duke of Medina Sidonia's ships ran ashore. Only two or three of the men were saved. They say that the Chief Admiral had left on board only five-and-twenty more barrels of wine, but little bread and no water. His masts had been so weakened by firing that he could not carry full canvas. The Duke had three English pilots on board ship. On the 10th day of September a further large ship of five hundred tons, *Maria della Rosa,* ran ashore off Ireland. On it were the Colonel Michael Oquendo, commander of part of this fleet, and also the Prince of Ascoli, the bastard son of the King of Spain, twenty-eight years of age. There were besides these ten noblemen, seven captains and five hundred soldiers. They all perished excepting one pilot who saved himself on a plank. He says that the King's bastard son came on board this ship off Calais. The vessel carried fifty cannon and twenty-five other metal pieces, as well as 15,000 ducats and silver reals and much gold. The same day two big vessels put eight hundred and fifty men ashore in Ireland, seven hundred of whom died, and the remainder were taken prisoner. The vessels were cast ashore. On the 12th day of September another big ship was wrecked. Thirteen noblemen were taken prisoner and four hundred men reached land. From yet another ship seventy-eight bodies were washed ashore. From a further wrecked vessel three noblemen, a bishop and seventy-nine mercenaries were taken prisoner. The others perished. On the 17th day of September two large vessels, the St. Joaquim and the St. Martin, sank. The admiral was de Ricaldo, and his ship was almost the largest in the whole fleet. There were on it eight hundred soldiers, sixty Portuguese and forty Biscay fishermen. They had starved for almost four days.

Finally another galleon of four hundred and fifty tons was wrecked with an Italian margrave and the old Naples and Seville garrison. On it were also Don Alonzo de Layba, Mestre de Campo of the Cavalry in Milan. On the 18th day of September there arrived news from Ireland that very many bodies had been washed ashore.

142. Mourning Prohibited in Spain

From Middelburg, the 14th day of November 1588.

It is said that news has arrived from Ireland that a further nine ships of the Spanish Armada have perished there. Sixteen hundred men are reported to be still alive, to whom the Irish are lending help. For that reason the Queen of England has dispatched thither six hundred men who are to take up hostilities against these people. From Sicily there comes information that the General Duke of Medina in Seville organized there a great procession to celebrate his return. Ninety ships of the Armada are missing, and every one has been forbidden to mourn his friends who were lost with the Armada. A forty days' fast has been ordered, hoping that thereby the return home of the missing ships will be obtained.

143. Peter's Pence

From Rome, the 16th day of December 1588.

During the last days the Pope has again deposited in the Castello a further sixty thousand gold crowns, so that now there are in all four millions in actual coin.

144. The Murder of the Guises

How the terrible butchery happened on the 23rd and the 24th days of December 1588.

On the 15th day of September last King Henri, the third of that name, convened Parliament in France that all the clerical and secular states might meet and take counsel with one another as to the attainment of peace and unity in matters of religion as well as in politics. But the States did not assemble until a good while later, and the Huguenots and the adherents of Navarre found means and ways to prevent this plan of the Catholics. It was their wish that the Pope's Bull of Excommunication should be put into force from Rome so that he and his successors might never obtain possession of the crown of France. But at this time many events are taking place at Blois. Each faction desires to draw the King over to its side. And the King, finding himself hard pressed by both parties, sanctioned the following terrible murder in order to regain his lost prestige.

On the 23rd day of September the King invited the Duke of Guise to Blois to discuss and settle with him matters of paramount importance. The latter goes to the King on that very day at eight o'clock in the morning. But as he enters the hall leading to the King's chamber, there springs upon him from behind the door one who has been hired for this purpose, and inflicts upon him two or three wounds in the back with a dagger. Thereupon several of the King's halberdiers hasten to the scene to do him to death. This all in the presence of the King. Thereafter the King gave orders for the assassination of the Cardinal de Guise, the brother of the murdered Duke, and for the arrest of other noblemen, and amongst them the provost of the Paris merchants.

164

145. A Miracle in Weimar

From Weimar, the 20th day of January 1589.

In this town there lives a burgess of the name of Nicolaus Walhelm, a glover. He has a stag's antler with six points, which had parted company with the stag's head twenty years before and has lain for almost all of that time in the loft amidst other antlers. This had been given to him as a present and at midday on the 18th day of September of the past year of 1588, he bored a hole through it with a clinching-iron and nailed it up in his room. The same night at eight o'clock the antler on the wall starts to bleed of its own accord from the largest horn. So it continues all night, also the following Thursday throughout the day and the night until Friday at 6 o'clock in the morning. The drops of blood fall on to a wooden seat below, and neither water nor soda can remove the stains from it, for the blood has eaten into it very deeply. In the end, the whole horn bled, and that to such an extent, as could never have happened with an ordinary antler. This has been witnessed with their own eyes by our pastors, as well as by many of the nobility and the citizens, all in all more than four hundred persons. The government have had the antler removed and the old Duchess commanded the antler to be brought to her, and there it still is. God knows what this portends.

146. France, Navarre, Poland, Sweden, Barbary and Morocco to join England against the Holy League

Brussels, March 16, 1589.

It is announced from England that envoys of the Kings of France, Navarre, Poland, Sweden, Barbary and Morocco have arrived to form an alliance against the Holy League. To all appearances nothing can come of this but a great and destructive war. It is confidently asserted that Don Antonio has been in Barbary with forty warships and has fetched these envoys. He seems to have been very courteously received by the King of Morocco, who expressed his readiness to favour the cause of the Queen of England. To oblige Her Majesty he will send an auxiliary force of 30,000 Moors, and furnish all supplies of food and munitions from his own country. All English vessels may get what they require in Barbary and put in there to recuperate.

It is said that this fleet will set out about 200 sail strong with the first favourable wind. There are stated to be ten to twelve thousand Englishmen and eight to ten companies of Hollander Lancers on board. It is pitiable that so much Christian blood should be shed and not against the hereditary foe.

147. English Raid on Corunna

Copy of a letter by an English Captain to the English Secretary in London anent Drake's raid on Corunna, written on the 6th day of May 1589.

Through God's help we arrived in Corunna on the 7th day of April, and the same day we set ashore, about two miles from the town, a number of our soldiery whom we divided into several detachments. They arrived in good battle formation about the distance of a musket shot from the fortress. On the following day at midnight we passed about one hundred pinnaces and barges with soldiery and cannon, between the ships and the fortress, disembarked the soldiery and fired with two big cannon upon the enemy. Soon thereupon the assault was made amid vociferous shouting and terrible firing, so that the enemy forsook their barricades and fled into the mountains. We then kept the enemy busily engaged with much continuous firing and shot down a large portion of the city wall with big cannon. In the harbour we found two galleons, one of them a marvellously big vessel with fifty-two big pieces. We set fire to the vessel, but removed the cannon. We further took a large ship from Biscay of about five hundred tons which was well equipped with copper and iron pieces, also a hulk of three hundred tons, likewise well equipped with pieces, and many more ships besides. Altogether we took from the enemy 140 big cannon. In the town we found in abundance wheat, flour, salted meat, fish, wine, oil, biscuits, powder, lead, anchors, sails, hemp and suchlike. All these stores had been deposited here for the provisioning of the Royal Armada which was to have sailed from here on the last day of this month. After that our people devastated the country-side for seven to eight miles around the town. Now and then they came upon a band of Spanish soldiers, in all over two thousand, who, however, took to flight. We hope to God that with His help we shall achieve the same success in other places, so that the Spaniards' arrogance towards the little island of England may be brought low. The provision and ammunition were of great assistance to us.

After having learnt during the last days that our enemies, about 8500 strong, had fortified themselves by a bridge some four miles from here, our general went to encounter them in good battle formation. After much skirmishing, he put the enemy to flight, killed four or five hundred of his men and pursued them for half a mile. They left behind them more than three thousand suits of armour and all manner of arms. Our people thus gained possession of a great number of horses and mules, and badly devastated the country-side by fire for eight miles round.

148. Drake at Lisbon

Madrid, June 10, 1589.

In our last letters we recounted how the English, after retiring from Corunna, put troops ashore at Peniche in Portugal. As it could offer no resistance, this hamlet surrendered to Don Antonio, who received it graciously and treated it with great considerateness. Then he passed further inland towards Lisbon without meeting any resistance, because the Portuguese all remained inactive and would not use their arms against Don Antonio. When he saw this, he took 10,000 to 12,000 men and marched straight upon Lisbon, and the ships followed him as far as Cascæs. So, on the last day of last month, he arrived half a mile off at Fuente de Alcantara, which is a suburb. When the Cardinal perceived this, he sent the Spaniards, about 2500 of them, four regiments of Portuguese and a few horsemen, to meet the enemy and stop him. But when they came outside the town and the Portuguese were required to fight, it was discovered that they had no stomach for it. So the Count de Fuentes retired again on the town with the Spaniards and Portuguese, in order to prevent the population from declaring for Don Antonio. Thus the English advanced to the suburb, and on the 1st inst. to the wall of the town. There they established themselves. They treated the Portuguese well and did them no harm. The town was completely held by the Spaniards and, to facilitate defence, women and children and other useless folk were put on shore across the river. The English thought to get into the town by Santa Catharina. They attacked twice but were thrown back by the Spaniards with a loss of 300 men and 30 or 40 prisoners. On their retreat, as they were passing over a hill, they were fired upon with heavy guns and much damage was done. The Duke of Braganza has marched to Lisbon on foot with 600 men, and many troops are coming there daily. From Castile extra help is coming with all speed. But when the enemy heard this he retreated on the 5th. On that same day the Duke of Feria was due with 1500 men and some cavalry, as also twenty companies of Spaniards and some more troops besides. So the English moved off in great haste and the cavalry pursued, in order to hamper their embarkation. We hope to hear every hour that further damage has been inflicted on them. It is believed that Don Antonio relied greatly on the Portuguese, because they would not fight against him. A Portuguese nobleman, they are called hidalgos, was caught trying to bring Don Antonio 15,000 ducats. He was executed together with a baptized Moor. This Moor, at the instance of Don Antonio, was supposed to shoot the Count de Fuentes, but he fired at the wrong man and hit him in the arm. He was hanged.

In their five days' skirmishing before Lisbon the English are said to have lost some 1000 men. It is doubtful whether their provisions will not run out, so that they will be forced to go home, especially as in Santander and other places ships are getting ready to resist them. The galleys are expected from Italy. Of the Moors we hear nothing at all. They seem, thank God, to be quiet.

149. Rumors from Seville

Seville, June 28, 1589.

News came this week by special messenger that the English Armada sailed away from Cascæs on the 18th inst. suffering from famine, dysentery and plague. They are said to have eaten their own horses. Two thousand Portuguese and 150 monks and priests were with them, but they refused to take them along and left them ashore. These Portuguese will soon be hanged, and it is to be hoped that half the fleet will die, so that it may not be able to come back here over soon. In the meanwhile all the fortresses are being equipped, and two galleasses with 1500 soldiers and five ships more from Sicily and many weapons and fighting men have come in too.

Letters of the 19th ult. arrived from Constantinople last Monday with news of the return of Hassan Aga, General-at-sea. He is ill seen, however, owing to his lack of success in the expedition against Barbary. Better measures shall in future be taken at Constantinople to prevent the Christian corsairs from doing so much damage. An ambassador from Persia is expected at Constantinople, and great preparations are being made for his reception. A big navy is also being equipped, and some say that peace between the King of Spain and the Grand Turk has come to nothing, because the King tried to include in the peace all the Princes of the House of Austria, especially the Emperor and the Isle of Malta. But the Grand Turk will consent to nothing more than the conclusion of peace with the King of Spain and all his territories, in whatever part of the world they may be. However, hope of a favourable result has not entirely disappeared. There is plague and great scarcity in Constantinople, and the poor are suffering grievously. Hassan Aga's galleys are in such bad condition that they would have succumbed if they had met the Spaniards on the way. They say here that the Queen of England is very ill; she is in danger of her life, and in the grip of some terrible disease.

150. The Murder of Henry III

Report of the murder of the King of France. (Undated.)

On the first day of the month of August, a young Dominican friar betook himself to St. Cloud where the late King sojourned, with a passport from the Count de Brienne, who is kept imprisoned in Paris. On his arrival he informed the guard that he had something which he wished to communicate to the King. The King ordered that he might be permitted to deliver his message on the following day. The Provost-Marshal gave the monk quarters at the King's request and entertained him right nobly. The monk said he was minded to do the King a great service. The following day the Provost-Marshal led the monk to the King's chamber. But, as there were several persons present, the monk demanded that the King might receive him alone. He led him into his cabinet and read various scripts which the monk handed to him. When the King had perused the last, he asked the monk whether he had any more. The latter thereupon replied "Yes," and, in place of the script, drew forth from his sleeve a short knife, the width of two fingers, which he thrust into the King's abdomen below the navel. He left it sticking in the wound. The King pulled it out himself and thus enlarged the wound. He then himself inflicted a stab upon the monk. At his calls for help several people came into the room, among them La Bastida, who helped to murder the late Guise, and he with his dagger slashed at the monk. Also one of the halberdiers thrust his halberd into the monk so that he was mortally wounded. He said that he had not hoped to come off so easily. After his death his corpse was dragged along the streets, rent asunder by four horses, and publicly burnt. The King did not expect to die of his wound. He walked up and down his room, and showed himself to his servants and to the soldiery at the window. But at four o'clock in the evening he felt great pains and when the doctors visited him they found the injury to be most grievous. They gave him an enema, and discovered that the intestine had been injured. The wound turned black and the King was informed of his perilous condition. He did not at first believe this, because he was feeling fairly well. But by and by he became weaker and a Capuchin was sent for to comfort him. But when he arrived the King no longer spoke. He died upon the 2nd day of this month at midnight. The body has not been interred as yet, and has been taken to Senlis. It is said that he has asked the King of Navarre not to take revenge for his death on the city of Paris. The story goes that the monk had delivered discourses not far from Paris and had then said that he would take the King's life. Even though he be burnt and quartered, he would feel no pain. The King of Navarre is still in St. Cloud and is besieging Paris to the extent of his power. He has made himself King of France and is thus acclaimed by his followers. He tries all ways and means in order to win to his side both the nobility and the common people. The Council of Paris has declared the Cardinal of Bourbon, who is held a prisoner in the castle of Chion, to be King. The King of Navarre intends to go to Rheims to be crowned there and to gain possession of the three royal cities.

151. Henry IV Ascends the Throne

From Rome, the 2nd day of September 1589.

From France confirmation is received of the fact that the King of Navarre has adopted the large coat of arms of France. He causes himself to be publicly acclaimed and styled King of France. The body of the young murdered King Henry he had buried in Senlis.

In all parish churches of Paris obsequies have been celebrated for Jacques Clément, who murdered the King. It is thought that the Paris people wish to erect a statue in eternal memory of him as the liberator of his country.

152. Another Burning of Witches

From Schwab-München, the 5th day of September 1589.

There again follows a confession given at Court by a monster who was burnt here yesterday. Her accomplice, who was also taken prisoner with her and who is said to be a

171

very rich peasant woman from Bobingen, died last Saturday in prison. It is reported that she has taken neither food nor drink for four days, nor given any evidence, for her devilish paramour has forbidden her to do so. She also continually called upon him to come and fetch her. She would listen to no mention of God or other holy matters. The witch, who was condemned yesterday, made a noose out of the straw on which she was lying and tied it round her neck in order to hang herself, but when food was brought in to her this was discovered and prevented.

Rumour hath it that the late sorceress was to have been burnt with the other witch, but neither I nor others did see anything of her. She must have been led away in secret and have lain hidden under the stake, and so both must have been burnt together. These monsters are said to have denounced many others who will in their turn meet their fate. Some one tells me that they brought another four such persons from Bobingen before dawn to imprison them. It is also rumoured that they will not spare the beautiful ones, once they have done away with the ugly and the lewd ones. One of the four brought in is reported to be a wealthy widow. The Bishop has made up his mind to exterminate all this vermin from his diocese. Dillingen also shows signs of this plague. The Bishop will probably have his hands full for some time to come with burnings and in the end, perhaps, even put part of the nobility in golden chains.

The present misfortunate female, Anna Schelkl, widow of Hans Schelkl of Bobingen, who has been produced in public, has permitted herself to be shamefully imposed upon and seduced by the accursed Satan, in contravention of the commands of God. She has repeatedly yielded herself to him in fornication and thus committed adultery in a strictly forbidden and sodomitic manner, and for over thirty years she has delivered herself to accursed witchery. She has denied God and all His Heavenly Hosts as well as Holy Baptism, and instead of the sign of the Lord she has allowed her body to be marked with the four signs of the Devil. She has thus beyond doubt permitted herself to be led astray from the divine mercy of God and to surrender herself to the sway of the Evil One. By means of the said witchcraft she has caused great harm and destruction and death to little children, people, horses and other animals and also assisted in spoiling and ruining the precious corn of the fields. Therefore the judges of this hamlet, Schwab-München, are unanimously agreed upon their verdict that Anna Schelkl be handed over to the executioner and be led by him to the common place of execution, there to be dispatched from life to death by burning on account of her loathsome and highly punishable misdeeds. Her goods and chattels to go to the Treasury of His Honour, the Venerable Herr Marquard, Bishop of Augsburg and Provost of the Cathedral of Bamberg. Let every one beware of such horrible sin!

Warning to those named hereunder:

I hereby give notice to all official persons, servitors, citizens, subjects and tenants, of whatever rank they be, who owe allegiance to my Gracious Prince and Master, and especially to those of this hamlet, on their oath and loyalty, to put this sentence into execution. Whosoever makes so bold as to hinder it by force is to be proceeded against and to be treated in like manner. Let all beware that they do not come to grief!

153. The Famous Alchemist Bragadini

From Venice, the 1st day of November 1589.

Your Grace will no doubt have learnt from the weekly reports of one Marco Antonio Bragadini, called Mamugnano. He is the bastard son of a nobleman here and was born in Cyprus. He is reported to be able to turn base metal into gold. Our government has had him conveyed hither under safe escort because the Inquisition has put him under ban. He is forty years old and was formerly possessed of no mean fortune, but spent it in riotous living. Then for a time he was mint-master to the Grand Duke Francis. From thence he came to the late Pope Gregory, who held him in great esteem. He thus obtained several thousand ducats. But when these too had been spent, he became a Capuchin and had taken his second vows. But since he could not subject himself to the strict rule of the order, he absconded without dispensation (hence the excommunication ban by the Holy Office) and betook himself to France. There he served several princes incognito.

Latterly he has returned again to Bergamo in Italy and has exhibited his art in Valcamonica and in a short time increased his fortune to over and above two hundred thousand crowns. He has expounded his craft to several persons and it had got so far that he was prevailed upon to come here of his free will. Such a host of princes and lords beleaguered him that he was scarcely safe, although he had a bodyguard of fifty archers. This man is now here in this city, holds banquet daily for five hundred people and lives in princely style in the Palazzo Dandolo on the Giudecca. He literally throws gold about in shovelfuls. This is his recipe: he takes ten ounces of quicksilver, puts it into the fire and mixes it with a drop of liquid, which he carries in an ampulla. Thus it promptly turns into good gold. He has no other wish but to be of good use to his country, the Republic. The day before yesterday he presented to the Secret Council of Ten two ampullas with this liquid, which have been tested in his absence. The first test was found tò be successful and it is said to have resulted in six million ducats. I doubt not but that this will appear mighty strange to Your Grace. It verily sounds like a fairy tale, but Your Grace will surely believe us, for everything is so obvious that it cannot be doubted. The confectioning of this liquid is, however, his secret, for in his letter of safe conduct he made express demand that he be not forced to divulge this. He also craves nothing more from this our Government but that it may exercise good watch over his life and his person. In return he will provide them with gold in sufficiency according to their demands. He has already made known that he is greatly amazed at the ignorance of the world, in not discovering this art before, considering that little is requisite for this achievement. This is truly marvellous and quite novel to all of us. The alchemists have taken heart of grace again and are working night and day. One hears of nothing but of this excellent man who, as already stated, has no other wish but to serve his country.·

From Venice, the 8th day of December 1589.

You have learnt latterly that the craft of the alchemist Marco Bragadini after being tested has been approved of. The tests have shown this sufficiently. The most noble personages here address him by the title "Illustrissimo" and

174

feast with him daily. The Duke speaks to him in the second person. By day noblemen attend upon him, by night he is guarded by armed barges. Whereas so many strange people have arrived here, the Government holds in readiness three fully equipped galleys.

From Venice, the 16th day of December 1589.

The alchemist is said to be at work now in making five thousand sequins per month at the request of our rulers. Thereafter he will make fifteen or sixteen millions more which he has promised to hand over to it. Day by day he shows himself in great pomp. He makes his friends presents of twenty thousand and more ducats at a time. Monday last he gave a banquet in honour of the Duc de Luxembourg, the French Catholic Ambassador in Rome, which, without counting all kinds of special confectionery, cost near upon six hundred crowns.

From Rome, the 16th day of December 1589.

The Venetian Ambassador has solemnly besought the Pope that Mamugnano, the alchemist, who now resides in Venice, may remain there without molestation by the Holy Office, on account of his being a former Capuchin. Thereupon the Pope made answer that he was not a little surprised at the afore-mentioned Rulers putting so much faith in that man. Though his art might be found to be successful, yet it only could accrue unto him by the help of Satan.

From Venice, the 4th day of January 1590.

It is said of our Mamugnano that his craft for transforming quicksilver into gold does suffice for small quantities, but fails to produce larger ones. It is reported that the night before last he made two ingots in the presence of some of our patrician aldermen, each one of the weight of one pound. There no longer exists any doubt in the matter. Discussion, however, is rife amongst some of this city's philosophers as to whether Mamugnano can renew the material wherewith he has made his gold, once it is used up. Some say yes, and others say no, so that it is doubtful what they really think about it.

154. Gold from New Spain

From Venice, the 12th day of January 1590.

News reaches us from Lyons that letters from Lisbon of
the 18th day of December of the past year report the
arrival in Seville from New Spain of the fleet with eight
millions in gold. More ships are expected to arrive shortly,
which had to remain behind on account of storms. They
are bringing a further four millions. This cause for the delay in the arrival of the first ships is the fact that they took
their course several degrees higher than is their wont in
order to escape the English cruisers who were waiting for
them on the usual degree. The other ships have probably
taken their course along other degrees for the same
reason.

155. Bragadini Works on

From Venice, the 19th day of January 1590.

Mamugnano changed a pound of quicksilver into gold
some days ago. But he is not satisfied with this weight,
because he has been asked by several persons to produce
a larger sum.

156. Letter from East India

*Tidings received in letters under date of 13th
January 1590, from Oriental India.*

When the last ships set sail in the year 1589, the following
exploits of war took place. The Armada, which Manuel
Continho and his brother Thomas de Sansa had dispatched to the coast of Melindo on the 19th day of January
1589, numbered five galleys and fifteen other ships. They
carried twelve hundred Portuguese. When, after heavy
storms, there arrived within sight the Estrecho de Moqua,
they noticed that four Turkish galleys had landed on the
coast of Melindo near a place called Mombassa. On this

island the Turks had built a fortress for their protection, not suspecting the coming of the Portuguese. The latter went ashore, and near on three hundred thousand natives banded themselves together in order to proceed to the island at low tide and to eat the people living there, which they had also done now and again on the mainland. For this reason the Turks had removed the cannon from the galleys for their protection, not apprehending any danger from the open sea. But the Portuguese Armada intervened, captured the Turkish galleys without resistance, and thereupon landed. When the Turks saw this they sought to take refuge on the mainland, but they were cruelly handled and eaten by the wild natives. Some of the Turks surrendered to the Portuguese, preferring captivity to being devoured by the cannibals. Thus the Portuguese took prisoner several Turks and Arab Moors.

The Portuguese general ordered the King of Mombassa, who owes allegiance to the King of Portugal, to be decapitated, because he had granted the Turks asylum in his territory. The fortress erected by the Turks was razed to the ground and the island pillaged. Then the Portuguese left the field clear to the Simbas, who killed and ate the people before the eyes of the Armada, so that within five days not a living creature was there left on the island. When they had cleared everything and had nothing more to eat, they again went to the mainland. They thereupon set out northward for the land of John, the Priest. Those of the Armada relate that the Simbas are well equipped with sharp arrows and eat all the men they can lay their hands on, and their wives they lead away with them alive. But they do not suffer a sick person among them. As soon as one falls sick, they kill and eat him. The Portuguese report that the natives were six hundred thousand strong when they set out upon their quest. Once they reach a place they do not leave it as long as they can find a man to eat, after which they depart. Victory fell to our Armada because the Simbas had caused so much trouble to the Turks that it was an easy matter to capture the galleys, which were taken into Goa on the 16th day of March.

Letters were sent with the ships from Santa Cruz to Portugal last January that two of our galleys and twelve galleots fought bravely with the blacks near Goa. The galleots withdrew into a harbour twelve miles from Goa,

177

whither the Governor dispatched a fleet. This fleet conquered the coast and drove the natives inland.

The fortress which our Armada destroyed in Malacca has been built up anew by the people there. The Governor, however, with three hundred Portuguese, once more drove the people away and tore down the building. All the ports of Malacca are of great importance, for it is thither the ships come to take in cargoes of pepper and other condiments and freight. It would be well to conquer the island of Sumatra. With four to six thousand Portuguese it would be possible to prevent all navigation to Moqua. The money, however, is lacking. Last year an English ship entered the Sunda Straits and took in a load of pepper. The captain had brought with him a letter and a present to the Bishop there, but the latter accepted neither. When the English made their way back towards England round the Cape of Good Hope they sailed forth with two more ships and took their course through the Estrecho de Moqua, where one of the ships was wrecked. With the other two they proceeded to New Spain and Mexico where they pillaged and took whatever they could lay their hands upon. From thence they sailed to the Philippines, where they loaded all manner of wares from China. One ship then sailed home, and another to the Sunda Straits to fetch a cargo of pepper. Navigation from New Spain to China has become an ordinary occurrence. Ships arrive there daily. Last year Don Juan de Gona sailed to Mexico, but when our Governor learnt of this he sent a galleot to fight him, for it would be India's ruin if he were allowed free passage. For there is a convention between the King of Portugal and the King of Spain according to which the Spaniards are not allowed to sail to the Philippines. By this the King, our Lord, vowed he would abide when he took possession of Portugal.

The Jesuits daily convert people in Japan to the Christian Faith. They have entire mastery of this island.

The Moors of Ceylon have taken a Christian for their king. He is the cousin of the last King. He asks for two hundred monks who are to baptize his subjects.

157. Further Successes by Bragadini

From Venice, the 26th day of January 1590.

Concerning the alchemist, Mamugnano, no one harbours doubts any longer about his daily experiments in changing quicksilver into gold. It was realized that his craft did not go beyond one pound of quicksilver, however much various persons begged him to produce more. Thus the belief is now held that his allegations to produce a number of millions have been a great fraud, in which he caused people to believe. For he who can make a small amount of gold should also be able to produce a large quantity. This is the question upon which learned professors hold dispute. Meanwhile he has cut down his expenses, also reduced his banqueting, and is seen about with a smaller suite than formerly. It is reported from Spain that the King has concluded an agreement with the Genoese for a loan of five millions towards the end of the months of March and April, one million during the middle of July and the last during the middle of September.

From Venice, the 26th day of January 1590.

The alchemist Mamugnano is making gold here for his needs. He is intending this Shrovetide to hold a joyous masque in the Square of St. Stephen, for which purpose he is having sent hither six fine stallions from Mantua.

158. Adultery at the Court of Saxe-Coburg

From Strasburg, the 7th day of February of the year 1590 *of the old calendar.*

John Casimir is said to be in sore trouble concerning his consort, for she has committed adultery with a Pole. The latter has had intercourse with her seven or eight times, and upon each occasion she presented him with a hundred crowns. When these things became bruited abroad, he was taken into strict custody to the Palace of Mannheim, about two miles distant from the city of Worms. Not long ago he escaped, but was caught again in the Palatinate. By order of the said Duke, several hundredweight of iron were fastened to his person, so that he may not be able to flee again. May God console him and all such as are afflicted!

The Princess has been divested of all her princely apparel and raiment. She is reported to be wearing the clothing of one of her former tiring women and to be in durance no less hard than her lover. Only an old woman is let in to her.

Otherwise information has been received that the alchemist of Venice has been instigated by the Grand Vizier to pass himself off as an alchemist and an artist in order thus to gain admittance to the city of Venice. This scheme has been, however, discovered, and the alchemist will not escape punishment.

159. Genoese Money for the League

From Venice, the 9th day of February 1590.

Tidings come from France that the Spinolas, wealthy Genoese merchants who did a large business in Paris, have collected a goodly part of the moneys owing to them from such countries as France, England and the Netherlands. Finding themselves possessed in Paris of so large a sum in cash as near on four hundred thousand crowns, they dared not remove it, because they were afeared that it might be taken from them. Still less did they wish to take it to Italy or Spain because trade there is at a standstill. They are now offering this sum to the League, and His Royal Majesty of Spain has promised its repayment in Spain. In Rouen there are other Spanish merchants, who possess a still larger fortune, which they also wish to offer to the League.

It is said that Mamugnano has won near on ten thousand ducats gambling with several noblemen, so that rumour hath it that he is as clever at gambling as at making gold. He is reported to have produced in these latter days ten thousand gold crowns at one sitting, which fact is confirmed by a credible witness, who was present on that occasion.

160. Probable Bankruptcies in Seville

Antwerp, February 13, 1590.

London letters of the 25th ult. have been received this
week. They mention that Lord Cumberland has come to
England with sixteen Indian ships which he has taken.
Rather a high figure. From another London source we are
notified that the Indian ships which the English have
taken had over 20,000 lbs. of cochineal on board. Also a
high figure. There were other goods on board, and gold
and silver as well. This is a serious loss for traders, and it is
to be feared that Seville will not get through without bankruptcies. In our business here things are none too good
either. God the Lord protect each one of us from harm!

161. A Scotch Alchemist at Prague

Venice, March 30, 1590.

We hear from Spain that the kingdom fears the Queen of
England will send her fleet again this spring to raid coast
towns. The King is taking useful counter-measures and
assembling many ships in Corunna harbour. A letter from
Prague states that a native of Scotland has arrived there
with thirty-five horses. He gives himself out as a real artist
who knows how to make gold, and is not inferior to Mamugnano in Venice.

162. Execution of Two Children

From Vienna, the 24th day of April 1590.

Yesterday two boys, the one thirteen and the other seventeen years of age, were put to death by fire and sword.
For some time they had caused much damage through
setting fire to property. May God guard henceforth all
the children of pious parents!

163. Another Burning of Witches

From Schwab-München, the 4th day of May 1590.

Last Wednesday the innkeeper's wife of Möringen and the baker's wife of Bobingen were tried here for their misdeeds in witchcraft. Mine hostess is a short, stout, seventy-year-old doxy, who had taken to her accursed witchery when eighteen years of age. This she has practised fifty-two years, and it is easy to imagine what havoc she has wrought in such a long time. As the result of fervent petitioning, her sentence has been lightened inasmuch as she was first strangled and then only burned.

The other was only seduced to this work of the Devil by Ursula Krämer, who was the first to be executed here. So far, she has not perpetrated any sore misdeeds, but so much has she owned to, that her life is forfeit. Even on her day of judgment she still thought she could vindicate herself, and even at the place of execution I myself heard her say that she was dying innocent. Most unwillingly did she submit to her fate. But in the end she was reconciled to it and prayed long to God that He might pardon her misdeeds.

This morn another woman was brought hither from Möringen. Only half a year ago she married off one of her sons to a widow, who is said to be of the same craft. Thus it is hoped that it may incriminate others here. To-morrow or next week some more are to be brought here, but no one knows from whence. There is much discussion here about the hostess of Göggingen. May the Lord grant that this be but idle talk.

164. Fresh Deeds of the Alchemist of Venice

From Venice, the 11th day of May 1590.

Whereas Mamugnano, the alchemist, passed some time in a village a certain distance from here, and several persons suspected him of making gold for other people, his rooms were sealed at the request of his creditors. By order of the Signori Capitani, however, one room was unsealed again.

During the last days a large fish was caught by the fishers near Malamocco. It weighs more than a thousand pounds, according to our weights, and measures twenty spans. It has two wide wings, eyes as large as those of an ox, and a round, small mouth with two teeth, one in the upper and one in the lower jaw. They are almost as thick as a finger and the fish has a strange colour. What kind of a fish it is the fishermen are as yet unable to say.

We have just learned that Mamugnano, the alchemist, has returned here. The Pope is said to have granted him absolution, but he had to make a donation of five thousand crowns and enter the Order of the Knights of Malta.*

165. A Miracle in Bohemia

Authentic tidings from Prague on the 6th day of July 1590.

In the town of Kaurim in this kingdom of Bohemia, five miles from here, there lives in the house of a widow a God-fearing, industrious man, Nicholas by name, with his wife and three small children. He was so poor that he had naught but four pennies. With these he went to a baker's on the morning of the 22nd of May and bought a loaf of bread. Carrying this home, he wondered oft, mid heavy sighing, how he should be able to provide further for himself, his wife and the children. He therefore entreated God in his heart that He might graciously maintain and feed them. He thereupon divided the loaf among the children, but after a little while they again demanded food. However, he neither had any money nor knew how it could be obtained, so he sent out his wife to borrow a few loaves of bread, but she accomplished nothing and came home with empty hands. Thereupon the man decided to go and dig loam which he might sell for money or barter for bread. He took a small pickage, and leaving the town behind, went to Brandschech Farm, near a village named Strzebovle, which belongs to the town Kaurim. As he

---

* Mamugnano or Bragadini, whose real name was Mamugna, eventually was hanged as a fraud and a cheat in Munich (1590) on a tinselled gallows.

reached the road near the estate of Herr Johann Lanna, Imperial Judge in the town of Kaurim, he discovered loam near it and thrust his pickaxe several times into the ground. Upon this, four large lumps of a snowy white substance were disclosed. He gathered these up and brought them home to his spouse, but was not aware as yet that they were flour. He ordered her to obtain as much bread for it as she could. She was absent a long while, as many people were greatly astonished, and some of them recognized this to be exceeding good flour. Since the aforesaid Nicholas waxed impatient and would no longer await the return of his wife, he set forth once more, taking with him a large napkin. After he had dug for a little while, he again found a great quantity of the white substance. He deposited it in the napkin and he had hardly begun to heap it on the cloth when the cloth was full, as he himself testifies. He thereupon carried it home. When he returned, his wife informed him that what he had found was not loam, but right good flour. He showed it to many people, who all recognized it as flour and bought it from him in lumps. Several gentlemen of the Council partook of it, and dumplings and baby's pap were also made therefrom. The bread is beautifully white, is of a sweet and agreeable flavour and of the fragrance of orris-root.

When this occurrence became known, many people went to visit the poor man and found his story to be true. The bailiffs, however, feared that the people might injure the corn, and therefore erected a fence around the place where the hole had been dug. In spite of this, many came from the cities, villages and hamlets to witness the miracle. They dug lumps out of the soil, small and large. Some poor people collected it in barrels. The flour is clean, and contains no earth or loam and easily separates from these substances. It is also slightly moist and holds together until it be exposed to the sun. It is of benefit to those who are God-fearing and especially such as use it for their own sustenance or that of their children. But, when unbelievers or scoffers touch it, it turns to sand. If it is allowed to drop to the earth, it becomes very white. The flour has also been brought hither, and many honourable persons have seen it with their own eyes and touched it with their own hands. They have thanked God profoundly for His boundless Wisdom and Mercy. May He feed those who are in poverty and of a believing heart now and through all Eternity!

166. Letter from Japan

From a letter written by Ægidius Matta, Priest of the Society of Jesu, to the General of his Order concerning the progress of Christianity, dated the 25th day of July 1590.

King Sapume, hitherto the most embittered enemy of the Christian Faith, demands that one of our brethren, who have come hither from the Spanish Philippines, be sent to Kangoxima, the most important harbour of his whole kingdom (whence I am writing), in order to hear confessions, preach and instruct his subjects. He also wishes that we found a settlement in the aforesaid port. He first did greatly insist upon this, but now has agreed to defer the matter till the arrival of the Father Inspector.

P. Caspar Celius, Vice-Provincial for Japan, who has lived the life of a saint and died immaculate, was taken to his grave in solemn state. This was marked not only by the numerous attendance of our Fathers, who chanced at this time to be present here, but by the presence of many Thomus-Christians who followed the funeral to Arima, where he was buried. His successor is Pater Gometius, who, despite his delicate health, is held in no less esteem than the departed. Concerning the position of Christianity in Japan, it is to be reported that three years have now passed since our Order was banished from this country. But by the protection of God we have met with no hindrance as the result of this banishment. Also the number of Christians in spite of this has not decreased, but, on the contrary, increased at a quicker rate than at the time when the Tyrant pretended to favour our doings. Several members of the nobility have become Christians and vie with their subjects in Christian zeal. D. Augustinus, a Christian, a vassal of the Tyrant, himself converted the Prince of Gotti to the Faith. It is of no mean advantage to the state of Christendom, that the islands upon which the said Christians are living, are situate far from the trading route of the Chinese. For this reason, also, all those who instruct in the Faith are removed far from the danger of a rebellion.

185

Nevertheless, in towns which are in closer proximity to the Chinese, such as Arima and Omura, the secrets of our Faith have been taught at all times openly and fearlessly and that with great success. In proof whereof there is the multitude of those who received the Blessed Sacrament. Apart from this, many crucifixes have been erected at various places, and frequented by servants of the Tyrant, without their being mutilated or pulled down. There are not many persons either who would easily consent to denounce us to the Tyrant, for they do not wish to cause him any annoyance, since he prefers to avoid trouble where he can. He likewise has the habit of passing things over in silence—although they be well known to him—when they appear to be vexatious.

The penalty of banishment is not so severely carried out in the case of the Japanese as it occasionally is elsewhere. It is therefore less strange, that we, though we be banished, yet continue our work with little hindrance. For all things that follow appear to the Japanese as banishment: the deprivation of the sight of that Mighty One, who has expelled us, and the avoidance of places that are greatly frequented, and the exhibition of grief and mourning in demeanour and attire, and a life fashioned on that of the Bonzes.

But now I revert again to the progress which Christianity has made here. One Ethnicus, or First Lord, of the name of Taikosama, a most violent enemy of Christianity, has not been able to hinder the spread of the Faith in his territory. Churches and crucifixes have been erected and all the inhabitants of a not unimportant town were baptized by me. A church was also built in many places—not only in those of great importance—and crosses were erected although the full time does not seem as yet at hand. Moreover a large number of those who have so far besieged our Port of Kangoxima now demand to be baptized. Further, also several Ethnici, who have been held prisoners by the Christians at various places, are also admitted to Holy Baptism, so that once the Tyrant Taikosama has been vanquished, we cherish the great hope—please God—that all those persons will adopt the Christian Faith. Our Ethnici here can scarcely recover from their wonderment at perceiving how little, if at all, we, who have been banished by the order of the Tyrant, allow ourselves to be frightened by his ordinances. Even three of the Thomi Ethnici extol our innocence, because, although all counsel us to do so, we cannot be prevailed upon to travel to China, leaving one or the other behind, in order to escape the present persecution.

They say it seems as though we were being detained by Providence, likewise as if we were endeavouring through our safety to demonstrate the might of God, Whose messengers we claim to be, as against the power of His enemies. As is men's custom they have taken this into their heads and firmly believe that we draw our strength from the enemies of Taikosama, so that our banishment from Japan may be rendered the more difficult. The Tyrant will imagine the same, when he hears that we are still in Japan.

We take credit to ourselves for hoping for the best. In the seminaries, which were instituted by Gregory XIII in Japan, a multitude of helpers grows day by day. This will be of the greatest importance for the growth of the Faith when Christianity is once more tolerated in these islands.

167. Famine in Paris

From Lyons, the 11th day of August 1590.

Although it was hoped that we should know before ending this letter how matters stand in the city of Paris, there have been no reliable tidings from that city since the 15th day of July. At this date, the Parisians still held out, but it is said that the troops of Navarre stormed the Faubourg St. Antoine on the 19th day of July. The Duc de Mayenne is reported to have received four thousand infantry and six hundred horse from the Netherlands together with a regiment of lansquenets from Lützelburg. There is great hunger in Paris; a pound of white bread costs half a crown; mutton, fore or hind part, legs or quarters for roasting, five crowns; ox or cow, one hundred and forty crowns; six sheep, one hundred crowns; a pound of horseflesh, five sous. Rumour has it that people are eating mice, cats and dogs, and also, that wine is very dear.

187

168. Frightful Apparition in the Sky at Vienna

From Vienna, the 11th day of August **1590.**

These days at 10 o'clock at night a most alarming wonder
has manifested itself in the skies. The firmament was rent
asunder and through this gap one could distinguish char-
iots and armies, riders with yellow, white, red and black
standards, moving as though to do battle against each
other. This awesome and unusual vision continued from
ten at night till about two of the morning, and was witnessed with alarm and dismay by many honest and trustworthy people. The significance thereof is known but to
God Almighty, Who may graciously prevent the shedding
of innocent blood.

169. The Plague in Rome

From Rome, the 15th day of August **1590.**

Since the month of July eight thousand people have perished from the plague which hath broken out in this city.
One of the brothers of our Governor died during one of
these last days, also his wife, who departed this life only
two hours before him. They were buried together. A great
number likewise have died in Pisa, and because of the
great mortality in Leghorn only a few are left there, for
many have fled.

170. Mighty Earthquakes in Vienna

From Vienna, the 16th day of September **1590.**

I cannot hide from thee that great havoc was wrought
here by an earthquake which began yesterday at 5 o'clock
in the afternoon. It shook the houses in the whole of the
town and lifted the people bodily into the air. At midnight
it caused several houses to collapse and killed various persons. Much brickwork and large pieces of masonry were

hurled from the steeples of the Churches of St. Stephen, St. Michael and the Church of Our Lady. Likewise in the royal residence it made stones, fragments, bricks and chimneys to split and break off. The roofs remained intact. The Schottenkirche is half destroyed. There was great terror among the populace, and it looked as though the Day of the Last Judgment was upon us.

The damage amounts to many thousand florins. At 2 o'clock after midnight there was another earthquake which was not so terrific. The people fled from the houses into the streets. A learned man, whose name is unknown, is said to have predicted that there will soon follow a much more terrible earthquake. May God have mercy upon us.

The lady of high rank who was possessed of the devil was exorcized yesterday in the Schottenkirche and thereafter became quite a reasonable creature. Last week when the priest was working upon her she remained in a trance for about an hour and life seemed extinct. When she came to herself she spoke many things that were passing strange and began to call out: "Woe, woe unto you Regents of Austria, woe unto Pappenheim, woe to the city of Pressburg, for it will be burned to the ground. Woe unto the city of Vienna, for it will perish!" She also related that the Angel Gabriel led her to the gates of hell and showed to her the souls of the condemned and their tortures. She pretends to have seen many great men, in particular Martin Luther, who pitifully cries out anent his teachings and sermons.

171. Valuable Prizes taken by the English

Antwerp, December 9, 1590.

It is confirmed from Zeeland that on the 17th ult. the English brought a big Venetian ship of 800 tons bound from Lisbon to the Barbary coast into Plymouth to be unloaded. It carried 1200 sacks of corn as stores for the Viceroy, and five barrels of gold for the payment of the garrison. From there this ship was to have sailed to Alicante to take in a cargo of Spanish wool. The ship has as well 544 bags of pepper, 388 chests of sugar belonging to Rafaele Fontani, and Giuliano Naso of Florence, and to Ludovico

Vesato. These goods will presumably be liberated, although the English had already unloaded 400 bags of pepper. But they have been ordered to put them in the Queen's warehouse. The ship *Maria Margherita*, likewise captured by the English, had on board 300 bags of pepper, 160 chests of sugar and 7 bales of raw silk. It is to be hoped that all this will be released. However, the cash and jewels belonging to the passengers and worth well over 15,000 ducats are probably lost. We have definite news too from the Portuguese that the ship called *La Capitania* has also been taken by the English. On board of it there seem to have been the Viceroy and 1500 nobles, an enormous quantity of money and much other merchandise. This ship left Lisbon last month for Portuguese India, but only got to the Cape of Good Hope and then sailed back to Lisbon because it was too late for it to complete its voyage to Portuguese India this year.

172. Disturbances in Prague

From Prague, the 24th day of December 1590.

During the past day a clamour was raised here that the Jesuits and the priests of the Pope are minded to take by force several churches of the Hussites on Christmas Eve, and retain them for the purpose of holding their services therein. It was also rumoured that the Jesuits have received outfits for war for some hundred men and have hidden them in their College. This alarm was raised by a monk, who said that he was awarded by the late Pope the privilege of obtaining possession of the monastery and church of St. Emaus, together with its revenue and appurtenances. This outcry came to the ears of His Imperial Majesty, who ordered inquiries to be made with reference to the matter. It has transpired that several artisans had spoken thus during a carousal. At the order of His Majesty they were examined by the councillors of the city of Prague. They were sent to court and questioned from whom they held such information. It resulted in a tanner being charged with spreading the rumour. He was put in prison in the Altstadt where he was questioned in kindly manner, but later put to the rack, as to where he had first heard these tales. But he pleaded ignorance. His journey-men were called and testified that he voiced such opinions before even they had partaken any wine. The aldermen condemned him to be executed with the sword. They submitted the sentence to the Emperor and asked him whether they should carry it out.

His Majesty issued a proclamation in the Bohemian language which was exhibited in all public places and, to some extent, has pacified the people, who were in an ugly temper. At first they had armed for resistance, although they had no grounds for so doing. In all parts of Prague there broke out disturbances. It has been ordered that a number of burgesses hold night-watch in all the suburbs of Prague. Likewise, a house-to-house visitation was carried out in order to ascertain how many strange guests there be with each citizen, how named, from whence, and of what nature their business. This had to be reported to His Majesty. Moreover, it was ordained that whosoever should know or hear of any danger should give tidings thereof to His Majesty or the Council. This scheme may lead to great bloodshed, theft and pillaging, if by chance a daring murderer or robber make use of this rumour to start an outcry and raise disorder in the town of Prague.

173. The Pope declares Henry of Navarre a Heretic

Rome, January 26, 1591.

After holding some Congregations about French affairs, the Pope has sent the Nuncio in Paris 60,000 crowns in addition to the monthly contribution of 15,000 crowns for the League. Besides this the Pope will send Briefs to Cardinals Vendôme, Lenoncourt and Gondi and to other clergy, and will excommunicate them if they do not abandon the King of Navarre. This latter the Pope is now calling a heretic, and a rebel against the Church of Christ who has forfeited his claims to the French Crown. Similar Briefs are to be addressed to all nobles in France and also to all the Princes of the League, reminding them of their duty and allegiance and encouraging them to pursue and utterly extirpate the heretics.

174. Extensive Recruitment in Germany

Düsseldorf, March 3, 1591.

It is confidently announced that representatives of the King of Navarre and of the Queen of England have received permission to recruit 6000 horse and 12,000 foot for Navarre and England in the territories of the Dukes of Saxony, Brunswick and Hesse. The representatives have brought over 160,000 ducats and have offered to deposit these with the Elector of Saxony. The Queen of England proposes to send 3000 lancers and 6000 Swiss to the Netherlands to prevent the Duke of Parma from taking a larger part in the war in France. The German troops are to be assembled and trained in the territory of Münster.

Thus we shall have a strange summer and no mention of the long-desired peace.

175. The Indian Fleet sails under convoy

Lyons, May 6, 1591.

On the 4th of April five vessels left Lisbon for India and one for Malacca. They are not taking much cash. They are escorted by eleven well-armed Netherlands ships with Portuguese and Spanish soldiers on board. But it is feared that they will be insufficient to protect the ships, and that in the coming summer the English will again worry us greatly. May the Almighty guard all from harm, bring safely in the two or three vessels due this autumn, and grant those outward bound a prosperous journey.

176. Rising in Saragossa

From Saragossa, the 15th day of May 1591.

Of news we have little that is good. To-day Antonio Perez, the King's secretary, was taken from the prison to the Holy Office. Thereupon the population of the whole town rose in arms with shouts of "Liberty." More than six thousand armed men forgathered, went to the house of the Count of Almenara, and broke down the gates, so that it became urgent to still the wrath of the multitude. This was done by the Justices of Aragon, who led the Count from his house on foot. The populace assailed him in such wise that it is a miracle that he was not torn to pieces. During this frightful affray, the Count received two wounds. He was taken to jail amid the shouting of the people, who wanted to put him to death as a traitor. Thereafter they all precipitated themselves into the court of the Inquisition, demanding the release of Antonio Perez and declaring that otherwise they would kill the Inquisitors. Two servants of the Inquisition were fired upon and perished. This riot lasted until the Viceroy and the Archbishop ordered that the secretary should be taken back to prison. There he remains and so the fury of the populace has somewhat abated.

The Archbishop has been in grave danger. For, although several counts and other noblemen came to comfort him, his life was not safe. I stood before him with a crucifix and perceived how sorely he was afflicted by this affair. We had the intention to hie to the Cathedral to fetch the Blessed Sacrament in order to assuage the fury of the population. But we feared that there might be attempts made on our lives and that of the Archbishop, for two of the Archbishop's servants who had been sent to the Cathedral were stoned.

177. Intercepted Letter to the Queen by her Ambassador in France

Translation of a letter to the Queen of England written by her ambassador. The letter was intercepted near Mouy by the garrison of Havre. (Original in French.)

Your Majesty has been informed of what happened up to the departure from Dieppe. He left me behind there with the King, Your good brother. Since this the Bishop of Rome, who supports the rebel party which fills his cooking-pot, has sent a Nuncio to the Duke of Mayenne with Bulls of excommunication against all classes, whereby the adherents of the League have grown more insolent than ever. But nevertheless this has greatly promoted the interests of our religion. For all the subjects of the King who call themselves Catholic have been urging him to declare himself a Catholic, and in order to preserve his realm he might finally have been forced, in common with his subjects, to practise idolatry and go to Mass. Without these absurd so-called Bulls of excommunication he would not have faltered from the right way. The King has faithful officials in his Parliament who have issued a warrant against the Papal Nuncio. This was actually done at the instance of the Papists themselves, who bethink them, as I hope, contrary to the opinion that I had of them, that God will cause the light of His Gospel to shine in this kingdom after it has been veiled for so long by Papal witchcraft. Madam, You will see the Papacy shrivel up sooner than You ventured to hope. We are about to destroy utterly the power and influence of the Pope by the creation of a Patriarch, with which the adherents of both religions are in sympathy. This is all that we can desire. There are still some bigots among us who are thought recalcitrant, but they will be brought to reason by fair promises which Your Majesty will understand. Louviers has been taken by surprise, and the Bishop of Evreux, one of the most obstinate partisans of the League, has been sent to Tours. There the wind is not favourable to the sacerdotalists. I am working in secret to have him arraigned, for such people as he are too dangerous, and I think that justice will not spare him. As for the true Christian Church, in all ways it is making wonderful progress in France. The King of Spain, that old foe of Your Majesty and of the Crown of France, is molesting us on his side, for he is sending quantities of money and of troops under the Duke of Parma. The King of France cannot resist these without the help which I have promised him on the behalf and by the instructions of Your Majesty. The Duc de Mercœur is awaiting him, Parma, but the Prince of Dombes will give him a fitting reception and will give our men such stout support that they will hurl their foes to earth. The Prince of Piedmont has gone to Spain with a small retinue to obtain money there, that he may make war against our comrades in Geneva. If he succeeds in this the Genevans will be supported by their neighbours. The indisposition of the King has made us anxious, but, God be thanked, he is out of danger. He has received £10,000 which were at once utilized for expenses of war and exhausted in less than a day. Cash and military stores are short here. Owing to lack of funds no auxiliaries can at present be drawn from Germany. The Duke of Saxony has shown himself very cold to God's cause. The Venetians put us off with fair words. Enthusiasm has waned everywhere. True believers in France rest all their hopes on Your Majesty. May it please You to give Your troops orders to advance without delay. It will be no small honour to You, Madam, to have overthrown the Roman Basilisk, and to have led the Gallican Church to the paths of truth. As for me I shall for ever esteem myself happy to be able to serve You as ambassador at so critical a moment. The King can get no support from the Turk, who might have sent a sufficient force into France but for the menaces of the Sophi. In this connection the Venetians have made a mistake which has delayed matters. But notwithstanding this the King is about to renew the alliance with the Turk aforesaid, because he hopes for great advantage from it. What will result I know not.

It was feared that the rebels would set up a King, which would not have been welcome to us, but the adjournment of the Parliament which had been summoned for May leaves us free to attend to our business undisturbed for a little while longer.

I write nothing to Your Majesty about the bearer of this letter, for I hope and feel assured that You know as well as I that he has lost no time since he has been on the continent, and that he has fully justified my expectations. He will above all give Your Majesty reasons for hastening to give Your aid.

I implore the Creator to grant You, together with good health, a very long and very happy life.

Given at Caen on the 15th June 1591.

Your most devoted and most obedient
servant and subject,
WALSINGHAM.

178. The English after the Fleet from Mexico: Essex ready to start

Middelburg, August 1, 1591.

Letters from London of the 28th July announce that the Earl of Essex is ready to start and is due to reach Dieppe before the end of the month with 4000 foot and 2000 horse. A conspiracy of courtiers against the Queen has been discovered. They are alleged to have intended to poison her. The accused have escaped and might well have lost their heads. The Spanish fleet has not turned up yet, for some of the English came upon two ships which had lost their way. They carried several thousand hides and some gold and silver. As it was not known where the other fleet was, vessels were sent from England to the Azores with provisions to meet the English ships there.

Two distinguished noblemen are said to have gone to the market in London in broad daylight and to have cried out there with a loud voice: "Woe, Woe, Woe!" Then they spoke to the people and told them to repent, for the Day of Judgment was at hand. One is said bitterly to have attacked the Archbishop of Canterbury and the Lord Chancellor. At this people wondered greatly and at length they were arrested, in order that they might be questioned as to why they did this. They answered they had heard Christ, who commanded them to do it. Others too should hear Him and do penance. The whole thing seems strange, and it appears as though God would now sit in judgment on these evil men. May the merciful God have pity upon us!

179. The Spanish Fleet gets through

Middelburg, October 17, 1591.

This week we have twice received letters from London to the effect that the English raiders are gradually coming home, bringing much loot with them. The fleet from New Spain is said to have reached Seville and to have fought its

way through the English fleet. In the engagement two of
the Queen's ships have been lost and many others
damaged. There is nothing in the tale about the Brazilian
ships which they are alleged to have captured. This is good
news which will cheer up the merchants here, after all
the losses they have suffered. The Spaniards have recently
taken seven English ships with fairly valuable cargoes.

180. Death of Pope Gregory XIV

From Rome, the 19th day of October 1591.

After every possible remedy had been employed to avert
the Pope's illness, his strength and speech presently forsook him. He departed this life on Tuesday last at 7 o'clock
in the palace of San Marco, where he had his abode. Although it was late at night, the Chief Chamberlain, Cardinal Gaetano, was sent for to come to San Marco. He
ordered the Papal Seal to be broken and took into custody
all papers and documents, as is the custom at the death of
the Pope. He also made all dispositions with regard to the
body. The latter was opened in the presence of the physicians and it is said that the right lung was affected and that
the kidneys were full of black and decayed blood. A gall-
stone was found likewise, the size of a hen's egg and
weighing two ounces. On the Wednesday in the early
hours of the morning the corpse was accompanied to the
palace by the Pope's nephews and his most intimate
friends, the Swiss Guard and the light cavalry. The Pope
lay in state in the Capella Vaticana, from whence the Canons of St. Peter fetched him and took him to their church,
where he still lies, so that the people may kiss his foot as
is their wont.

181. But it has lost heavily and spices will be dear

Lisbon, October 19, 1591.

God be praised! Perhaps before receiving this letter you
will have heard by special messenger of what has happened to our Armada and the fleet from New Spain, which

wintered in Havana. On the 8th inst. some of these ships, both from the Armada and from the fleet, and on the next day some more, came in here damaged and badly knocked about. General Don Alonzo de Basan came in likewise. Some of them are still missing, but perhaps have shaped a course for other ports. Of the Havana fleet 30 ships are still missing, but 18 have come in here and 30 to Seville. But altogether 70 ships left Havana. Our Armada had a collision with some English ships, but they soon took to flight. The Captain's ship escaped badly mauled, though it is thought she sank afterwards. The flagship, one of the Queen's best vessels, of some 60 guns, was surrounded and fired at all night till she surrendered the next day. But our ships hit each other too and two of them were sunk. However, the crew of one was saved. Immediately afterwards the fleet from New Spain came up. Of this 13 ships were already missing, and if our Armada had not cleared the English out of their way they would have had a very bad time. They intended to sail to Lisbon in company; but from the 26th to 29th September they met with such unprecedentedly bad weather that all the ships were separated. Some ran to Isola Terzera and San Miguel, and in sight of Terzera 11 ships were wrecked, among them the English ship, out of which, however, the guns had previously been taken. They have survived very great dangers, and it is hoped that some ships may yet have got to safety at San Miguel, or that the Armada has gone to Corunna. We cannot yet estimate the loss. The Havana fleet is not yet unloaded, and we must await the report of the casa de contractation in Seville. Altogether 14,000 arobas of cochineal seem to have been shipped. Nothing is known about ginger, as so many vessels have been lost. All the silver and gold for the King and the merchants has remained at Havana. The English captured some vessels close in here after they had weathered the storm, but their best haul was made between Santo Domingo and Havana. There they took a ship with a lot of silver on board, some say less than 500, others more than 700,000 reals. This will ill suit the people at Seville after the heavy losses they have been suffering for some years. It had been hoped that by means of the Armada the spices from Malacca which had been loaded up in 1589 would be saved and brought here. But the stuff has been left in the Azores. Those interested now want to bring it here in caravels, but as winter is at hand this cannot be done before next year. If no ship comes in from India till then, spices will get dearer every day. Cloves cannot now be got for 5000, but if the galleon comes from St. Thomas the price might fall again.

182. Election of Pope Innocent IX

From Rome, the 2nd day of November 1591.

On the morning of the past Sunday, the 27th day of October, which day had been fixed for the entering into Conclave, Mass was said at the usual place in the Chapel of St. Peter. Cardinal Gesualdo, as Deacon of the Sacred College, celebrated the Mass of the Holy Ghost and the Bishop of Bergamo delivered a solemn address. Thereupon the Cardinals entered in procession into Conclave—and this was only closed at 16 o'clock in the evening, in order that they could be provided with everything that was needful to them. On the Sunday the Cardinals held a congregation in the Capella Paulina. There the fourth Papal Bull with regard to the Pope's election was read out and the Custodian and the civic officers had to take the oath of allegiance and obedience until such time as the new Pope should be elected. The other prelates and ministers were instructed to guard the Conclave with the utmost care.

The ambassadors of the various sovereigns did not omit to remind the Cardinals at this time of their several interests. It was rumoured on the ensuing day that Cardinal Madrucci had said that for divers reasons he felt that he could not become pope and wished therefore that no notice should be taken of his name, but that the claims of those only should be considered whose election demanded less thought and deliberation.

183. Festivities at the Court of Dresden

Concerning the recent christening of the child of the Elector of Saxony and the accompanying festivities, in the year 1591.

The tilting-ground at the palace of the Elector in Dresden has been prepared in such magnificent and gay fashion, as

I have never beheld before. The seats have been covered throughout with sprigs of green fir, and between the arches and the lists there have been dug into the ground about one hundred mighty and lofty firs. These were daintily hung with fine oranges, pomegranates, large pumpkins and other luscious fruit. All kinds of large and small live birds fluttered about betwixt the fir-trees. Likewise many red and black squirrels flitted continually from one tree to the other. His Grace the Elector marched up three times with his miners, to the sound of fine music and the miners' songs. It was right wondrous to listen to these, and to see such a procession as had never been witnessed before. The last time, His Grace led one hundred huntsmen into the lists. They were all clad in green and made beautiful music, singing and blowing their horns. The huntsmen carried a very large, transparent and beautifully decorated cage, containing four bears, six boars, four wild wolves, two lynxes, several foxes, many hares and other small animals, such as martens, badgers, squirrels, rabbits and wild fowl. These were released on the tilting-ground, and whosoever contrived to catch one of them was allowed to keep it. The four bears, the wild boars, the wolves and the lynxes were let loose in the tilting-ground, where they roamed to and fro. The people stood in the courtyard. But the dogs kept good guard over the animals and the people took no harm. Only the wild boars charged among the populace and many fell to the ground. But the dogs gave them no quarter, so that, thanks be to God, no one was hurt.

The jousts were continued throughout four days. The mantenators were barons. The races were run for money. The sponsors were the Elector of Brandenburg, his spouse and the Administrator; the latter, however, was unable to be present because he had fallen from his horse when attempting to tilt at the ring, and broken his shoulder blade. But by good fortune he was not greatly injured and he is right well once more. The Landgrave, Maurice of Hesse, the old Duke of Brunswick, Philip by name, and a Count von Rolinz were also sponsors. Otherwise no strange guests have we had here.

His Grace the Elector has had the little Princess christened, omitting the exorcisms. This has highly pleased the

Calvinists and it looks as though a change of religion would occur here.

184. About half the Spanish Fleet is lost
Bankruptcies

Antwerp, December 14, 1591.

According to one letter from Seville about the Indian fleet only 34 ships have arrived there and 44 have either been lost or been captured by the English. Others again hear that 40 ships have come in and 40 are lost. However this may be, it is a very heavy loss which, both in Seville and in other places, will cause great confusion among traders; moreover, serious failures are to be feared.

185. Disputes between Calvinists and Lutherans

From Frankfort, the 12th day of February 1592.

We are advised thus from Leipzig: the common mob of artisans and shop-apprentices have caused a riot following upon the death a few days ago of Christianus Schütz. He was formerly Chaplain-in-Ordinary at the Court of Dresden. He was dismissed during the lifetime of Duke August, because of his adherence to Calvinism. The crowd ran with yells and clamour to the house of the deceased and broke the windows of the afflicted widow, shouting therewhile that he should be buried under the gallows. He and his following had caused the death of the young princely offspring and the common folk likewise regarded their destitution as due to him. Since the demise of our Sovereign of blessed memory near on seventeen hundred persons have been dismissed; this has caused a large number of wicked and evil-minded ruffians to be about. As the persons living in Schütz's house feared to be molested by that vulgar concourse, the widow of the Elector had to post halberdiers in and outside the house, so that order might be maintained till the funeral. When this was about to take place the next day there was no one to be found willing to carry the deceased to his grave. He had, therefore, to be laid upon a cart and drawn by a horse. Some rapscallions then banded themselves together, causing such clamour with howling, yelling and whistling that it defies description. They pelted the mourners, of whom there were few, with mud so that these had perforce to retire.

Another case occurred here this week. Dr. Gunderman, formerly pastor in this town, was cast into prison at the castle a few weeks ago. His wife was greatly mortified thereat. She was on the point of confinement and was seized by such melancholia that she hanged herself on the roasting spit of the kitchen. These will be terrible tidings for the doctor when he comes to hear of them.

186. War upon the Bandits in the Papal State

From Rome, the 14th day of March 1592.

A few days ago a father and his son who had given refuge to the bandits were arrested and taken to the Castello.

The bandits had given chase to the new Nuncio for Naples, Monsignor Aldobrandini, in such wise that he had hardly been able to save himself. Only a short time ago, a day's journey from here, they plundered a castle and a market and robbed goods worth over sixty thousand crowns. They led away with them many men and women and set fire to the market. The Pope has issued orders for the enrolment of four thousand soldiers and granted sixty thousand crowns for this purpose.

187. Birth of the Antichrist

From Venice, the 14th day of April 1592.

This week a News-letter has been circulated here which is said to have been written by the Grand Master of Malta and divers other Christian princes. This News-letter reports that in a certain province of Babylon there has been born to a woman of evil repute a child whose father is unknown. The child is reported to be covered with cat's hair and to be a dreadful sight. It began to talk eight days after its birth and to walk after a month. It is said to have intimated that it is the Son of God. At its birth the sun grew dark at midday and on the previous night a mighty flame of fire appeared above its house. Many mountains opened, and in one of these there was seen a column covered with Hebrew script reading: "This is the hour of my birth!" On the next day there fell from Heaven a goodly quantity of manna and precious stones; at other places, howsoever, snakes and other horrible creatures. When the child was questioned as to the meaning of this, it made answer: that the precious stones stand for the supreme delight of those who will keep his commandments, the snakes for the martyrdom and castigation of the disobedient. Adoration of this infant has already begun because it has performed great miracles, awakening the dead and making the blind to see and the lame to walk. The populace is being encouraged by a bare-footed friar, who alleges that this is the true Son of God. For the sake of brevity I must omit further reports which do not sound very credible. It is said that the Rabbis have come to the conclusion that this is the Child of Perdition, the Antichrist.

188. War on the Roman Bandits

From Rome, the 25th day of April 1592.

When Mario Sciarra, the noblest chief of the bandits, arrived at a village not far from Velletri and found no victuals there, he petitioned the towns of Piceno and Norcia to supply him therewith. They sent answer that they wished to negotiate with Mario in person; but he sent one of his nephews to them, and him they shot dead. For this reason Mario went into Piceno, killing most of the inhabitants and sacking the whole place. He has also pillaged several of the neighbouring villages, and in one of them he caused the burgomaster to be hanged. In the vicinity of Tivoli, Mario Sciarra met a company of soldiers and fought with them. Thirty of their number stood their ground and as many again were caught and hanged. This is the reprisal for refusing to recognize Sciarra as King of the Campagna. For this reason on Tuesday last Don Francesco Aldobrandino and the son of Marchese Malatesta set forth from here to Frascati with a goodly gathering of the inhabitants, and there joined forces with a number of soldiery to take the field against the bandits. They showed themselves fearlessly in the open with flying banners, drums and rack-waggons in fair number. Some were on horseback and others afoot. Near Libreto there appeared three hundred bandits who did some skirmishing with Delfino. He is reported to be sorely wounded. Leonessa in the Abruzzi, a place belonging to the Duke of Parma, was likewise invaded by the bandits, secretly assisted, so the rumour goes, by the peasantry. But, when this became known, those who had given help were thrown out of the windows as traitors to the country.

From Rome, the 9th day of May 1592.

The bandits who have been marauding in the Papal States for some time past, have finally made their escape in the direction of Aquila and Ascoli. Presumably the Spaniards, who were to have held the passes at the frontier, put up no resistance. The tale goes that a papal captain permitted himself to be bribed with money and allowed the bandits to escape. The Pope has issued orders that they must be refused passage throughout the Papal States, so that they do not return at the time of harvest and devastate the corn in the fields. To that end the Romans have offered to supply the money for three hundred mounted cavalry to fight them.

From Rome, the 16th day of May 1592.

Last Saturday a vast number of soldiery proceeded from here to Tivoli in order there to join issue with other armies against the bandits who are making great depredations. They descended at night on Luparella in Apulia where they murdered six hundred people and the Bishop, and made off with their spoil, which is estimated at over a million. In Sessano they commandeered food and drink, driving the cattle away with them. Civitanova they burned to the ground, slaying about sixty persons. From there they pursued their way to Foggia, where they intended to steal the large sums of money that were kept at the tollhouse. Had they succeeded in their enterprise they would have come away with great booty. Another band of brigands marched to Ascoli with their captain, Bachieratto, so that they might capture the Governor Visconti by night. This they failed to achieve, but they invaded a place near Montalto, where they did seventy persons to death in a gruesome fashion. Mario Sciarra is for the nonce near Norcia with a strong contingent of his bandits.

189. Nuptials at the Court of the King of Poland

Letter concerning the Royal Wedding in Cracow, which is to be held on the 26th day of May 1592.

From Breslau. This day a merchant arrived here from Cracow, where he has been staying for a fortnight. He reports that the future Queen of Poland is at the time resting in Pless, but will arrive in Cracow the coming Tuesday, the 26th day of May. The Queen is diligently practising Italian dances, as the King, likewise, is being instructed therein daily by a Polish gentleman who has lived for a long time in Italy and France.

His Majesty has ordered a masquerade which will cost over sixty thousand ducats. Fifty persons have been commanded to appear therein. They are to have their faces disguised in such fashion that each one shows that of another person and not his own, in order that none of them may be recognized. The Queen *in persona* will perform Italian dances, and gold-embroidered robes only will be worn for the masque.

All the burgesses and merchants will appear in the German dress, which is in many colours. Their coats, ornamented with silver and white loops and buttons, will be a gay sight. They will all go out in procession to meet the Bride, and the nobility will follow on horseback. So far neither the nobility nor the merchants have allowed themselves to be seen arrayed thus. Six black and six white bears are to draw the bridal coach. Another coach is to be drawn by six stags. The white bears will be made to dance and thus there will be sufficient drollery with the wild animals. The merchant also reported that he had been in the King's bedchamber. It is very spacious and the royal bedstead is in the middle thereof. It has a velvet curtain and velvet-covered chairs stand around it. On the bed there lies a sleeping-rug lined with velvet and sables. The Royal Bride is portrayed in this chamber, wearing a white and silver robe, and she looks at you with a laughing mouth, so that the King, as he looks at her picture, has to laugh likewise.

190. Injunction against Merry-Making

Extract from an Order written by the Most Excellent Count Octavian Fugger, issued by him on the 6th day of October 1592 with regard to the abolition of all festivities.

In the present grievous times, with death rampant, wars, disunion and tribulations, the perversion and decay of the land and the people as well as the shedding of Christian blood wax ever more disastrous. The monstrous undertakings of the Arch-Enemy of the name of Christ show that the prayers we have been offering up for the averting of these dangers and misfortunes do not suffice. It therefore behoves and well befits every one of us, as it is only meet that all should abstain from all worldly luxuries and joy. It is therefore my command that at the very earliest moment you should affix in my name (forasmuch as authority is vested in me) mandates on all the church doors with the sexton's seal thereon, forbidding most forcibly, at the risk of chastisement, all public festivities, such as singing, whistling, dancing, masques, promenading in the streets and other worldly merry-making. For all these my permission is withdrawn until further notice. With regard to weddings, I will herewith agree to their celebration provided this be done with all modesty, to the accompaniment of muted string music. I request you to call together all priests in my name and inform them that on the Sunday on which they shall have the aforementioned mandate, it is to be affixed and published and that they are not only to read it out from the chancel, but also to exhort their parishioners seriously to live according to its injunctions. Transgressions will be punished firstly with admonitions, and should these fail with other adequate measures. With this, God speed.

191. Executions in Saragossa

From Saragossa, the 11th day of November 1592.

On the 19th day of October at 5 o'clock of the evening there were executed here: Juan de Luna, Don Diego de Heredia, Francisco de Ayerbe, Dionysio Perez de San Juan and Pedro de Fuerdes. In the first place, according to old usage, they were led, all except Fuerdes, through the streets of Saragossa on horseback. Don Francisco and Don Diego were in black woollen penitential garb and long black cloaks, the horses being swathed in black saddle-cloths. Ayerbe and Dionysio Perez were also led on horseback in black penitential robes, but their steeds had no saddlecloths. Pedro de Fuerdes was dragged in advance of them on a bundle of straw by two horses. On the market-place a scaffolding had been erected out of boards, and in the midst thereof a small railing; before this they were made to kneel. This scaffolding was covered with black cloth. Don Juan de Luna had his head cut off from the front and Don Diego from the back, Ayerbe and Dionysio Perez merely had their throats cut, then they were laid down and left to die by inches. Pedro de Fuerdes they strangled with a rope. When he was dead he was quartered and the four quarters hung out in the streets of Saragossa. Don Juan de Luna's head was affixed to the royal town hall, that of Don Diego on the city gate, that of Francisco de Ayerbe at the prison, because he had removed Perez by force from there and led him away. Don Pedro de Fuerdes' head was fixed on one of the city gates.

Upon the ensuing day, the 20th, the Inquisition held its examination in the market-place. This lasted from 7 o'clock in the morning until 8 o'clock in the evening. Eight people were arraigned for sedition and condemned to death. They were executed on the 24th. At the same time the portrait of Antonio Perez was brought to this trial and on account of his heresy and sodomy burnt with prisoners who had been sentenced to the stake. Besides these, twenty to twenty-five other persons from Saragossa were also tried: some of them were flogged, others expelled from the country or sent to the galleys.

207

192. Christening at the Court of Poland

From Warsaw, the 7th day of July 1593.

Last Sunday, on the 4th day of this month, the royal christening was held in Warsaw after Vespers as follows: First the guests and all the officials of the Court went into the church, then the King followed. On his right hand there walked the Papal Nuncio, on the left the Envoy of His Imperial Majesty. Then came the Swedish Princes, the King's sister, who held the child in her two hands in a cradle most beautifully and daintily covered. On her right she had the Chancellor and on her left the Wojwode Adamovski. Since the Swedish lady found some difficulty in carrying her burden, the two said gentlemen assisted her. Thereupon followed the Queen. On her right walked the Envoy of Graz and on her left the Wojwode Woyzelinski, then came the young Queen, who had been confined but six weeks before; accompanied by Cardinal Count Radziwill on her right, and the Treasurer of the Polish Crown on her left. Then followed all the ladies-in-waiting of the three Queens, and as it was a beauteous day, all was most gay and sumptuous to behold. In the church the Royal Princess was given in baptism the names Anna Maria by the Cardinal Radziwill. The sponsors were: the Roman Imperial Majesty, who bestowed a necklace valued at fourteen hundred thalers as a christening gift; and the other godfather, the Envoy of Graz, who has presented, in the name of the mother of the Queen, another necklace which is nearly equal in value to the former; and the third sponsor, the old Queen, has given a bracelet and a rosary, which, surely, was of more worth than a wreath of marjoram. After the christening a short address was given, after which they all returned from church in the same order. Thereupon there took place a private banquet which was over so promptly that every one came home by daylight.

193. Henry IV becomes a Catholic

From Lyons, the 13th day of August 1593.

We have received tidings in what manner the King of
Navarre on his birthday, the 28th day of July, was pronounced at St. Denis to be a member of the Church of
Rome. Thereupon, it was urged on the Princes of the
League by the common people in Paris as well as by Parliament that peace should be made. Although the Spanish
Ambassador and the Legate of the Pope had declaimed
against this, nevertheless a general peace for three months
was declared. It is supposed that peace will become effec-
tive thereafter. Preachers shout and rave against this from
the chancel and make an outcry that the King will not
keep faith with the Catholics. In Vivarais, Languedoc and
other places round here this peace has already been
hailed with great rejoicing. The King had arrived at his
country seat of La Roquette near Paris, which belongs to
the former Chancellor, and the Princes were agreed to
come to meet him from Paris. But the Spanish Ambassador
and the Papal Legate like it not and were ready to depart.
A courier has been dispatched hither from Madrid reporting that the fleet from New Spain and Peru has safely
reached port on the 28th of last month. The treasure is
priced all in all at ten and a half millions, but nothing whatsoever is heard about the two missing ships from Calicut
and the galleon from Malacca, so that it is feared that harm
has come to them and that they may well be lost. This
would be a great disaster to many. May God grant that
good news may still be obtained with regard to them.
The Spaniards and the Portuguese will then flourish exceedingly, especially if the ship that is awaited from India
also arrives safely.

194. Henry IV will do his best against Spain

Antwerp, September 12, 1593.

They write on the 9th inst. from the Hague that the Na-
varrese envoy has announced there and also to the Queen

of England that now as before the King may be expected to spare no effort. He has received assurances to the same effect from the States General and the Queen of England, and supplies of munitions and military equipment will continue to be sent to France to drive the Spaniards out of the King's dominions.

195. The Dutch go to India

Antwerp, September 3, 1594.

At Amsterdam, besides the three ships which recently sailed for India, three other large vessels are being got ready, also to go to India, in order to see if they can arrange a harbour for Indian trade, and somewhat diminish the King of Spain's traffic with the East Indies. If they find a good passage it will be very profitable for this country. Towards this voyage the States General have granted 2000 Rhinegulden and ten of the chief men of business the same sum. If the voyage is successful, the money will be repaid to the States General.

196. Wondrous Tidings from Berlin and Leipzig

From Berlin, the 23rd day of December 1594.

Dear Lady Mother:
I cannot hide from you that a few days ago the ten-year-old daughter of a God-fearing burgess had a vision by night in her sleeping chamber, which was suddenly filled with a great radiance. Shortly thereafter there appeared unto her the form of a beautiful youth, all clad in white, who held a sword in his hand. He quoth: "Listen, child of man, and fear not nor be horrified! I am a good angel sent by God to the intent that thou mayest preach before the high authorities and bid them know that the Lord will afflict the German lands as He hath done to those of His people the Jews, when they would not abandon their great conceit, their lust and their sins. For just as He is gracious, longsuffering and pitiful, so does He come in His wrath and anger to punish mankind."

This child had but the day before been for the first time to the Lord's Table and although she did not speak much otherwise, she fearlessly repeated this angelical command before many people. Thus do the good angels preach that we must do penance and eternally offer praise to the gracious Lord for this consoling warning. On the other hand the bad angels preach most fearsomely and horribly in the Neumark. In a small town, Freiburg by name, evil spirits have possessed over one hundred and fifty persons, to which the preachers and also our friends testify.

Some few days ago a bad angel was also in Spandau, hardly two miles from here. There he made seven persons to be possessed, out of whom spoke the evil enemy. Many God-fearing people have heard this.

When the eclipse of the moon took place on the night of the 19th to the 20th days of October at five of the morn, there were seen in the skies strange rays and likewise other signs. Through this it can well be assumed that God will punish us with various plagues, unless we do become converted in time and do real penance for our sins. May the Almighty provide for us in His fatherly fashion, not according to our deserts, but according to His Mercy. Your beloved son, MAGISTER HERMANUS LIPHORPIUS, RECTOR.

From Leipzig, the 25th day of December 1594.

What my brother wrote from Berlin and Spandau is, alack, but too true. The burgesses of Spandau have since then collected all high collars and burned them in the open market-place. In Berlin, likewise, it has been forbidden to wear high collars and the bows which women flaunt on their skirts. Two days ago, one of our servitors arrived from Silesia and he says that three weeks ago a mountain erupted close to a little town, Goldberg by name. Smoke issued therefrom and rose into the air; it turned upon the town, lifted the roof from two houses and a piece of the church, and then receded into the mountain. In the Striegan various people who were dead and buried have reappeared. They torment and frighten the people. It was decided to exhume one of them, cut off his head and bury him under the gallows, which was done, but it proved of no avail; he appeared as heretofore. It was then decided to exhume him once more and to burn him. After this he appeared no longer, and all the others did likewise vanish.

211

197. The West Indian Fleet fears to leave Havana

Lyons, October 27, 1594.

A messenger from Spain for Italy rode through here just lately. He brings news that the Indian fleet with its very valuable cargo is to winter at Havana. It cannot get out, as English ships are there. They are said to have carried off 15 small vessels from New Spain containing leather and other goods.

198. Attempted Murder of Henry IV

From Antwerp, the 2nd day of January 1595.

A letter from Paris of the 29th brings news that the King of Navarre all but perished in the palace of Madame de Lioncourt. For as he was returning the salute of one who had made obeisance to him, a youth between seventeen and eighteen years of age essayed to stick a knife into his throat. But the thrust went too high and pierced the right cheek, whereby the King has lost two of his teeth. The handle of the knife remained cleft between the teeth. How this is going to develop we shall know by the following letters.

199. Copy of the Judgment and Sentence passed by the Parliament in Paris upon Jean Chatel, a scholar who studied in the College of Jesuits, on account of the horrible murder which he dared to attempt against the King's Person. Also the sentence passed upon the Jesuits, who have been banished from the Kingdom of France as Corrupters of Youth, Destroyers of the Peace and Enemies of the King and State.

The Parliament has examined the criminal suit, which was begun by the Provost of the Royal House and thereafter was continued at the request of the Royal Procurator-General against Jean Chatel, who has studied in the College of Jesuits at Clermont and now lies in jail. Parliament has given hearing to the confession of Jean Chatel and of the Priest of the Society of Jesu, Jean Guerette, former tutor of Chatel, as well as that of Pierre Chatel and Dionysia Hasdrat, his parents, and to the charge of the Royal Procurator-General and has found: Jean Chatel has been recognized guilty of the crime against the divine and temporal Majesty and is condemned as follows: He must make public penance before the doors of the church in Paris, naked in a shirt, lie on his knees, and hold in his right hand a burning candle, two pounds in weight. He must say and confess that he planned the inhuman and horrible murder against the King, in most malicious and treacherous fashion, and did wound him in the face with a knife. He must likewise confess that during his trial, he did say, according to false and cursed instructions which he had received, that it was permissible to kill kings, and that Henry IV did not belong to the Church as long as he had not received confirmation thereof from the Pope. He must manifest remorse and sorrow and crave forgiveness from God and the King. When this shall have taken place he will be conducted to the Place de la Gréve in the cart of infamy, and there be riven with tongs in the arms and the legs. His right hand will hold the knife with which he was desirous of committing the murder, and this will be lopped off. Then he will be rent asunder by four horses, his members and his body shall be thrown into the fire and his ashes strewn to the winds.

Moreover, Parliament has declared that all his estate is to be confiscated and surrendered to the King. Parliament likewise forbids any one, of whatsoever condition he be, by fear of punishment for lese-majesty, to repeat publicly or privately the offensive and rebellious words of Jean Chatel, which are not according to the word of God and have been condemned through the holy decrees as heretical and accursed. It further recognizes that the priests and alumni of the College of Clermont, and all others who call themselves followers of the Society of Jesu, destroyers of the peace and enemies of the King and of the State, have, within three days after the promulgation of this judgment, to leave the city of Paris and all other towns and places wherever they may have their colleges, and within fourteen days to leave the kingdom. Should they still be found within the confines of the kingdom after this time has elapsed they shall be punished for the crime of lese-majesty, their movable and immovable property to be employed for works of charity and distributed according to the findings of Parliament. Moreover it is forbidden to all subjects of the King to send students to other Jesuit colleges outside the kingdom. Parliament recognizes further that the present decree is to be executed by all the courts and prefects of this district. It also orders all the prefects and governors to carry out the execution within a fixed period. The representatives of the Procurator-General are to keep the matter under their control and to report within a month to Parliament, on fear of losing their office, as to their success.

200. Moratorium in Spain

Rome, February 11, 1595.

Spanish letters of the 1st January confirm that His Majesty on request of the traders has forbidden all payments at fairs and other places of business till after the arrival of the Indian fleet, on condition however that those who owe bills and demurrage fees must pay interest on them monthly. It is thought that this measure would not have been resorted to unless there had been a risk of many failures in Spain and elsewhere.

201. Why cannot the Pope help to pay for the War?

Rome, March 15, 1595.

The King of Spain has had the Pope informed that he does not oppose the pardoning of the King of France, and that the Pope should act as he thinks best for the honour of God and Holy Church. Nevertheless His Majesty is resolved to wage unceasing war against Navarre. Concerning help from the King against the Turks, His Majesty asks to be excused, owing to the delay of the Indian fleet, and begs the Pope to draw temporarily on the Treasury of the Church in the fortress here till the above-mentioned fleet comes in.

202. The Pope's Pardon for Henry IV

From Rome, the 5th day of September 1595.

Last Sunday morning at 8 o'clock the Pope caused himself to be carried in pontifical vestments to the square in front of the church of St. Peter. Nearly all the Cardinals present and a great number of prelates and gentlemen followed him thither. When he had taken his place with the Cardinals, there soon appeared the proxies of the King of Navarre, Messieurs Duperron and d'Ossat. They prostrated themselves before the Pope, kissed his feet and tendered to him their letters of introduction, in which the absolution which had oft been craved before, was submissively craved once again. The Pope showed himself favourably inclined to this petition, but he first commanded that a document be read out to the said proxies, in which it was declared that he was right willing to absolve the King, but that after receiving absolution the King was to say his rosary daily, attend Mass and conform to other spiritual exercises. Thereupon the aforesaid proxies first foreswore all heresies in the name of His Majesty, and publicly professed themselves to be of the Roman Faith. They likewise promised to carry through the conventions which had been agreed upon, and accepted the penance imposed on them.

Thereupon the two Psalms *Miserere* and *De Profundis* were sung and the Pope gave the absolution and added that he had permitted the King ingress to the Church Militant, and was willing to allow him likewise to be received into the Church Triumphant, after he had shown himself proficient in the spiritual exercises that were pleasing to God. Then the Cardinal Sancta Severina conducted the proxies to the church of St. Peter, which had been closed hitherto, and there they knelt before the high altar, took their oath and made their prayer and their act of thanksgiving. They likewise swore that His Majesty would himself execute all that he had been bidden to do before an apostolic Legate. They then took leave of the

Cardinal, betook themselves to the church of St. Luigi and heard Mass there. Afterwards they gave a stately banquet in their quarters to the gentlemen who had accompanied them. On this and the following days a cannon was fired on the Castello degli Angeli and various other joyful entertainments were likewise arranged.

203. Peasants' War in Upper Austria

From Vienna, the 13th day of November 1595.

With regard to the Peasants' War in Linz the tale goes round that the soldiery has again been skirmishing with the peasants near Freistadt. Six hundred men on both sides are said to have fallen, but victory remained with the peasants, who pursued the lansquenets as far as Freistadt. The Upper Austrian province is reported to have craved help from us in foot and horse. Two couriers arrived yesterday bringing with them a script according to which, if no help is sent, the nobles of Upper Austria will be in the utmost peril. For this reason Herr von Königsegg will be dispatched thither to-morrow with a troop of horsemen. Herr von Starhemberg is said to have lost three hundred riders in this affray.

There be posted up everywhere notices for the levying of troops, for the peasants are waxing ever stronger. They are said to be encamped not far from here, forty thousand strong, near the Danube. One cannot wholly blame them, for they are sorely pressed with the new taxes which they cannot afford to pay. They have most stately and experienced leaders who keep strict discipline, so that much might be learned by us from them. Since all the towns in the country must needs send troops, those of Wels were but a short time ago attacked by the peasants and soundly trounced, but not killed. Only their armour and weapons were taken from them, and they were sent back. If this war were to continue the country would be ruined and fall into decay. May God prevent this upheaval!

204. Drake at Havana

Amsterdam, January 27, 1596.

News reaches here that Captain Drake has arrived at Havana. They are greatly annoyed at this in Spain and 28 ships are sailing there from Portugal, as well as some from Spain. So there may well be blows in that locality, and the Queen of England will doubtless send warships and troops there.

205. Dysentery in Drake's Fleet. Drake dead

Antwerp, May 18, 1596.

They write from Middelburg on the 16th inst. that five ships have arrived from Spain reporting that dysentery has broken out among the crews of Captain Drake, and that Drake himself and his second in command and many of his men have died of it. Upon this the troops left Havana and all the forts and sailed back and ran into the Spanish Armada. They were so completely encircled by it that not more than three ships of their number got back to England.

Others say, however, that Drake has captured an island near Havana called Santa Martha, has fortified Havana and been joined by many Indians. The English Armada, 100 warships and 50 storeships strong, is said to have sailed for Plymouth and to be awaiting a fair wind there. With the fleet are 14,000 veteran soldiers, and many nobles who have volunteered. Colonel Vere has arrived here from Holland with 2500 well-equipped soldiers, who are also to sail.

Rome, June 22, 1596.

Letters reached here recently by a Spanish messenger to the effect that the King has had definite news of the death of Drake and that fifteen large English ships which Drake had with him are lost. His Sacred Majesty was extremely delighted at this news and some Spanish ships fell upon the English, who at once fled. But the Spanish General sped after them and took two, finding on board 60 soldiers and 20 nobles.

206. Panic at a Bull Fight

From Madrid, the 6th day of July 1596.

A few days ago, the inhabitants of Toledo, according to their custom, have held a bull fight before His Majesty. A great multitude having collected, some evil young rogues suddenly set up the cry: "The houses are falling!" Thereupon such panic arose among the people that they rushed out of them and betook themselves to the tablados or tribunes. This caused one of these to collapse, and several persons were hurt. The others fled without caps, hats or coats—the women without capes or slippers, only in scanty attire. In the meantime, some graceless ruffians arrived and carried off all they could lay hands on, especially plate and golden trinkets. This turmoil lasted for over an hour.

207. The Funeral of His Most Serene Highness Ferdinand, Archduke of Austria and Tyrol

From Innsbruck, the 20th day of July 1596.

First of all there stepped forth various craftsmen and their guilds from the local Presbytery. In front of them strode the Custodian of the Hospital, holding a candle protected by a shade. Then came one hundred patriarchs in black coats and smocks, each carrying a burning candle in his hand. Then came the venerable Council of Hall in mourning garb, with burning candles. Then came the honourable and wise Council from the princely town of Innsbruck, likewise with burning lights. Then followed the Town Clerk of Freiburg and the Town Clerk of Enzenstein. Then all the officials and the regimental and civilian scribes, together with the valets of His Most Serene Highness, the regimental secretaries and the gentlemen of the Capuchin Order, twelve of whom bore aloft a silver cross. They were followed by the Franciscans, the barefooted friars and the monks from Wilten. Then came the whole of the clergy with several of their vicars, twenty-four in all. Then the choristers and musicians of His Most Serene Highness, the Court Chaplain, the Court Preacher Antonius and the Father Almoner. Then nine prelates, the Suffragan Bishop of Brixen, the doctors and secretaries, the nobility, the military and financial Councillors, the Provincial Diet and the dapifers and grooms of the chamber of His Serene Highness, also the army kettledrums, swathed in black cloth. Then the flags—a light blue flag with the Hapsburg escutcheon and a stately black charger caparisoned in black with the coat of arms of Tyrol hanging on both sides. Then a yellow flag with the coat of arms of Tyrol; a beautiful red flag with the coat of arms of Württemberg and Swabia; a green taffeta flag with the coat of arms of Carniola; a fig-brown flag with the coat of arms of Carinthia; a rose-coloured flag with the coat of arms of Styria; a double-width white taffeta flag with the coat of arms of Burgundy; a blue flag with the coat of arms of Austria; and an entirely golden flag with the full coat of arms of His Highness of blessed memory. Then there was led past a magnificent horse with silver-gilt trappings and a red velvet saddle. It was decked in front and behind with white feathers. Then came Herr Siegmund von Welsberg carrying a long black flag which trailed on the ground; then Herr Christoph von Welsberg bearing on a black velvet cushion the Golden Fleece. Herr von Kolowrat as a former Master of the Horse carried the gilt helmet with gorgeous peacock feathers. Then two gentlemen carried a large shield with different coats of arms embossed thereon; next was borne a beautiful gilt sword, and the Count of Hohenembs came next, carrying a silver-gilt sceptre. The Count of Nogarol bore the hat of the Archduke. Then came the ducal bier. It weighed about seven hundredweight, and twenty-eight noblemen supported it with much strain. Then followed His Eminence the Cardinal, the son of His Highness, the Archduke Mathias and the Ambassadors to His Highness. The Count of Lodron and Herr von Vrintz led the Archduchess, then came the young Archduchesses, their governess and the tiring-women. Then followed the Commander of the Life Guards, and the bodyguards of the Archduke Ferdinand. The procession lasted five hours and passed through the town, the suburbs, the fortifications and then into the new burial-ground.

208. Capture and Looting of Cadiz

Middelburg, July 30, 1596.

On the 27th inst. I reported what news had come in about the English fleet. Since then another eight vessels, 22 days out from San Lucar, have come in. They bring not only confirmation but also plenty of details of events up to their departure. When the English arrived before Cadiz on the last day of June they found there four big galleons with 1000 to 1200 men on board, together with 20 to 22 galleys. These vessels moved up in crescent formation. The English Vice-Admiral advanced against them and, after an exchange of shots, he anchored to their right. In this position the two fleets fought furiously for a long while, but as the wind was unfavourable for the Spaniards they fell into disorder, and the English burnt the two galleons *San Philippo* and *San Andrea.* They also sank several galleys which could not get away. Then the Englishmen rapidly entered the harbour, where they found 36 ships with mixed cargoes for New Spain. On the next day they landed troops and captured the town, but they met with much resistance so that there was great loss on both sides. The Spaniards defended themselves for a long time bravely, but the English were 20,000 strong, including 300 horse. The English subsequently sailed to Santa Maria and there and at San Lucar plundered and burnt. Some nobles in the fort at San Lucar in expectation of relief held the place for five days, but in the end they had to surrender. The fear now is of the English going on to Seville where they could completely devastate the open country. God protect the unhappy country folk, already in such fear and terror as prevail all over Spain. In company with the English were five galleys from Barbary. They relate that the King of Arsinoe has armed also and raised 40-50,000 men. He is said also to have given permission to the English to put into Barbary and obtain provisions and other military stores. The English have already sent some captured ships to Barbary, and the outcome is awaited with great anxiety as heavy losses are feared amongst the traders.

209. Spanish Financial Policy

From Lyons, the 19th day of September 1596.

King Philip of Spain intends to confiscate and keep for his own use and purpose the share of gold and silver belonging to different persons, which the fleet has just brought home. This comes to nearly ten millions, as shown below, and its confiscation will be detrimental to many.

A record of what is due to each individual from the incoming fleet, which will be kept back by the King for his own profit:

	Millions of Ducats
Malvenda	1.7
Suares	1.05
Ambrogio Spinola . . .	0.4
Nicolo Fornari	0.6
Nicolo Doria	1.0
Sinibaldo Fiesco, Giovanni Battista Guidetti	0.8
Simone Luic and Allessandro Sauli	0.5
Battista Serra	.0.5
Fuggeri	2.0
Detto Fuggeri per una partida fatta in Fiandra	1.3

Total: 9 millions and 800,000 ducats.

210. The Peasant War in Upper Austria

From Linz, the 1st day of December 1596.

Our peasants behave as if possessed by the devil. They collect in all four quarters and it is believed that the day before yesterday there were eighteen thousand of them in Kremsmünster. They did no violence, for food and drink were proffered to them at their first demand. Of this, however, they refused to partake. They seem bewitched, for as soon as the word is given, even in this cold, they leave their wives and children, hasten from their houses and farms, yet attacking neither towns, castles, nor even villages. They tell the populace, whom they drag along with them, that for all they care, horses, oxen and cows, even the women may perish, and they pawn their cattle with the inn-keepers and drink away their gold.

To-morrow we expect a great number of them, in spite of the fact that the Proclamation which will be read to them has already arrived from Prague. I learn that by this Proclamation His Majesty grants them his pardon, though by their rebellion they have forfeited all their possessions, as well as their lives. Before next Tuesday His Serene Highness Archduke Mathias should come to Linz, for his retinue is already arriving hourly.

211. King Philip defaults

Rome, December 7, 1596.

Last Tuesday night four messengers from Genoa sent by the merchants there rode through here on their way to Naples. The same number are riding to the Netherlands and two to Milan. All this because the King of Spain is withholding payment of the money brought by the fleet, and requiring its use as a loan for the war against England and the Netherlands. The King will repay the money with interest in three years, or take it as an advance on the 30 millions promised him by the Kingdom of Castile for the English war. Genoa reports that there is consternation among merchants. Everything is in confusion and there will be many failures.

212. Spanish Financial Policy

From Venice, the 13th day of December 1596.

The King of Spain has sternly commanded that no gold or silver should be exported from the kingdom, or used for the purposes of trade. He has ascertained that this gold is recoined into the currency of foreign princes and that great profit is derived therefrom. It is also rumoured that a large sum of money for all sorts of merchandise has been dispatched to the Levant, where it has flown into the coffers of the Turkish Emperor. It seems that His Majesty is resolved to fit out a fleet out of the four or five millions of gold which are to be paid out yearly to the merchants as interest. Through this his bills of exchange will circulate slowly, causing much bankruptcy for money is very dear among the merchants.

212. The English Doctor of the Prince of Juliers

Cologne, January 23, 1597.

The English Doctor who is to attend the Prince of Juliers is here. The Councillors demand that he should first give proofs of his skill on others. They also wish to address a question to His Imperial Majesty, so as to get His Majesty's opinion.

214. Birth of a Monstrosity at Vienna

From Vienna, the 15th day of March 1597.

In the New Market here a poor lansquenet's wife gave birth to a child who had a head on his back just like an Indian cock, and legs which were turned the wrong way at the knees so that it hit itself in the belly when it wished to bend them. It soon died, but not before being baptized.

215. Philip II Borrows Again

From Rome, the 29th day of March 1597.

It is written from Madrid on the 4th day of the month that the King has published a decree whereby no silver coins are to be exported from the realm. He has also ordered that the reals, which before were worth thirty maravedi, are henceforward to be changed for forty maravedi. The King has also signed with his own hand the deed of the loan of Herr Fugger, and confirmed it by a decree. But for the other merchants the situation is still unfavourable.

216. The Peasants' War in Lower Austria

From Vienna, the 15th day of April 1597.

The rebellious peasants have not as yet been pacified, and lie a few thousand strong near Melk. But many of them are being killed, hanged and made prisoners by the cavalry. Only yesterday more than twenty of them were brought into the Government House, amongst whom there were many ringleaders, also their commander, together with his lieutenant. The horsemen take everything they possess away from them, sending away daily whole shiploads of bed linen, bacon, dripping, all sorts of household goods and much money, and thus they collect great riches, as the peasants here are very wealthy. Last Good Friday there came here a ship laden with such like things, among which were two big casks of forty buckets each of wine, besides a chest and a few coffers filled with money. The journeymen seized them, tapped the casks and allowed all the wine to flow out. They broke open the chest and robbed it. The two small coffers, which no one could carry by himself, were taken away in a skiff by the fishermen, who shared their contents. On the following Wednesday such a ship again arrived and the people wished to treat it in the same manner. The horsemen who accompanied this vessel sent warning to the judge, who thereupon betook himself with his servants and other varlets to the river. They caught the thieves, dragged them off to prison and on the next day hanged four of them; although one of these had but taken a pailful of wine and the other two hens from the ship, one of which fell into the water. Of the fishermen who had stolen the small coffers with the money, twenty-five were caught. Of these some were let free, but they have to pay a fine of five thousand florins. What it is intended to do with the others time will show. If they are not punished people's possessions will no longer be safe. Since the vintagers of

Mödling, Petersdorf, Baden, Inzersdorf, Gumpoldskirchen and other places have refused to work any longer for their old wages, they have become rebellious. They collected about two thousand strong, and the nobility and all landowners were commanded to gather with their horses in as great numbers as was possible to them. Thus were raised about three hundred horses and a troop of infantry. So they broke up camp last Friday and marched on Mödling, Baden and Pfaffstätten. There they fell upon the rebellious vintagers before daybreak and immediately hanged a drummer and six ringleaders. When the rest saw that they were outnumbered they at once consented to parley and themselves delivered their ringleaders, of whom more than fifty were brought in by the horsemen, and, as a punishment, forced to work in the town moat.

217. The Prince of Juliers and the English Doctor

Cologne, May 1, 1597.

The Prince of Juliers has submitted to the care of the English Doctor. If he cures him he will gain great honour.

218. The Prince of Juliers incurable

Cologne, June 12, 1597.

According to all appearances the English Doctor will not manage to restore the Duke of Juliers to his senses. So he will lose greatly in credit and reputation. If he had been able to help His Serene Highness it would have been a useful thing, as he would thus have been able to keep together the Duchies of Juliers, Cleves and Berg with all their dependencies.

219. A Rain of Blood in Vienna

From Vienna, the 18th day of July 1597.

At noon to-day, in a few places in front of the Schottentor, it rained blood. This was witnessed by many people, and many basketfuls of stones covered with blood were carried into the town.

Vienna, undated.

An order to the Mayor of this our town—Paulus Steyrer—to be delivered on the 19th day of July 1597.

It is made known to the Mayor of this town, Paulus Steyrer, by the Government of Lower Austria, that, according to trustworthy reports, yesterday in front of the Schottentor in Siechenals, also Hernals, Döbling, Sievering and near these places there fell a rain of blood. The stones which were sprinkled by it are said to be in existence. In order, however, to have a precise report thereon, the command goes forth from the Government that the Mayor should at once set an inquiry afoot as to the way in which this took place and that he should send information to the Government about the same before noon.

Given in Vienna, the 19th *day of July* 1597.

The faithful report of Paulus Steyrer, Mayor of this town, in obedience to the above Decree. The enclosed Decree I have received with due reverence, and in order to obtain special information regarding this matter, I betook myself in my own person, accompanied by a burgess of the Outer Council, Georg Hesch by name, to certain villages, namely Hernals, Währing and Unter-Döbling. In Döbling I found out from the judge that a butcher in Nussdorf had last Friday bought on the oxen market three oxen. These he ordered his servant to drive home. As, however, one of the oxen was very lazy and hard to drive, the butcher's man cut his tail with a knife and made him bleed. Thus the blood flowed into the hairs of the tail, and the ox splashed it about, whisking his tail this way and that, thus sprinkling the whole road. Wherever then the blood fell upon a stone there it remained. Thereupon I went with the above-named Hesch to Nussdorf, where I found both the ox and the butcher's house; I have also, with my own eyes, seen the ox sprinkling the blood. Except for this no blood fell on any one's body or clothing, and also no blood was found in the foliage of the trees or in the vineyards. So much have I to report obediently to Your Honour.

From Vienna, the 22nd day of July 1597.

It is still impossible to find the right explanation for the rain of blood. The Mayor reports of a wounded ox, others tell otherwise, among them Herr Streinz, keeper of the door of His Serene Highness, and a ducal halberdier. These report that the town is full of stones covered with blood, but that the drops of blood are as small as a raindrop or as large as lentils. As Herr Streinz has it, both may be right. We shall, however, investigate still further.

220. An Indian Rising in Peru

From Venice, the 15th day of August 1597.

It is rumoured that five hundred Spaniards and fifteen thousand Indians have risen in Peru against Don Pedro de Valasco on account of religious dissensions. This is bad news not only for Spain but also for the merchants, as gold and silver arrives from Peru, conveyed hither by the fleet, and this will now be prevented by this rising.

221. The Execution of the Rebellious Peasants in Vienna

From Vienna, the 25th day of October 1597.

I can report nothing new except that yesterday the chief ringleaders of the rebellious peasants, the cooper and the tailor, together with two others, a provost and a commander, were executed in this town in the place called Hof, on a scaffold. The cooper was quartered alive, and the two others were beheaded. The tailor and these two died in pious, Christian and Catholic fashion, confessing their sins before death and partaking of Holy Communion. The cooper died unrepentant and in his Lutheran heresy. This is a fearsome example, and all rebels should take warning therefrom. Four more ringleaders have been made prisoners here. They will be taken to Waidhofen and one especially, Schremser by name, who was a colonel, will be quartered there, but the other three will be put to the sword.

222. The Jesuits assign England and Scotland to the King of Spain

Rome, October 4, 1597.

As the Pope is again ill in bed all business is at a standstill. Even though His Holiness trusts Cardinal Aldobrandini, the latter is unfamiliar with the affairs of the States of the Church, and there are only a few people who do know anything about the matter. Accordingly the Spanish ambassador has complained to the Pope about His Holiness having accepted a document delivered to Him. This document states that the King of Scots is to succeed the Queen of England on her death; but the Pope is adjured to use every effort to restore these two Huguenot kingdoms to the Papal religion. Against this document the Jesuits have composed one assigning the succession in the above-mentioned kingdoms to the King of Spain and his heirs.

223. Marriage of Emanuel of Portugal with Emily of Nassau

Brussels, December 27, 1597.

The marriage of the sister of Count Maurice of Nassau to the son of Don Antonio of Portugal, who calls himself a Prince from Portugal, has been celebrated. The ceremony was performed at the house of Admiral Egmont of the Hague in presence of that Admiral and of many other Huguenot gentlemen. Count Maurice was not present, and bride and bridegroom have fled to Wesel as he is in pursuit of them.

224. Excommunication of Cesare d'Este.

From Rome, the 27th day of December 1597.

In the Consistorium held here last Monday, in the presence of the Pope, the Bull of Excommunication against Don Cesare d'Este and his associates was read out in a clear voice by Cardinal Peretti, as Deacon, before the full assembly of the Holy College. After that the Pope fell on his knees, kissed the candle which he held between his hands and thereupon spoke the anathema against Don Cesare and his followers. Then he returned to his customary place.

His Holiness wishes likewise to include in this excommunication all those who hinder the proclamation of the Bull and such as did not permit the transit of provisions for the papal troops. At the same time there goeth forth a decree, addressed to the Imperial and Royal Majesty, as well as to all the Christian Princes, that no help whatsoever is to be vouchsafed to Don Cesare and his vassals. Whoever opposes this command also comes under the Bull of Excommunication, and preachers exhort the people to guard themselves against it. Twelve days' grace has, however, been granted to Don Cesare.

225. The Prince of Juliers still not cured, Doctor useless

Cologne, February 12, 1598.

The Prince of Juliers is still at Hambach, and the English Doctor has accomplished little so far with his drugs. The Estates think of holding a session at Essen to consider whether they shall make His Serene Highness marry again.

Letters from Dordrecht report that at Scheveningen, near the Hague in Holland, a whale has been caught, 20 ft. long and 16 broad. This the Hollanders consider a good omen.

226. He is much better, so the English Doctor is some good after all

Cologne, February 12, 1598.

The Duke of Juliers is getting on so much better as regards his mind that it is thought the Councillors of His Serene Highness will soon permit him the use of sidearms again. It looks, therefore, as though the English Doctor who is still always with His Serene Highness would accomplish something useful.

227. Danzig Ships for the Polish-Swedish War

Antwerp, May 5, 1598.

We hear from Amsterdam that some ships have arrived from Danzig and report that all ships at Danzig are being detained. It seems that they are to be used for the war of the King of Poland against Sweden. They also report that four English cloth-ships have arrived in the Sound but have been confiscated for not showing their goods to the Customs. This will cause many failures among the English.

228. A Present for the Mistress of Henry IV

From Venice, the 8th day of May 1598.

The Duchess of Mercurio has presented Madame Gabrielle d'Estrées, the favourite of the King of France, with beauteous pleasure grounds and a park with animals in Brittany, worth more than sixty thousand crowns.

229. Report of Peace between France, Savoy and Spain

Middelburg, May 14, 1598.

This time we have nothing particularly fresh to write.

We hear from Antwerp that peace has been concluded between France, Savoy and Spain. The text of the treaty has been sent to Spain and to the Pope for ratification. But about our country and England we cannot yet know. The whole story has been thought untrue in default of any report from France. We hear from Moscow that the Prince is dead and the English there have had to leave the country. They seem to be attacked just now on all sides.

230. Peace between Spain and France not to include England or Holland

Middelburg, June 4, 1598.

It was announced a week ago that the French had arranged a separate peace with the Spaniards, and that England is excluded. The Frenchman is to get back all his towns, including Calais, but the Spaniards are to be allowed to move in and out. And so our countries will have to carry on the old war with the Cardinal again. It will last a long while, for so long as this King of Spain lives no peace can be expected on our side; we must go on with the war. As the Frenchman is going to sit there neutral and do nothing for our country the English will have to be careful. After lying outside Lisbon for some weeks and stopping ships from sailing, the Earl of Cumberland has gone off to Brazil. Yesterday and to-day many ships have come out from San Lucar, Lisbon and Portugal and made for Holland. Two vessels also have arrived from India with hides, woods, gold and pearls. Vessels are likewise daily expected from Spain. The people of La Rochelle have carried off two ships from Spain. The English do not yet know where to go to with their ships. Their representatives arrived from England yesterday and have been magnificently welcomed and entertained at the Town Hall. They are now to go to Delft to have a look at the place. If they can find a port that will do for their ships they will choose it, but at present it is not known what place they will take.

231. English Cloth for the Continent

London, July 5, 1598.

As for the peace between us and Spain it is universally talked of even at Court. All depends upon what Her Majesty's representatives bring back from France, and their return is awaited with great eagerness. If they bring good news, then various great Lords and Earls of the Council will be sent to France to continue negotiations with that country.

Two vessels have just come from Zante and two from Patras laden with currants and muscatel and two from San Lucar with 200 casks of wine. They say that the Earl of Cumberland has taken the island of Teneriffe in the Canaries. Whether this is true time will show.

Three vessels have arrived this week from Venice laden with currants, muscatel and the like.

Up to now the English merchants have not yet decided what place to select for their cloth trade, for the deputies they sent for this purpose to Holland have not yet returned. Last Thursday four ships with the usual cargoes left here for Staden and Hamburg, but they are still lying off the mouth of the Thames, as an express messenger was sent after them yesterday to stop them. The reason is this, that the Merchant Adventurers have heard that they are not wanted at Hamburg and will not be allowed to send foreign goods there. How this will be settled we shall know in time. A finer crop of corn stands in the fields than has been seen for twenty years, thank God. May the Almighty grant a continuance of fine weather so that we may be freed from the scarcity!

232. The Death of Philip II

From Madrid, the 13th day of September 1598.

After our King had lain ill for some time, he died here in the monastery of the Escurial on the 12th of the month at 5 o'clock in the morning. May God have mercy on His

Majesty. Immediately thereafter a courier was dispatched to the Imperial Court. His Majesty had been three weeks in his bed and could not be moved on account of large ulcers which had broken out. He was also forced to lie prone always.

233. Large Sales of Cloth at Middelburg

Cologne, October 7, 1598.

The English have already sold 12,000 pieces of cloth to Holland alone, and English cloth comes here every day from Holland. The patterns designed for Germany, however, will probably remain on their hands, as import is universally forbidden, even through Hamburg.

234. The Attempted Murder of Maurice of Nassau

From Antwerp, the 15th day of October 1598.

It is confirmed that an attempt has been made to stab Maurice of Nassau with a long weapon which looked like a pointed dagger, the interior of which was full of holes and poison. The assassin, however, betrayed himself and confessed in prison that some years before he had been persuaded to do this by the Jesuits, who had sworn to pay him a large sum of money. They had already paid him in advance one hundred Flemish pounds, and the remainder he was to receive after he had committed the deed. Whether this will further the peace negotiations, time will show.

235. Porto Rico taken by the English

Antwerp, October 10, 1598.

News comes that the English have taken the island of Porto Rico in India, but that the fort is still apparently holding out.

236. The War in Sweden

From Danzig, the 18th day of October 1598.

I enclose the news which we have received from Sweden from His Royal Majesty of Poland. Duke Charles had petitioned through the Electors and the Ducal Ambassadors to be allowed to appear in person before His Majesty in order to justify his mode of government and to refute the calumnies of his adversaries; but safe conduct was not granted unto him. It was required that he should surrender at discretion, disband all his troops and await submissively the verdict of the King. This the Duke was unable to accept; he thanked the Ambassadors for their trouble and resorted to other means. On the 17th September he advanced with all his troops, twelve thousand infantry and one thousand five hundred cavalry, to within one and half a mile of the King's camp and there pitched his own. He himself appeared about a quarter of a mile from the King's camp with six hundred men and sent a herald to the King with the request that he should be allowed to parley with four of the latter's Counsellors. These the King sent to him and to them the Duke expounded his fruitless efforts to obtain a personal interview with the King, in which he could have justified himself. He begged the four gentlemen for their mediation. Though they answered him in a churlish manner, yet they carried his petition to the King, who, however, rejected it and once more reafirmed the above-named grievous conditions. In the meantime a skirmish had arisen between the six hundred Swedes of Charles and the four hundred Hungarians, in which the Swedes were defeated. Through the personal intervention of the King and the Duke the fight was suspended. Thereupon the Duke again inquired for the conditions in order to settle the whole dispute. He was informed that he must make his submission, disband his troops, retreat and appear before the appointed Diet at Stockholm. In view of his danger the Duke accepted these conditions as he wished to display his goodwill and avoid further bloodshed; he also withdrew, but only in order to occupy a more favourable position before the Castle of Stangeborg, which he was able to bombard as well as the King's camp. When the King's army became aware of this the next morning, it lost heart. Thereupon Duke Charles rejected the old conditions and put forward new ones which were hardly more acceptable. New negotiations were begun, which the Duke prolonged on purpose because he was expecting his Armada from Finland where it had scattered the royal troops. He also learned that the King's fleet had been driven from its course to Stockholm by storm, and that it had lost part of its crew. He determined to strike at the King by land and by sea, as soon as his fleet had arrived. The King, however, retreated secretly by night, no one knows where, forsaking all his provisions. When the crews of the Royal Fleet, which was lying off Stockholm, went ashore the following morning, in order to receive their pay, they found the camp empty. As now, however, the news of the approach of Charles's Armada began to spread, and as they had orders to take aboard the large stores of provisions and ammunition, they quickly weighed anchor. But only twenty-five of the sixty ships arrived in safety to the port of Danzig. Two were sent to the bottom, the flagship together with two others, which were overladen, ran ashore and their precious cargo was plundered by Charles's ships. The others, about thirty in number, mostly Scotch and English, did not put up any sort of defence and remained quietly at anchor. Duke Charles sent them a message that it was known to him that they had but agreed to convoy the troops under compulsion, and that no harm would befall them or the goods aboard, did they but willingly surrender. This they did. Thus Duke Charles obtained considerable booty and a great victory. Nothing is known about the King's fate. The King's mistake is that he did not defeat the Duke and take him prisoner as some of his Counsellors had advised.

237. Philip's Lack of Money

From Madrid, the 20th day of November 1598.

The new King of Spain, with his cavaliers, on the 8th of this month held his entry in most magnificent fashion into

San Hieronymo, not far from here, under a canopy which was carried by twenty men, and on this occasion there was a display of much gold and silver and precious stones. Now the King is preparing to sally forth to Barcelona with his sister and his mother. This is due to take place next December. But there is great penury. And whereas the fleet is expected in January with gold and silver, His Majesty had countenanced negotiation with the purveyors of the Court for a sum of four hundred thousand ducats to be paid out at different dates in the Netherlands.

On the 7th day of November on account of the plague, which is spreading more and more, several streets in Lisbon have been barricaded and in the Palace all gates have been closed excepting one. Also in front of this palace a whole street has been walled up and so has a house in which there were many different articles of value; the people who lived in it were also driven out. But some daring youngsters assembled and carried everything away at night time. In Galicia as well death holds sway.

238. The Edict of Nantes

From Lyons, the 21st day of March 1599.

Fresh letters from Paris of the 15th of this month report that the Edict about religious peace was published in Parliament on the morning of the 25th of February. On the same afternoon the King's sister started on her journey to Lorraine, but on the way stopped to visit His Majesty at Saint-Germain. The Edict has, however, not yet been published in the city, as it appears that once more something has happened to prevent this.

239. The Dutch in the Straits of Magellan

Frankfort, April 15, 1599.

It is confirmed from Holland that the States General have forbidden all trade and navigation to Spain. They have also ordered that all merchants and skippers who have sustained loss through the detention of their ships and wish to avenge themselves should report to the States General and take out Letters of Marque so that they may be enabled to attack and plunder all Spanish ships and property at sea.

Amsterdam reports that their three warships which sailed from Rotterdam to the Straits of Magellan with a Frenchman have already seized a vessel from East India with a very rich cargo of gold, silver and general goods, and thrown overboard every Spaniard they found. The booty has been divided. The Rotterdamers have sailed back to the Straits of Magellan, and the Frenchman has come to La Rochelle. This has spread terror among the Spaniards.

240. Old Mexico

Venice, April 30, 1599.

Of the Indian fleet only one galleon with two millions in gold and a large quantity of cochineal has remained behind. The newly arrived fleet informs us also that the Spaniards have conquered a new kingdom in India called Old Mexico. It is inhabited by intelligent people who are to be instructed in the Christian faith. Very rich gold and silver mines exist there also.

241. The English allowed to trade with Spain

Antwerp, May 1, 1599.

There is a lot of talk here about peace developments between Spain and England, and the Queen of England has already announced that any one is free to go to Spain with merchandise. The English are very anxious to go there.

Further news comes from London that the Earl of Essex in person and his Armada have gone to Ireland. The rebel Earl of Tyrone is said to be a fugitive, and to have suffered a great reverse from the Viceroy of Ireland.

242. The Baptism of Jews in Rome

From Rome, the 15th day of May 1599.

Early last Sunday the Pope celebrated Mass in the Chapel of San Giorgio. There were there seven Jewish persons, three men and four women dressed all in red. These the Pope baptized himself in the presence of nineteen Cardinals, seven of whom he appointed as godfathers. He named the men after these and gave the women other names, and then caused them to be confirmed and immediately to receive Communion.

243. A Plague of Dolphins in the Mediterranean

From Rome, the 10th day of July 1599.

Two canons have just arrived here from Marseilles in order to recount to the Pope that in the Sea of Provence there is to be observed such a conglomeration of dolphins that not only do they interfere with the fishing, a most valuable source of revenue, but also with ships sailing on the sea. A Papal Brief has been bestowed upon the canons addressed to their Bishop, in which it is ordered that the matter should be taken in hand by means of prayers in the churches, processions and much fasting. Moreover, the Pope anathematizes this vermin, so that, with God's help, it may perish.

244. Holland becomes a Colonial Power

From Amsterdam, the 24th day of July 1599.

Out of the eight Dutch ships which left fourteen and a half months ago for India to obtain spices, four arrived here this week. They are richly laden. Their most important consignment is nearly three hundred loads of pepper, which should come to over four thousand packets. The remaining cargo consists of other kinds of spices, such as cloves, nutmeg, cinnamon, etc. The ships have a capacity of two hundred and twenty-five, two hundred and fifteen, seventy and forty loads respectively. The other four ships with soldiery have been left at Banca. These have set sail for the Moluccas and are to follow in a few months. This is considered here as great tidings, and much wonder is expressed that they should have taken such a short time over the journey. It took them seven months to make the East Indies and they lay two months in Banca. There they procured all their cargo, and have returned in five and a half months. Never have the Portuguese accomplished such a journey.

The Indians of Banca traded with them in most friendly spirit, and the Dutch paid the inhabitants of Banca for all the damage they had caused them three years before. In the meantime, the Portuguese attacked the town of Banca, but with the help of the Dutch, the Indians have killed eight hundred of these and captured the rest with the ships. Whereas the Dutch have succeeded so greatly in this sea journey they will undertake others, and if the King of Spain does not beware and put a stop to them, in time great harm will befall the kingdom of Portugal and the Venetians.

These ships are valued at three hundred thousand Flemish pounds. They will make yearly a great trade in spices and cause many others to alter their course. The Dutch States wish to go out again to India with these ships and to send an envoy to the King of Banca. They will never relinquish this desire unless the King of Spain prevent them by force.

245. The English must send Ships to India too

London, August 7, 1599.

From the sea and from Ireland there is nothing of importance to chronicle this week. The wild Irish take to the bush and the woods so that they cannot be got at. Orders come from Court to get ready 12 warships and 3000 men at once. Their destination is unknown.

The arrival of the four ships at Amsterdam has caused great astonishment in England, so merchants here are thinking of fitting out 12 vessels at once and sending them to the East Indies to import spices.

246. Divorce Plans of Henry IV

From Rome, 12th day of September 1599.

To-day, on account of the request of the King of France for a divorce, a meeting of Cardinals was held, in which the following three considerations were put forward:

1. That the King and Queen of France were blood relations and that they had no dispensation.

2. That King Charles IX had, out of fright, almost by violence, compelled them to marry.

3. That at the time they were of different religion.

Therefore this divorce is to proceed with all celerity. From this it is gathered that the marriage of His Majesty with the Princess of Tuscany will surely take place.

247. Family Tragedies in Rome

From Rome, the 12th day of September 1599.

Cenci's children were executed here yesterday. The eldest son was rent asunder with two tongs, beheaded and quartered, the daughter was beheaded. The youngest son was forced to watch all this. He was brought from prison and straightway taken back to it. He was pardoned on account of his youth. A nobleman of Rome, Paulus de Santa Croce, stabbed his own mother who was fifty-four years old, because he surprised her in adultery. The murderer, however, escaped through the window. A lawsuit has already begun against him and property of his will be confiscated to the amount of seventy thousand crowns.

248. The Dutch Harass Portuguese Trade

From Antwerp, the 22nd day of October 1599.

Letters from Amsterdam report that a Dutch ship, which had sailed with thirty-six other ships from the Canaries to

India, had separated from these and joined two English pirates in robbing a few ships in the Spanish Main. This ship made fast in Texel, which is not far from Amsterdam, but it is not known as yet what goods it has brought. Two Dutch ships have likewise called at Emden with fifteen hundred cases of sugar. Three other ships are expected from Brazil. Dutch navigation to the Indies is becoming ever greater, which will cause the Portuguese heavy damage in their trade.

249. Armistice in Ireland. Arrest of Essex

London, October 23, 1599.

All I have to chronicle is that our Queen's Commander-in-Chief in Ireland, the Earl of Essex, has arrived here, having arranged an armistice with the recalcitrant Irish. Her Majesty is displeased with this, and has had the Earl arrested and placed in safe custody in the mansion of the Lord Chancellor. There is a strong rumour that the Queen is about to enter into negotiations for peace with Spain, but no envoys have yet been dispatched.

250. The Counter Reformation in Austria

From Steyr, the 30th day of October 1599.

As already announced, His Serene Highness Ferdinand of Austria and Lord of the Manor of the three countries of Styria, Carinthia and Carniola, holding a hunt soon after St. Jacob's Day at Eisenerz, forthwith displaced two pastors and appointed in their stead two Catholic priests. When, however, His Serene Highness had left for Graz, the two above-named priests were again driven out of the parish. His Serene Highness was very much displeased and immediately dispatched some commissaries to reinstate the two priests. He also gave them six hundred troopers from Croatia and Slavonia, in order that, should the inhabitants of Eisenerz prove obstinate, they might enforce his will with an iron fist. These arrived here fourteen days ago and the community and the miners wanted to oppose them in arms. Thereupon the commissaries promised them that no harm should befall them from the soldiers, and that the desires of the inhabitants of Eisenerz should be respected.

The Commissaries were then allowed to enter the town, and they won the game, for immediately thereupon they arrested the heads of the municipality, the aldermen, burgesses and others. Also every one had to deliver his arms in the market-place and the soldiers were quartered in the town. Thereafter the two priests were reinstated by force and seven gibbets were erected in the market-place, of which two were just in front of the Town Hall.

On the next day the provost with his retinue also betook himself there, so that he could begin with hangings, beheadings, impalings and other torments, tortures and agonies, to find out by means of suffering whether there was an understanding between them and other places and districts. Altogether it is a grievous state of affairs. Every one who can, flies from the parish. Women with their children are driven from their houses and are obliged to watch in terror and pain the miserable existence of their husbands. Although it was intended to execute the ringleaders and the heads of the town at once, it is said that Imperial Commissaries have arrived these last days, who have sternly forbidden, in the name of His Majesty, any harm to be done unto any man or to put any one to the rack or torture. It is greatly hoped that His Majesty will show mercy.

The Commissaries are also due to travel these days to Aussee, Schladming, Gröbming, Neuhaus and Rottenmann, in order to proceed with this matter everywhere. That this should take place with more speed, the governor, Count Wolkenstein, has collected three hundred of his own peasantry in the field one mile from here so as to unite with the other troops. As, however, most of them belong to the Evangelical faith, they are not reliable. When the need for action comes, they will not yield obedience. Three weeks ago His Highness had the collegiate church in Graz forced and caused the chairs, the altars, the company flags and the gravestones of former sovereigns to be pulled out and hacked to pieces and the whole church emptied. For what purpose he now wishes to use it is uncertain.

The secretary of the local council of Graz, Herr Gabelhofer, is still imprisoned in the castle in that place. None of his acquaintances are allowed to see him. The secretary of the Carinthian Council, Herr Kantelberger, has died of torture, after great agony. The motive of this was to find out the intentions of the local council; but he would divulge nothing.

251. The Monastic Life of Pope Clement VIII

From Rome, the 12th day of February 1600.

The Pope is quite determined to lead a monastic life as an example to the whole world. On account of this he has already ordered all carpets and ornaments to be removed from his rooms and especially from his sleeping chamber, allowing nothing to remain therein except a bedstead, a table and several skulls, as he wishes only to lie between four walls. Near him sleep two Benedictine monks, who stand in very good repute. He has summoned them to his presence, in order to pass his time with them and only to think of spiritual matters.

252. Joyful Return of the English East Indian Fleet

Cologne, June 9, 1600.

The arrival in England of four ships from the East Indies, and besides these of two from the West Indies, has been announced quite recently. Two of them have already come to Middelburg and were met by two companies of trainbands with music playing and welcomed with joy bells as well. Although these vessels have brought a quantity of spices they had not enough money to load their holds right up. One of the vessels, worth more than the two that have come here, was lost near England. Their cargo consists of 90 loads of pepper, 7 loads of cloves, 8000 lbs. of mace and a small amount of nutmegs. They took 14 months on the outward, 6 on the homeward voyage, and lay still seven months loading.

253. Clement VIII hears Confessions

From Rome, the 8th day of April 1600.

Last Saturday the Pope sat in the chair of the Chief Penitentiary in the Church of St. Peter with a white rod in his hand, and heard confessions there for three hours, granting the people absolution. Among these were many pilgrims, such as the Viceroy of Naples and the Duke of Sessa, as well as the bandit chief and the former most intimate adviser of the Sciarra. These the Pope touched on the forehead with the white rod.

On Tuesday the above-named Viceroy and his wife, also the Princess of Castelvetrano, dined with the Pope, and the day before yesterday Cardinal Aldobrandino gave the Viceroy a sumptuous banquet served at five tables. After dinner a hunt of all kinds of deer was held in the courtyard of the palace.

254. Conferences of Philip III of Spain for Purposes of obtaining Credit

From Rome, the 17th day of June 1600.

The gentlemen we named recently who a short time ago were resolved upon arranging a new financial transaction with the King of Spain, are now, for lack of ready money, no longer wishful to lend him these sums. For this reason they have begged the gentlemen of the Monte San Giorgio to pay the deficit required to complete the needed amount, in return for which they have offered to place in the Monte as much fine gold and silver as would be necessary as a security. This, however, was refused, and therefore His Majesty suffers from some lack of cash. Although the Spanish kingdom had declared itself prepared to advance six more millions as Assignation on the fleet which is due to arrive, and to pay the royal debt therewith, this money has not been found to be sufficient. The merchants, who are concerned in this, have offered to withhold their loan in the meantime, in order that the intended Assignation may be extended until the arrival of the fleet.

255. England and Holland Conquer the Trade of the World

From Antwerp, the 2nd day of July 1600.

From Holland and Zeeland we get written tidings that four ships from the East Indies and others from the West Indies have again sailed into Plymouth in England heavily laden with spices. Altogether they have brought ninety loads of pepper, which are estimated at about 324,000 lb.; also cloves and mace. Besides these there are nine other ships expected in Zeeland, Amsterdam and Rotterdam. The consignment of the two ships which have recently come from the Moluccas amounts to 620,000 lb. of nutmeg, 65,000 lb. of mace, 35,000 lb. of cloves and 700 lb. of pepper, which altogether is estimated at 230,000 Flemish pounds. In exchange these two ships have carried away with them 300,000 Flemish pounds in cash. It is said that six more ships are due to sail for the East Indies, namely four of the old and two of the new Company. This route becomes therefore of universal use, which is very harmful to the Spaniards, because it has been decided in Holland and Zeeland that this journey should be made through Portuguese and Spanish waters. It is announced from Emden that a ship has come here from Pernambuco in Brazil, the sailors of which report that the fleet of the United Provinces with seven ships have captured two forts in Brazil, and that afterwards they attacked the town and carried off between seven and eight thousand cases of sugar.

256. The Dangers of Sea Voyages

From Cologne, the 18th day of August 1600.

Two ships the *Lion* and the *Lioness* belonging to Balthasar Monseron in Zeeland have arrived home from Madagascar with thirty loads of pepper and with some white ginger. They have had a bad voyage and have endured great dangers both afloat and on land on account of the savages.

These gave them to drink of an intoxicating beverage, which they took full of trust. Owing to this they all became unconscious and for three whole hours the ship was besieged by the savages and nearly lost. But those on board the *Lioness* fought the savages so bravely that the latter had to abandon her. However, eighty men who had landed perished. These savages, therefore, should not be trusted.

257. The Execution of the Earl of Essex

From Antwerp, the 23rd day of March 1601.

It is written from London that Lord Essex, together with one of his most distinguished companions, belonging to the nobility, has been beheaded there in the Tower. This, however, is kept quite secret, as the causes of the conspiracy against the Queen likewise are not yet divulged. It is also said that the Queen has not confiscated the estates of the Earl, but has given them as a present to his young son, whose godmother she is, from which it is gathered that she is graciously disposed towards this young Earl.

From Cologne, the 4th day of March 1601.

Letters from Amsterdam report that the executioner who carried out the sentence on Lord Essex with the axe was frightened to such an extent, that he first of all slashed the Earl through the shoulder, then through the head and lastly through the neck and this in most grisly fashion. Great sorrow has been excited thereby not only in England, but also in Holland and Zeeland among the common people, for the said Earl was greatly devoted and attached to his religion.

258. Persecution of Jews in Prague

From Prague, the 5th day of April 1601.

A short time ago there died here the Jew Meisel. Notwithstanding that he had left His Imperial Majesty ten thousand florins, and much cash also to the Hospital for poor Christians and Jews, His Imperial Majesty on the following Saturday, viz. the Sabbath of the Jews, ordered Herr von Sternberg, at that time President of the Bohemian Chamber, to enter the Jew's house forcibly and to seize everything there was. The widow of Meisel handed this over willingly, for she had already set aside and hidden the best part of the treasure. That which was taken away came to forty-five thousand florins in cash, besides all manner of other things, such as silver plate, promissory notes, jewels, clothes and all kinds of coins. After this, however, the President, against whom the Jewess and the sons of the two brothers of Meisel had raised a strong protest to the privy councillors, was not satisfied with all this money and booty, and no doubt at the command of His Majesty, once more broke into the house at night. The son of one of the brothers was taken prisoner, secretly led away and tortured in such guise that he confessed to the executioners, as a result of which the following substance was handed to the Bohemian Chamber:

80,000 ordinary single ducats of 2 florins apiece make	160,000	florins.
5,000 pure golden Portugalese of 20 florins apiece make . . .	100,000	florins.
15,000 pure golden Rosenobles of 4 florins 5 kreuzer apiece make .	61,250	florins.
30,000 turnip ducats of 2 florins apiece, make	60,000	florins.
10,000 Styrian ducats of 2 florins apiece make	20,000	florins.
60,000 silver thalers of 7 kreuzer apiece make	70,000	florins.
Together with the above-mentioned .	45,000	florins.
Make altogether	516,250	florins.

259. A Lansquenet Bears a Child

From Piadena in Italy, the 26th day of May 1601.

A weird happening has occurred in the case of a lansquenet named Daniel Burghammer, of the squadron of Captain Burkhard Laymann zu Liebenau, of the honourable Madrucci Regiment in Piadena, in Italy. When the same was on the point of going to bed one night he complained to his wife, to whom he had been married by the Church seven years ago, that he had great pains in his belly and felt something stirring therein. An hour thereafter he gave birth to a child, a girl. When his wife was made aware of this, she notified the occurrence at once. Thereupon he was examined and questioned as to how this had come to pass. He then confessed on the spot that he was half man and half woman and that for more than seven years he had served as a soldier in Hungary and the Netherlands; in proof whereof he produced his genuine passport. When he was born he was christened as a boy and given in baptism the name of Daniel. In his youth he learnt the handicraft of a smith, which until this day he had practised simultaneously with his soldiering. He also stated that while in the Netherlands he only slept once with a Spaniard, and he became pregnant therefrom. This, however, he kept a secret unto himself and also from his wife, with whom he had for seven years lived in wedlock, but he had never been able to get her with child. When the aforesaid Captain heard of this he informed the Church authorities, who thereupon sent a notary to ascertain the facts and report thereon. After this event had been proved in this wise, the christening of the child was finally ordered to take place. Herr Reitner, Ensign from Wenigarten, in lieu and stead of the Captain, stood sponsor with several noble ladies at the christening of the child, which was named Elizabeth. This christening was celebrated with many ceremonies and in the presence of soldiery, such as drummers, pipers and three trumpeters. Many noted men and women in the nobility as well as five hundred soldiers accompanied the child home again from the christening. The aforesaid soldier is able to suckle the child with his right breast only and not at all on the left side, where he is a man. He has also the natural organs of a man for passing water. Both are well, the child is beautiful, and many towns have already wished to adopt it, which however, has not as yet been arranged. All this has been set down and described by notaries. It is considered in Italy to be a great miracle and is to be recorded in the chronicles. The couple, however, are to be divorced by the clergy.

260. The Spaniards besiege Ostend

Antwerp, August 3, 1601.

We do not hear that His Serene Highness has thus far accomplished anything of value before Ostend. He has apparently taken a trench, but this is not much use, as the States General have thrown up an entrenchment outside the fortress, which they hold with 3000 men. His Highness has not been able to block the harbour either, as four English warships are lying off it on guard. Any day 4000 English soldiers may come to Ostend and 500 nobles at their own expense, so that the capture will be arduous for His Highness and cost him dear in time and men. His Highness is not yet lavishly provided with troops for the siege either. An Englishman disguised as a farmer recently went to Mestricht, to find out whether the town could be captured by treachery, but he was caught and brought a prisoner to His Highness in camp.

261. 50 per cent Profit for Dutch Shareholders

Cologne, September 9, 1601.

We are advised from Amsterdam on the 3rd inst. that the profits of the four East Indian vessels recently arrived are to be distributed to shareholders. Each one is to receive 50 per cent. Pending the arrival of the other two vessels belonging to this Company, three more ships are to sail for East India this autumn.

262. Fresh Troops for Zeeland together with Peace Overtures

Antwerp, March 14, 1604.

Letters of the 5th inst. from London report that the King, in order, like the late Queen, to maintain friendship with the States General, is continuing to afford them assistance.

249

For this purpose he has sent 3000 soldiers to Zeeland, and some thousands more are to follow. But he has no objection to the King of Spain raising as many troops as himself.

Moreover, His Majesty has published a decree that all Jesuits, Seminarists and Popish priests must be gone from the country by the 20th inst. on pain of death. Whether this will promote peace remains to be seen. It is not known whether Parliament will meet this month.

The Constable of Castile is making great preparations for his journey to England, and the King of Spain seems to count on peace between himself and England as a certainty. The King of England has said too that he is no foe of Spain, and that therefore the matter is not pressing, as the only problem is the confirmation of the ancient friendship, and the Constable will be welcome whenever he comes. But the King of England will insist that his subjects have the right to go to East India and other places outside the dominions of the King of Spain.

Also, despite frequent requests, the King of England has not consented to give an audience to Antonio Perez, or to allow him a ship for his journey to France. The King has had him informed that as he found people to bring him over to England without the King's knowledge, they may as well take him back again. So he will have to depart without an audience.

The Dutch, who offered to hand over East and West India to the King, have received the answer that His Majesty does not desire this, that he has enough of his own, and that his only wish is to possess his countries in peace and quiet.

263. Peace Negotiations. The Spaniards ask too much

Antwerp, July 2, 1604.

London letters of the 10th June announce that the Spanish envoys and five of the King's Commissioners have been meeting to discuss terms of peace. The Spaniards began by asking what kind of peace the English required. The English replied to this that it was the business of the Spaniards to explain themselves on the point. The Spaniards demanded a peace offensive and defensive against the

King's enemies. This the English refused. Then the Spaniards asked merely for a defensive peace, whereby if one side or the other were attacked the other must come to his aid. Thereupon the English declared that it was more to the point for them not to be at enmity with anybody than to be in need of aid from Spain, for they had no intention of breaking the peace in any direction. The Spaniards asked to be informed whether the only wish of the English was that neither side should harm the other. The Spaniards desired that the English should give no assistance to rebels against the King. This the English took very ill, saying that it was contrary to the honour of their King. However, this point will be further considered.

264. Peace concluded but terms not yet published

Antwerp, September 10, 1604.

We have letters of the 1st inst. from London stating that on the 29th ult. the conclusion of peace between Spain and England was made public. The King gave the Constable of Castile and all the other gentlemen a very magnificent banquet, and presented them with some 100,000 carlins* worth of silver plate and precious stones. But the text of the peace is not to be printed until the King of Spain has personally sworn to observe it. Therefore the King of England has despatched an envoy to Spain. The Spaniards are to come back here again in a week.

265. The Fall of the Fortress of Ostend

From Antwerp, the 24th day of September 1604.

The fortress of Ostend, which had been beleaguered for three years and two and a half months, has just been surrendered by agreement into the hands of Spinola. Upon the 22nd day of this month, at 10 o'clock of the forenoon, two thousand five hundred soldiers of the General States marched, with all their arms and four pieces of heavy

---

* Karlsgulden, carolini or carlins were coins minted by the Popes and the Dukes of Florence valued in England at fourpence.

ordinance, upon the town of Sluys. Although Count Moritz of Nassau, as is reported in letters from Middelburg dated the 14th, set forth by ship with twenty thousand men on horseback and on foot as well as with twenty-four cannon, for which journey twenty thousand loaves had been supplied to him in Zeeland, he was unable on account of a head wind, and also of the heavy firing from Spinola's palisade, to land in the port of Ostend, in which there were most of his men.

Since the troops of the General States, terrified by the constant firing, were unable to resist any longer, they were obliged at last to surrender.

266. Skirmish at Sea between the English and Dutch

Cologne, October 22, 1604.

In Holland and Flanders there is much talk of peace, and envoys have arrived in Holland from England, Denmark and the Saxon Princes, who are strongly urging peace. A general assembly of the States General has been called for the 18th. They want to repay the money lent them by the Queen of England on the security of Flushing and Briel and to get rid of the garrisons there. So peace cannot be entirely relied on.

It is reported from Brussels that the English and Dutch ships met at sea off Zeeland. When the English would not pay the Dutch the customary courtesy of the sea by firing a salute, the Dutch fired at them in earnest. The others did the same, and so a regular skirmish resulted, but who won is not known at present. On the other hand, the King of England is said to be very solicitous about Spain and His Highness, so that it seems almost as though he would like to withdraw his support from the States General.

267. Rejoicings at Antwerp

Antwerp, November 5, 1604.

The peace with England was made public last Sunday, and then at nine o'clock in the evening all sorts of bonfires were lighted, *feux de joie* let off, and a great peace celebration was held with drums and fifes and discharge of cannon.

268. Extraordinary Occurrence at the Imperial Court of Prague

From Vienna, the 8th day of December 1604.

From foreign parts comes the news that, a short while ago, His Imperial Majesty wished to betake himself to his apartments through the corridor at his right hand. Thereupon the eagle, who has his stand in the courtyard by the cistern of the fountain, flew towards His Majesty through the corridor and into his own chamber. There, upon a table a snow-white dove was to be seen, whereat His Majesty was greatly surprised, for it was unknown to him that white doves were bred in that part of the country. When this was bruited about, elderly people were heard to remark that during the lifetime of the second Kaiser Maximilian a white dove had also shown itself in his chamber, coming from the blue, and this just before His Majesty had travelled to Regensburg to the opening of the Diet, where he gently passed away in the Lord shortly hereafter. But since nothing of this matter has been reported from Prague, it cannot be easily believed.